Robert Somers

The Trade Unions

An Appeal to the Working Classes and Their Friends

Robert Somers

The Trade Unions
An Appeal to the Working Classes and Their Friends

ISBN/EAN: 9783743410541

Manufactured in Europe, USA, Canada, Australia, Japa

Cover: Foto ©Suzi / pixelio.de

Manufactured and distributed by brebook publishing software (www.brebook.com)

Robert Somers

The Trade Unions

By ROBERT SOMERS.

"A book, not a small one, might be made up of the strange doings of Trade Unions Monopoly is hard to teach, and I fear the working men will only learn through suffering, and may do mischief which cannot be afterwards repaired."—RIGHT HON. JOHN BRIGHT. *June* 3, 1875."

𝕰𝖉𝖎𝖓𝖇𝖚𝖗𝖌𝖍:

ADAM AND CHARLES BLACK.

LONDON : LONGMANS & CO.

1876.

LONDON:
R. CLAY, SONS, AND TAYLOR, PRINTERS,
BREAD STREET HILL.

PREFACE.

THE Author has taken the liberty to place on the Title-Page a sentence or two from a published letter of Mr. Bright, expressing with eminent authority much the same idea and aim as had suggested the composition of this Book; and he may here add a few words from the speech of Lord Derby, on receiving the freedom of the city of Edinburgh in December last, pointing as directly to the main sources from which he deemed that the materials of such a work, if the discussion was to be preserved within recognised bounds, should be derived. Lord Derby, without reference to this subject in particular, said :—

" Look at the number of Royal Commissions that have been appointed, and of Committees in Parliament that have sat in the last twenty years to report upon various administrative matters. How many of these Reports have been acted upon ?"

Trade-Unionism has had seven or more years of most eventful history—of history on the largest public scale of affairs. This history is printed in volumes of Hansard, in scores of Blue-Books, in millions of newspapers, in innumerable decisions of Civil and Criminal Courts, and, it must be feared, in many details of private woe and desolation of which there has been no recorder. But even of what has been printed on this subject under the authority of Parliament itself, how much may not be as completely buried for all practical purposes as the Reports of Royal Commissions and Select Committees to which Lord Derby has referred in general, and which he almost despairs, not without reason, of Parliament being able to overtake?

To endeavour to analyse the abundant materials, and to present, within brief compass, the subject of Trade-Unionism as a whole, and in the connexion of its various parts, would thus appear to be a desirable undertaking.

CONTENTS.

Royal Commission of Inquiry on "the Labour Laws."

THE TRADE UNIONS.

I.

INTRODUCTION.

THE subject of this book may be best introduced by a few interrogatories not difficult to answer.

Have any societies, companies, or organised bodies of whatever kind, acted so conspicuous a part on the public field of affairs in this country as the Trade Unions during the last ten years?

Is any one conscious of a day during the last ten years on which the proceedings of the Trade Unions, often the most unpleasant to themselves and to others, have not been recorded in the newspapers, and attracted the attention of the kingdom?

Has any disturbing action in industrial affairs been more constantly felt those ten years than the action of the Trade Unions?

Have any sectional parties in the State, during that period, been so active politically, or been found so frequently in the lobbies of the House of Commons, interviewing members, and demanding changes of the laws as the Trade Unions?

These questions can only be answered in one way, and the questions themselves have only to be stated in order to prove the great importance of the subject to which they refer. They show that the Trade Unionism of present times

B

is a novelty in this country, and like all novelties of such
magnitude, it is more or less portentous, requiring much examination in the interest both of the Unionists themselves
and of the public.

The history of Trade Unions in this country may be said
briefly to have passed through three well-marked stages.

If we go back a century, we find a state of common law
adapted to the social and commercial circumstances, and
to the ideas of public policy, and of right and wrong at the
period, under which the systematic action of many of our
Trade Unions would have been impermissible, were it even
possible to conceive that such action could have occurred
to any of the working men of that time. But this state of
the law did not prevent the formation of Trade Unions to
support each other in brotherly membership of the same
trade, to require full apprenticeship, to promote the utmost
skill in the trade, and to urge, in harmony with employers,
every means by which the interests of the workmen could
be advanced, short of violence, or of any acts that could
render the procedure of the Unions a political or legal
question. Many of the Unions of that ancient standing
remain in full vigour to the present day. They are seldom
heard of in the noisy movements of recent times ; but,
adhering to their traditions, they have never lost their integrity, and have never fallen below other bodies of skilled
workmen in rates of wages, in full demand for their labour,
or in any advantage which a skilled workman most prizes.
It is to these older Unions we owe the doctrine, long
familiar, but now more than half exploded, that a Trade
Union is a non-political body, and that as an association it
has nothing to do on the high but perilous stage of politics
or revolution.

Advancing along the course of history, we come to the
second stage of Trade Unions, or rather of the manifestation of a new form of Unionism, which may be called
Tumultuous Unionism, when erratic leagues of working people broke out, no doubt under desperate motive, but under
equally desperate ignorance, in the destruction of machines,
incendiarism, and other fell outrages. This was as unlike

as possible to the Unionism that had grown up under the
wing of the eight or ten incorporated trades which form the
Middle Age constituents of all our cities and boroughs.
New manufactures had arisen ; the introduction of machine
power was more or less modifying all trades ; masses of
working people had gathered round new centres of employment far beyond the bounds of ancient cities and boroughs ;
and great international wars, diverting in their absorbing
passions both Parliament and people from the study of social
and industrial questions, had brought their usual severe reaction on all the springs of labour and subsistence. These
circumstances account for the uprise of Tumultuous Unionism, but this revolt of Labour was an extremely formidable
affair in its time, and Acts were passed into the Statute
Book, striking at the existence of such combinations, and
placing all societies of workmen in their outward procedure
under severe restrictions.

The third stage in the history of Trade Unions began at
least fifty years ago, when the Legislature repealed all the
anti-combination Statutes, retaining only some statutory
provisions against acts of a definitely criminal character ;
and this stage extends to our own times, in which the Legislature, so far from calling in question the right of combination, has been labouring to give, and has successfully given
this right the utmost legal sanction and protection consistent
with that equal right of all under the law which must prevail in this country. It might be supposed that the legal
history of Trade Unionism would here end, and that the
proper and honourable traditions of the Unions would re-
vive and acquire irresistible force. But this, so far, has not
been the experience. The Trade Unions that have had the
most ample notoriety of late years are found to be as dissatisfied under every successive effort of the Legislature as
they were before, and, throwing away the idea that Trade
Unions are non-political bodies, boldly proclaim that they
must have more power over the law, and that the votes of
every M.P., to whom they have given support, or who expects their support, must be cast in favour of some imaginary supremacy of Trade-Union labour, and the exemption

of Trade-Union procedure from the ordinary equity of the realm.

With this state of affairs, so far as the past is concerned, it would be vain to found any reactionary dispute. It is the result in substance of the growth of public liberty; of a large extension of the franchise without more than the ordinary guarantee that the newly-enfranchised, or the new candidates, would know at once the proper use and responsibility of the franchise; of a liberal sentiment common to all parties in favour of any measure that may really improve the condition of labour; and, last though not least, of a demagoguery in the Unions themselves which often miscalculates both its wisdom and its power, and speaks loudly in the name of its followers without any adequate authority. But facts and reason may have some sway, as regards the future, in checking the progress of whatever may be impolitic or destructive.

There was for some years a general public satisfaction in the success of strike. That a body of Union workmen had beaten their employers in a fair struggle was as popular as anything that could happen; that wages were rising, that labourers in one corner of the vineyard after another were becoming more comfortable, that labouring classes long so unduly depressed as the colliers, for example, were raising their heads, and that Parliament was busily engaged in providing for them at the expense of employers and of the State greatly improved conditions of health, safety, and justice in their avocations, were all facts in complete accord with public sentiment; and there can be no doubt that the Unions under proper guidance might have laid at this stage a foundation of stable improvement for the working classes. But when it was seen that one successful strike only prepared the way for other strikes in rapid succession, keeping large masses of working people out of employment, and in increasing poverty; and that under the operation of economic principles which neither Unions nor Parliament could alter, a rise of wages, arbitrarily propagated by successive strikes, brought no real relief to labour, but only placed the whole working population under greater

straits of living, besides obstructing and diminishing legitimate trade, there naturally came a change of opinion, and
people began to perceive that an interminable struggle between capital and labour, such as the more demagogic
Unions would precipitate in large masses and in endless
detail, is about the worst calamity that could befall the industry and the industrial classes of any country.

The last, however, to share the public conviction are
probably the more active Unions themselves. They are
propelled some length in a course of combat against unequal forces, and it is the courage of our race, when hostilely
engaged, to brave every extremity. How many sad proofs
do Unionists give of their determination to sacrifice their
present and future interests to the barest chance of gaining
some trivial advantage over their employers! Yet this question, in all its gravity, is surely not beyond the reach of
ordinary reflection and inquiry. The Unions, and the
working men who are the life of the Unions, may examine
for themselves, in the light of their own experience, how far
their policy has been prudent or imprudent, capable or incapable of success, and what changes of their policy may
be necessary to place themselves in tolerable harmony with
the radical circumstances of law, civil and natural, in which
they have to operate. As for the politicians outside, who
look upon the Unions simply as an existing force to be con-
ciliated by smooth compliances, and used to the best advantage for their own ends, it is equally within their power to
lay aside so superficial a view, and, rising to the comprehension that Trade Unionism is in reality a great web of
policy of the nature of an *imperium in imperio*, in which the
most intricate mechanism is not uncunningly contrived towards specific ends, and is put into action by what is often
a most formidable force, to see and judge clearly how far
this great web of policy is calculated to answer its own purposes, or consists with the interests of the working classes,
and how far, in fine, it can be treated without the most
desperate folly as an undetermined and merely playful element in party politics.

The materials of judgment on this subject are now so

ample that there can scarce be any apology for evading the main points of consideration. Within the last seven years there have been two Commissions of Inquiry under the Royal Seal, at the instigation mainly of the Trade Unions themselves, by which have been elicited not only such volumes of evidence, but such careful analysis of the evidence and such full deliberation on the part of the Commissions, as have only very seldom been displayed on other subjects. There is thus no want of means of information on this Trade-Union problem. The only *lapsus* to be feared is that the vast body of materials available may not be sufficiently examined, and that the Unions, and the masses of working men passing and repassing under their influence, will pursue their accustomed way, heedless of the light which so much inquiry and experience have thrown upon it. Nor is it quite certain that many present and future M.P.'s will not be tempted to take the same light and easy course.

The labours of the Royal Commission, appointed in 1867 " to inquire into the organisation and rules of Trade Unions " and other Associations, whether of workmen or employers, " and into the effect produced by such Unions and Associa- " tions on the workmen and employers respectively, on the " relations between workmen and employers, and on the " trade and industry of the country," extended till 1869, and were recorded in eleven blue-books and two or three supplementary documents.[1] The political sentiment of the time was specially favourable to the Trade Unions, and to their most adventurous projects, whether of combination or law-making. Trade and finance had passed through a severe crisis in 1866, and industry was slowly recovering from a state of depression in which Trade Unions have little opportunity of being aggressive, and when the common regret, indeed, is that there is not more demand for labour, with more liberal wages. The "working man," moreover,

---

[1] The members of the Commission were Sir William Erle, the Earl of Lichfield, Lord Elcho, Sir Edmund Walker Head, Sir Daniel Gooch, Mr. Herman Merivale, Mr. James Booth, Mr. Roebuck, Mr. Thomas Hughes, Mr. Frederic Harrison, and Mr. William Mathews.

in view of a large extension of the franchise, had become
the cynosure more or less of both the great parties in the
State. The Unions were strong in numbers; and to establish pleasant relations with their leaders, and hold a certain
dalliance with all their schemes, however crude or adverse to
the interests of labour, seemed to many politicians the
readiest means of securing great numbers of votes in all
the town constituencies of the kingdom. This speculation,
indeed, did not prove ultimately profitable; for it happened
that nearly all the Trade Union leaders were candidates for
seats in Parliament in their own proper persons, and at the
last General Election the Union candidates and their Parliamentary patrons came into awkward collision, and in not
a few instances destroyed each other's chances of being anywhere but at the bottom of the poll. But it is necessary to
refer to the advantageous conditions under which the Trade
Unions passed through the great inquest of 1867-9, chiefly
because there is a habit of the Unions, after moving elaborate
inquiries of this kind, to give little heed to the conclusions
to which the inquirers come, and to pass on, demanding
more inquiries, in an obscure and headlong purpose, which is
most disheartening to many who, without selfish interest or
political ambition, have long studied and advanced the condition of the working classes, and who desire to see the
various questions brought to a regular and just solution.

The only cause of anything in the nature of prejudice in
the public mind anterior to the Inquiry of 1867-9 arose
from the ranks of the Unionists themselves. A series of
most infamous Trade Union outrages at Sheffield had, a
year or two before, greatly shocked the whole kingdom, and
disconcerted even the most sanguine of the Trade Union
politicians; and the Royal Commission had not well entered on its labours till it was found necessary to give power
by a special Act of Parliament to examine witnesses on oath
in regard to a long train of less notorious but equally inveterate outrages on trade and labour at Manchester, casting a
most lurid reflection on the ultimate issues of Trade-Union
policy. These events had a certain reactive effect, but as
they had been at once universally condemned by the Trade

Union "authorities" as utterly opposed to "the rules," they were soon treated as the merest local and transient exceptions to the uniformly peaceable and wholesome action of the Unions; and the Inquiry pursued the even tenour of its way with little or no loss of its original Unionistic impulse. The political Unions were in full activity and in high working order. The employers were unorganized; non-union workmen were totally unrepresented; and these classes made little or no rebutting effort. The Commission was left with scarce any evidence as to the effect of Trade Union action on the industry and commerce of the country— a branch of the investigation that has grown to great dimensions during the intervening years—while, on the other hand, the Commission was abundantly supplied with all manner of evidence that could place the Unions in the most favourable light. It is improbable that the Trade Unions can ever have a more choice opportunity of stating their own case; and it is equally improbable that they can ever have a Commission of Inquiry more disposed to give the most generous interpretation to whatever they have to advance, whether in self-defence or in self-assertion. The Earl of Lichfield and Lord Elcho had distinguished themselves by a decided sympathy not only with the working classes, but with Trade Unionists as appearing to them the most active embodiment of the working-class interest. Mr. Hughes and Mr. Harrison were avowed advocates of Trade Unionism in its fullest and most doubtful aims. In Sir William Erle, Chairman of the Commission, there was a venerable impersonation of reason, of profound knowledge of public law and polity, and of that unquestioned benevolence of character which, when combined with reason and knowledge, is the sum of excellence. Other members of the Commission might be named without a shade of disparagement in the view even of a Trade Unionist. Working men, in short, may freely purge their minds of all suspicion that the questions affecting their interests do not receive in these high Inquiries a thorough and impartial examination, and may revert to the conclusions of successive Commissions, and to the ample records in which these proceedings have been embodied as to a fount of wise understanding and suggestion as regards the rights, the obligations, and the conditions of all true and possible prosperity, of labour.

The Inquiry of 1867-9, and the attending legislation of 1870, in which various important recommendations of the Commissioners were quietly ignored and set aside by Parliament in favour of provisions more indulgent and pleasing to the Unionists, had not been more than a few months completed, when, upon cases emerging in the Courts—particularly the case of London gasmen, who were found not entitled to commit a breach of contract in large bodies without rendering themselves liable not only to ordinary fine or damage, but to criminal consequences as conspirators in an unlawful purpose—the Unions at once began an agitation for a new Inquiry into what seemed to them gross inequalities of the civil and criminal law. This gave occasion for the appointment of the Royal Commission on the Master and Servant Act, the Criminal Law Amendment Act, and the common law of Conspiracy. This Inquiry simply brought up anew the critical questions that had been investigated to the core by the Royal Commission of 1867 ; and there was little or nothing to be expected from it but some amendments of statutory detail, in which the plank of reform was so narrow that, in giving an inch of right in one direction, there might be danger of giving an ell of wrong in another to the working man. This second Royal Commission has just completed its labours, and has been followed by legislation in which, as in the former case, the conclusions of the Commissioners have been again set aside in favour of something or other deemed more satisfactory for the moment to the Unionists.

It would be idle here to anticipate what shall afterwards have to be more closely examined. But no doubt can remain that in these two Inquiries there is a full exhibition of the Trade-Union Question in its various phases, of the state of law to which the agitating Unions aspire, and of the principles of equal right and liberty, and of public good, by which such aspirations on the part of clubs and societies of workmen are bounded. It would seem desirable, therefore,

that the great body of evidence, and of legal and practical
reason, thus collected and recorded in an authentic form,
should be popularly understood, and should be so duly
reflected upon that its wholesome uses may be realised in
public opinion and in the future course of affairs. The
chief question is how far the Trade Unions have of late
years been pursuing a right or wrong course; and the chief
duty is to distinguish the right course from the wrong. It
will be observed that the bent of the new type of Unionism
is to look upon the redress of labour as a matter chiefly of
politics and legislation to be overtaken by a system of Trade-
Union agitation on the largest scale. But experience runs
much counter to this current of Unionism, and fully estab-
lishes, indeed, the fact that the redress of labour depends on
conditions and laws over which politics and legislation have
little control. The Union wrecks of the last two years, and
the vast amount of funds squandered in hopeless strivings
against an ebb of commerce, over which Queen, Lords, and
Commons have no more power than Canute had over the
flowing tide, are sufficient proof that there is much more
implied in the redress and good of labour than our cotemporary Trade-Union philosophy has apprehended, and that
Trade-Union leaders going in and out of Parliament,
fomenting and upholding these desperate struggles as if
the relations of capital and labour could be solved by any
action of theirs or of Parliament, are about the most ghastly
spectres that could flit across the path of the working
classes. If the following pages, proceeding in the light of
the two Royal Commissions of Inquiry referred to, and of
such other indisputable *data* as there may be occasion to
adduce, should help to make this more clear, they will have
served a good, and even a great, purpose.

It is difficult to avoid speaking in a general way of " the
Trade Unions " as if these bodies were all amenable to the
same remarks; whereas the fact is that there are many
Trade Unions in the kingdom—and these some of the oldest
and most successful Unions—to which much that has to
be said is scarcely in any degree applicable. This is a consideration which the reader will be able to carry along with

him. The distinction between a right and wrong course of Unionism is to be observed throughout.

To any one, indeed, who can carry back his recollections and his sympathies with the working classes thirty or forty years, there is a fragrance pleasant to recall in the benevolence and *esprit de corps* of the trades. There was the friendly aid to a brother member of the trade in sickness or distress ; the care to maintain the skill and efficiency of the craft ; the welcome and support given to fellow-workmen out on travel for work. Now-a-days one is not apt to associate much dignity with "the tramp ;" and no doubt in the olden days, as now, there were some who tramped too much and too long. But in past times a young man bred in a country town or village was seldom deemed master of his trade till he had visited some of its chief seats and had worked in some of the most renowned shops. However poor he might be, he could set out on this tour of improvement, under difficulties of travel not conceivable by the present generation, yet confident that his trade would sustain him, and that his fellow-craftsmen would everywhere secure him a spell of work if they could. Many a British workman, when there were neither steamboats nor railways, wayfared to most of the capitals of Europe, and brought back an insight and practice in his handicraft that was not only an armour to himself, but improved his fellow-workmen, and enriched the industrial art of the country. There was a " freemasonry " in the trades that enabled working men with scarce a coin in their pockets to accomplish such feats ; and though it may not be recovered in its old forms, yet the spirit of it is undying, and may be as useful to British industry now as ever, if our workmen should only choose to give it a sound and wholesome development. But those were times when the trades looked forth with a free, bold, and generous glance over the whole sphere of commerce ; when they had not yet learned to regard every employer as an enemy, and had not ceased to esteem every workman, from whatever quarter he might come, as a brother ; when the action of the Unions was centrifugal and self-preserving, without being exclusive or inhuman, and had not assumed the violent centripetal force of recent times, rending and stripping up the largest centres of employment at home, and smiting down every workman seeking employment from the next town or the next street as a "black-neb," a "knob-stick," or any other term of reproach which it is so easy for one workman to cast on another.

Trade Unionism has undergone of late years a great transformation in the features of it most familiar to the public ; and on the nature and tendencies of this transformation there seems strong ground of appeal to the collective Unions, to the members and leaders of the Unions, to the working classes in general, and to the whole body of public opinion.

II.

OBJECTS OF THE UNIONS.

THE Royal Commission of 1867-9 had to inform itself fully of the organisation and rules of the Trade Unions. The constitution and laws of the Societies were produced in many cases when called for in the course of the Inquiry. But in addition a series of questions were addressed to 332 secretaries of Trade Unions, intended to elicit the same kind of information, and to this official circular answers were returned by forty-five Societies in the list. These and other documents of a valuable character have been printed, and form an essential part of the evidence to which it is necessary to refer.

Nevertheless a Royal Commission of Inquiry has chiefly to do with personal witnesses of more or less authority, who, coming forward of their own accord, represent the active interest taken in the questions under consideration; and the first point of the Inquiry, as practically unfolded, was to discover the objects which the Trade Unions propose to themselves, and to take the definition of these objects from the lips of their own chief officers, who thus appeared in an active and representative form. Unless we can know what the deliberately proposed objects of the Trade Unions are, we can know nothing of these Societies; and readers must here exercise some patience if they should wish to be informed from the only authoritative source.

MISUNDERSTANDING AS TO OBJECTS.

Now, it is remarkable that the first witness called, Mr.
Robert Applegarth, general secretary of the Amalgamated
Society of Carpenters and Joiners, placed the objects of his
Association on a wholly benefit basis. Support of members
in case of sickness, accident, or superannuation ; burial of
members and their wives ; aid to emigration; loss of tools
by fire, water, or theft ; relief to members out of work or in
cases of extreme distress, are the only objects which Mr.
Applegarth, quoting from the constitution of his Society,
could assign to it. Of course, there is the deceptive particular here of relief to "members out of work," which in a
bye-clause is made to signify 15s. a week out of the funds
to "any free or non-free member or members leaving his or
"their employment under circumstances satisfactory to the
"branch of executive council," and which may receive a
most elastic interpretation when strikes are in question. But
no one reading Mr. Applegarth's preliminary evidence could
imagine that the Amalgamated Carpenters and Joiners was
more than a mutual benefit society of a most praiseworthy
character. The second witness, the late Mr. William Allan,
secretary of the greater Society of Amalgamated Engineers,
and who is entitled to be named with all respect, gave
practically the same account of the objects of that Association. The contributions of 33,600 members, of which
there was so far an accruing surplus, were obtained for relief
to sick and superannuated members, funeral expenses, allowances to widows of members, and allowances in cases of
accident. There was also a large disbursement to members
"out of employment ;" but strikes and self-inflicted idleness,
according to Mr. Allan's evidence, were strictly guarded in
the Society of Engineers. His account was, that a number
of men going out on strike in any town must not only have
the approval of the district committee, but must obtain the
sanction of the Executive Council before they could have
any access to the funds. The question of " out of employment," according to the rules of the Amalgamated Engineers, has to pass through several stages of deliberation

before it can obtain final authority, and this is a wise enough provision. But Mr. Allan implied that if the strike was intended to resist a reduction of wages in any locality it would receive a much more easy authorisation than if its object were to enforce an advance of wages; and there are communistic features in the interior regulations of the Society,—such as hostility to piece-work; heavy fines imposed on any member doing piece-work who fails to share his earnings with others working on the job; and a strong action of the Society to secure the employment of its members in preference to, and in exclusion of anybody else,— which have a curiously monastic aspect. Yet no one could infer from Mr. Allan's preliminary evidence that the Amalgamated Engineers are more than a mutual benefit society, or extensive cloister of people bent on providing for their wants by leaning on each other in a legitimate way, in so far as it may be voluntary, and satisfactory to themselves. It is equally characteristic, however, of the evidence of Mr. Allan and Mr. Applegarth that when further questioned as to the financial sufficiency of the funds of their Societies for the purposes in view, they at once lowered the " benefit objects " so prominent in the constitutions of their Societies, and declared them to be altogether subordinate to the " trade objects " of which the constitutions say little or nothing at all. The Amalgamated Society of Engineers, according to Mr. Allan, could not afford its advantages to the members if the trade and benefit funds had to be kept separate. " The union in " one society of trade and benefit purposes." he said, " is " beneficial. The latter soften men's minds. and render " them more careful with respect to the former." Mr. Allan was a man of some thinking power, and in these words undoubtedly touched a philosophical conclusion, viz., that any large body of men of ordinary intelligence, who have accumulated by laborious saving considerable funds for benefit purposes, will in proportion as they appreciate these purposes be softened or tempered in mind as to any loose squander of such funds on other purposes, and on what may prove the " cast of a die." That Mr. Allan's wisdom has found some practical response in the action of the Amalgamated

Society of Engineers there may also be no reason to dispute.
But it failed to reach the financial obliquity of raising funds
for one class of purposes, and leaving them open to be
expended on impulse for a wholly different class of purposes.
Mr. Applegarth also said, though in contradiction of what
he had before described from the written constitution of the
Society of Carpenters and Joiners to be its sole objects,
that theSociety, strictly speaking, should not be regarded as
a benefit society at all. "It is 'pure and simple' a trade
"society, although members support it the better on account
" of its benefits unconnected with trade purposes." There
is thus considerable confusion, even in these highest types
of Trade-Union organisation, as to what the constitutional
objects of these bodies are. A certain class of beneficial
purposes, known and measurable, are put in the fore-front of
the rules, and yet found on cross-examination to be subordinate in practice to other purposes that are left vague
and undefined ; so that to arrive at the objects proposed to
themselves by Trade Unions, as the Royal Commission experienced, becomes at the outset a task of unusual difficulty.

The next witness, Mr. Richard Harnott, secretary of the
Friendly Society of Operative Masons, carries us a little
farther into the subject. Mr. Harnott, though secretary of
a Union of 278 branches, which puts "Friendly" into its
title, and in which one would expect to find the benefit
purposes in great practical predominance, gives at once a
frank statement of the real objects of his society. The
members pay 4_d_. or 7½_d_. per week to the common fund of
the Union. Those who pay 7½_d_. are entitled to 10_s_. per
week when they are sick in addition to the trade advantages ; those who pay 4_d_. are entitled to the trade advantages only. The separation of trade and benefit objects,
and of trade and benefit funds, which appears from the
evidence of Mr. Allan and Mr. Applegarth, to be so difficult
or impossible, or so injurious to the Unions, had not presented itself in the same light to the Friendly Society of
Operative Masons. When asked what the objects of his
society were, Mr. Harnott answered,—" To protect the
" members from all encroachments by employers, as well as

" to maintain the rate of wages generally ; that was the origin
" of it, and is still the object of it." There can be little
doubt that in this answer there is an honest, and at the same
time temperate statement of the principal object of many
of the Trade Unions. Mr. Edwin Coulson, secretary of
the London Operative Bricklayers' Society, gives the same
reply :—" The objects refer to trade purposes, with burial
and travelling relief to members." Mr. George Houseley,
general secretary of the Sheffield Bricklayers' Society, also
in its title " Friendly," gives the priority to " trade purposes," and adds, " partly for accidents and deaths."
When asked whether it was originally established for the
friendly purposes, he answered, " I am unable to say." But
out of a yearly income of 5,964*l.* there were paid for deaths
alone 1,362*l.*, and yet the society's reserve fund was only
3,649*l.* Mr. Houseley would not allow that all the money
thus unaccounted for went for " trade purposes "—one delegate meeting cost 1,088*l.*,—but the " friendly " finance even
with this explanation being unexplainable, on the question
being put, " Is one purpose of the Society to raise wages
and lessen the hours of labour ? " he at once replied,
" That is it." Mr. William Macdonald, honorary secretary
of the Manchester Operative House-Painters' Alliance, embracing forty-four towns, gave as the objects of his Union,
" the general objects of a Trade Society, combined with an
accident and burial society," with little financial reserve for
the latter purposes, but with considerable experience in
" strikes " and " negotiations with employers " conducted on
an exceptionally small weekly subscription of 3*d.* during
nine months and 1*d.* during three months of the year.
Mr. Robert Last, general secretary of the Operative House
Carpenters' and Joiners' Society, with 150 branches and
10.000 members, a yearly income of 15,000*l.*, and a reserve
fund of seldom more and sometimes less than 500*l.* in hand,
had no hesitation in saying that while his Society existed
both for trade and benefit purposes, its prime object was
" to enable the members to resist the encroachments of un-
" principled employers." Of such encroachments he gave
as example a " discharge note " in the Midland counties,

C

which, as may be gathered from the evidence, was a cer-
tificate that a workman required to take with him from one
employer to another, and may have had some disagreeable
incidents. The large annual income and the small reserve
fund of this Society would seem to indicate an almost
frantic warfare for "trade purposes," in which employers as
well as workmen may have become much excited. The
examination of Mr. Last, ended in a controversy between
h m and Mr. Applegarth, the more national representative
of Carpenters and Joiners, as to the value of foreign
" doors " imported into the Midland counties, of which
Mr. Applegarth averred that they were good work, and of
which Mr. Last, proceeding on what he had inferred from a
previous conversation with Mr. Applegarth, maintained the
contrary. Though this dispute was settled amicably between the two in a somewhat Pickwickian sense, yet it was
not without a certain grave significance ; because if such
articles as doors, whether of good or bad quality, should be
imported from abroad under the pressure of trade disputes,
nothing could prove more certainly that there is a loose
screw in the Trade-Union procedure.

The Royal Commission had not only great difficulty in
ascertaining the precise objects of Trade Unions in this
inextricable blending of " trade " and " benefit " purposes,
but when the " trade " element appeared clearly from the
evidence to be the predominant object of Trade Unions,
the difficulty of the Commission became scarcely less to
discover what this predominant trade object really implied.

Mr. Charles Williams, general secretary of the Plasterers'
Society, centre in Liverpool, 128 branches, and 8,000 members, on being asked what the objects of his society were,
replied—" Protection of trade, burying of our dead, and
relief in case of accident." As there was nothing in this
case to show for burial or relief fund, Mr. Thomas Hughes,
Member of Commission, appears to have given up further
query, and Mr. Roebuck assumed the examination, which,
in the concisest form, was as follows : —

What do you mean by " protection of trade ? "—Protecting it in the
same way as I would protect property.

That explains nothing—what do you mean?—Making the best of my property I can by all legal means.

That is protection of property, but what is "protection of trade?"—Simply seeing that there are no undue encroachments upon it.

What do you mean by "undue encroachments upon trade?"—A man taking away from me something he has no right to.

But I want to know, without illustration, what your property here is?—I have learned a trade, that trade is my capital, and I have a right to protect it.

Is there any capital in labour?—Is there not? It is my capital.

Out of this *cul-de-sac* there was obviously no escape by further question or answer, the line of catechism having passed by successive leaps, without practical sequence of any kind, from "protection of trade" to "protection of property," and from that to "protection of capital," in which ultimate position Mr. Williams settled down confidently in the conviction that he and others having learned a trade, were entitled to look upon the trade as their "property" or their "capital," without respect to others engaged in the trade, to the successions of capital and skill invested in the trade, and, in short, to all in the trade who had gone before or might be coming after them. Mr. Frederic Harrison, another Member of Commission, in this dilemma put the question—"Do you mean by 'protecting trade' maintaining "the old advantages, and endeavouring to acquire new "advantages for the operative plasterers?" To which Mr. Williams readily replied, "Yes, as near as that is possible."

MR. A. MACDONALD AS TO OBJECTS.

Mr. Alexander Macdonald, President of the National Miners' Association, and now M.P. for Stafford, admitted that the Colliers' Unions in Scotland were established, as a rule, for trade purposes only. The objects of his National Association were—" First, legislation for the better manage-" ment of mines; second, compensation from employers for " accidents; third, assistance to all members and districts " when unjustly dealt with by employers; fifth, to make the " hours of labour not more than eight in the twenty-four for " all miners in the United Kingdom; sixth, relief allowance " to aged and infirm members, and members permanently

" injured in the mines." Mr. Normansell gave a similar account of the objects of the South Yorkshire Miners' Association, "better legislation" and "assisting miners in deal- " ing with their employers, by securing them allowances when " out of work," being at the head of the list. Mr. Macdonald testified that in the Scotch Colliers' Unions the place of the benefit funds in other trade associations had been supplied by workmen having private benefit societies of their own. Mr. William Garner, Secretary of the West Bromwich Millmen's Association, stated the same fact in regard to that body. The proposal to establish "sick-benefit" was quashed, because of the members being connected with other benefit societies.[1]

To elicit distinctly the objects of the Unions as assumedly reasonable bodies of men, is a matter of the first importance in all that regards the Trade-Union question. The curious and involved mixture of benefit and trade purposes, and the perversion of funds subscribed for definite benefit to indefi- nite trade purposes, form the main source of all the diffi- culty of the Unions, not only among themselves, but as regards the law. Because when the Judges, in any case affecting more especially the finance of the Unions, find that the funds of the association have, of system and with apparent consent, been squandered on purposes not defined in its rules, there is no basis of law or reason on which they can give judgment. The matter wears on its face a form of outlawry, and the parties present themselves in the courts as a congregation of fools and knaves between whom it is impossible to adjudi- cate. How deeply this disorder penetrates the Trade Unions may be seen in the case of the Amalgamated Engineers and the Amalgamated Carpenters and Joiners, which do on a considerable scale carry out their benefit obligations and have very large financial interests at stake to that end, and yet when brought to question through their chief officers de- clare that benefit objects have but a secondary, and that trade objects have the first place in their scheme of action. This equivocation runs in various gradations through all the

[1] Farther on, reference shall have to be made to "question and answer" in the Minutes of Evidence, but for the foregoing see *Eleventh and Final Report of the Royal Commissioners*, vol. ii.

Unions till it comes to Mr. Macdonald and the colliers, and there it is honestly confessed that trade objects are the sole objects of the combination.

FINDING OF THE COMMISSIONERS.

The Royal Commission in its Report, defines the objects of Trade Unions to be " in general of a twofold character :— " First, those of an ordinary friendly or benefit society; " secondly, those of a trade society proper—viz., to watch " over and promote the interests of the working classes in " the several trades, and especially to protect them against " the undue advantage which the command of a large capital " is supposed by them to give to the employers of labour." But of these twofold objects the Commissioners observe that " the last referred to are, in the great majority of exist- " ing Unions, the main objects of the members in asso- " ciating together;" and that it has simply been " found " desirable by the promoters of Trade Unions to combine " with these objects the functions of a friendly or benefit " society. Additional members and additional funds are " thus obtained;" and a stronger hold is acquired over the obedience of the members " to the orders of the Union issued in what it deems the interests of trade"—disobedience involving expulsion, and forfeiture of all the benefits to which a member would be entitled, " it may be, " from a long course of subscription, continued with the " very object of securing to himself those benefits." This is as strictly accurate a definition of the " Objects of Trade Unions" as can be attained from the evidence of the leaders and chief officers of these bodies themselves ; and there can be little error in the conclusion that to resist reductions of wages, to enforce advances of wages, and to shorten the hours of labour, are the main objects of all the more active and enterprising Trade Societies. Round this stem there is a garnishing of mutual benefit insurance, more or less developed, and more or less cultivated or neglected in the various Unions, but on the whole purely auxiliary and subsidiary to the main designs.

III.

METHODS OF THE UNIONS.

HAVING cleared up sufficiently the "Objects of Trade Unions," the next step is to inquire into the " Methods" by which the Unions propose to attain, and do endeavour to attain, the purposes for which they are constituted. The objects are twofold—viz., trade objects and mutual benefit objects. But though the latter in many cases are either the only objects set forth, or are given the highest prominence in the constitution of the societies, yet by general admission the trade objects are the principal objects, and substantially the only objects, which the more active Unions care to pursue. In this respect, they require the first attention. The trade objects, as defined from the evidence, are " to resist re- " ductions of wages, to enforce advances of wages, and to " shorten the hours of labour." [1] Besides these, there are many minor objects of trade regulation promoted and en- forced by the rules of the Unions, but generally they are intended to operate towards the three results above-named, and are in themselves mostly of the nature of " methods," or means to an end, and will come up in ample specimen, and in their proper relation, in the course of the subject.

INVOLUTION OF METHODS.

What, then, are the methods by which the Trade Unions endeavour " to resist reductions of wages, to enforce advances " of wages, and to shorten the hours of labour," with other objects of the same general and ultimate tenour? The

---

[1] See *Report of the Royal Commissioners*, par. 28. The Commis- sioners report that "a further object is to bring about a more equal division of work among members of the trade." But this passes into detail, which, however questionable, need not be pressed into the general "trade objects" of the Unions.

Royal Commissioners in their Report define the action of /
the Unions as of two kinds, viz., direct and indirect—the
direct being the strike or the combined demand with strike at
the back of it, and the indirect being gradual but systematic
attempts (1) to limit the number of workmen employed in
any branch of industry, so as "to create a monopoly of
labour," and (2) to repress competition among the privileged
workmen themselves. The distinctions thus made by the
Commissioners are both exact and comprehensive enough
to be generally followed in an analysis of the subject. The
truth is that there is a positive method, recognised and
practised by the Unions, of taking a stand for an object,
whether it be to resist reduction, or enforce advance of
wages, or to shorten the hours of labour, or to accomplish
one, two, or all three of these objects; and, if the stand
under threat of a strike be not at once successful, of going
at once into strike or cessation from labour, whether the
sphere may be large or small, local or general, in which the
stand has been taken. And there is also a negative method
of the Unions, more important even than the positive, because
it is more constant, minute, and elaborate, and is preparatory
of the positive method, viz., "limiting the number of workmen
" in any branch of industry," and " repressing the competi-
" tion of the limited number of workmen among them-
" selves," as the Royal Commissioners report to her Majesty,
yet branching out into such a great variety of minor regulations to these ends as the Commissioners could hardly be
expected to follow in detail. But, in point of fact, this
negative—or restricting, prohibiting, and regulating—method
of the Unions cannot be separated by any hard-and-fast line
from the positive method of combined demand and strike,
because at any point of the long chain of regulations the
positive method may be, and in practice is, systematically
applied. The discrimination of "direct" and " indirect"
methods of the Unions by the Royal Commissioners can only
be recognised, therefore, as a didactic distinction. In practice
they are completely fused into one. The " direct" is ever
ready to come to the assistance of the " indirect" on the
smallest scale; and the " indirect" is always attempting to

prepare a sphere for the action of the " direct " on a larger
scale.   Union workmen throw down their tools, and go
into strike, because of some breach of Union regulations in
a shop or work, which must appear to them and to their
councils to be important as some infinitesimal part of a
general policy, but which, to all but themselves, appear
utterly silly, or, as sometimes happens, utterly noxious.

DIRECT METHODS SHORT OF STRIKING.

With this preliminary understanding of what is really imported by such terms as "direct and indirect," or other
terms, by which the methods of the Trades Unions may be
distinguished, it is necessary to advert to a potent form of
the " direct " process of the Unions seldom noticed, because
it applies for the most part to individual workmen, whether
Unionists or non-Unionists, and is generally successful without resort to anything so formidable as a combined demand
or strike.   When a combined demand is made, or a strike
is either threatened or takes place, the world hears of it ;
but there is a constant direct action of the Unions, with
strike in the immediate background, by which individual
workmen are injured or ruined, and employers are over-
borne in their sense of right, and in their good feeling
towards the victims, of which the world never hears, though
such cases may be of weekly occurrence in every workshop
or place of employment under Union regulations in the
Kingdom.   Whatever occurs in this way is the result of
Trade-Union bureaucracy, and proceeds silently and un-
observed, however cruel and unjust it may be, like the procedure of other bureaucracies.

On this point take, first, the evidence of the late Mr.
Allan, secretary of the Amalgamated Society of Engineers,
which must be admitted to be one of the most intelligent
and well-disciplined Unions, and in its action may be believed
to present the Trade-Union policy in its most reasonable form.
To question 787, Mr. Allan replied : " We have no rule
" which fixes the rate of weekly wages between the masters

" and the men, but if a member believed that he was not
" getting a proper rate of wages, the society would encour-
" age him in objecting, that is to say, would pay him his
" benefit while out of employment." In other words, the
man would be told to strike, and to draw his strike allowance in the meanwhile. But as this could not go on for
ever in individual cases, on the question being put, supposing the man to be willing to work somewhat under the
Union scale of wages, rather than live on "strike pay,"
what then? Mr. Allan replied, " He would stand a good
chance of being excluded." In short, of being dismembered, disunionised, and bereft, without reason or equity, of
all part or lot in his contributions to the friendly funds of the
Amalgamated Engineers. In a prior examination, Mr. Allan
had said, with respect to the relation of his Union to non-
society men and ejected members, that "there are such
" things, for example, as not interfering with a man, but at
" the same time refusing to speak to him, or hold intercourse
" with him. If the party had committed himself in some
" way in connection with the trade we should put him into
" ' Coventry.' " [1] The result of which plainly is, that no
non-society or excluded society engineer can hope to live or
work with any comfort among the truly amalgamated
confrères; and that if, as Mr. Allan bore testimony, "from
two-thirds to three-fourths are members of the Union," all
but the whole trade must be closed against the unhappily excluded third or fourth of its members. This can only be
deemed a mild type of the silent and comparatively occult
operation of the " direct method " of Unionism, because it
is well known to every reader of the newspapers that the
presence of a single " black-neb " or "scab " in any place of
work is frequently the cause of a cessation of work. Mr.
George Smith, of Smith & Taylor, contractors for the new
India and Foreign Offices, indicated, from the employers'
point of view, the effect upon workmen of this elaborate
effort of the Unions to maintain what Mr. Allan called " a
" proper rate of wages" to all in the employment. He says,[2]
" One consequence is that when a reduction takes place the

[1] Q. 628.   [2] 2832-51.

" books are gone through, and all men who are incapable of
" earning as much as others are picked out and discharged.
" The uniform rate thus throws out a vast number of men
" who might otherwise be receiving fair wages, and who are,
" as it were, a sort of outcasts, who go from shop to shop,
" and ultimately pass to the workhouse." If a workman in
the Union thinks he should have 2s. or 3s. a week more, and
the council approves, he may make the claim, and have 15s.
out of the funds, much less probably than one-half his actual
wages, till he succeeds in the other object. If he should tire of
this purgatory, and be disposed to resume work at his old rate
of wages, it will be at his peril as a member of the Union, and
he will be in danger of being "excluded." This is a form of
the case when wages are rather on the rise, and the Union is
straining its diplomacy to pull up all its members to a higher
and more general uniformity of wages. But, on the other
hand, when employment is on the decline, and reductions
have to be made, the effect pointed out by Mr. George
Smith occurs, and all the less efficient workmen find themselves at once discharged by their employers, and disbanded
by their Unions, outcasts from their trade on both sides,
waifs wandering about between shops and the workhouse in
the most pitiful helplessness. It is to be conceived, therefore, that under the fair exterior, even of the Amalgamated
Engineers, the bureaucratic operation of that body may be
trampling down many members and non-members into
pauperism, whose sad fate is never heard of.

But, proceeding farther into the Union evidence, much
more pronounced views are expressed on this point than are
to be found in the evidence of the late Mr. Allan. Mr.
George Howell, of the bricklayers, for example, on being
questioned[1] whether his Union would refuse to work with a
non-Union man who was receiving less than the Union rate
of wages, replied, " Yes, they would," which means, of course,
a throwing down of tools, and a strike. On being reinterro-
gated by Mr. Mathews to the same purpose, Mr. Howell
adhered firmly to his "Yes." Mr. W. Macdonald, of the
Manchester House-Painters' Alliance—a trade in which there

[1] Q. 1744.

is scope for much variety of talent, and the competent members of which appear to have objection to labourers and hobbledehoys being brought in to do even slap-dash work—on being asked[1] whether a superior painter, willing to work at lower wages than the society was driving at, would be equally objectionable, replied, " Yes," the same. " We interfere with him because he interferes with us. We have as much right to refuse work as he has to work." ' The same idea has still cruder forms ; and coming down, for example, to the Colliers' Unions, where the question of wages pursues a mysterious way of its own, and the rate of pay at which it may be the desire or interest of men to work has little or no place, any one "black-nebbing" is suppressed simply by physical force. But taking the more consolidated Trade Unions, in which constancy of purpose and self-control may be believed most to prevail, and of which the Society of Amalgamated Engineers has been our starting-point, there can manifestly be no correct apprehension of what the Royal Commissioners call the "direct method" of the Unions, without taking into account the daily and habitual exercise of the power of the Unions in the case of individual workmen, dismembering society men and excluding non-society men to the end of extruding both from the field of labour, which is all the more effective because it is noiseless, and noiseless because it is seldom or never resisted. The battle here is one against a thousand, and the one, of course, falls without a struggle or a cry. The pretexts on which this power is exercised are usually small ; they are often not important enough in any workshop to stir the most combative of employers to resistance ; and the smaller they are the more certain it is that the deputation from the Union, or the simple notice from its Executive Council will succeed. This action of the Unions operates with the steadiness of a machine not only over the general domain of the trades, but in every separate shop or employment of each trade ; and the direct action of the Unions, and its bearing on the interests of the working classes, cannot be understood without taking this form of it fully into view.

[1] Q. 2363.

Mr. Edward Hughes, a deputy from the Master Builders'
Association of Liverpool, and a witness before the Royal
Commission on the Labour Laws, setting aside the causes of
general strikes in the country, gave the following enumera-
tion of the grounds of local and sectional strikes in his own
trade, which obtain little or no publicity, and may not issue
even in strike, but which express demands constantly urged
by the Trade-Union bureaucracy with strike as their compelling force : —

(1.) Advance in one degree or other of wages.
(2.) Reduction of hours.
(3.) Objection to foremen.
(4.) Objection to non-Union men.
(5.) Objection to Union men in arrears to the Union.
(6.) Objection to work with men receiving extra wages for efficiency,
termed " blood-money."
(7.) Objection to machine work.
(8.) Objection to work imported from other districts of the country,
such as quarry-worked stone.
(9.) Objection to machine-made bricks, and bricks made by non-
Unionists.
(10.) Objection to a Clerk of Works taking a plumb-line in his hand
to try if a wall be plumb, the Unionists contending that they have the
right to use the plumb-line, and that the Clerk of Works has the right
only to look on.
(11.) Objection to the number of apprentices, and to apprentices not
being sons of men in the trade.
(12.) Objection to having two ladders, one for labourers to ascend,
and the other to descend.
(13.) Objections to piece-work.
(14.) Refusing to allow tile or brick floors to be laid by any but
brick-setters.
(15.) Objections by labourers to the employer appointing his own
foreman. *Et cetera.*

One may stop here almost as much aghast as Macbeth,
when seeing Banquo's progeny :—

" Another yet ! A sixteenth ! I'll see no more ! "

But, looking in the most serious frame at this finicalness
of Trade-Union rule, and its intensely explosive power of
producing disagreements, strikes, and miseries in petty but

infinite detail, is there anything in the whole realm of literature or tradition to be likened to it, unless perchance it may
be such undivine interpretations of the Sabbath law as
were indulged by the Jewish doctors two thousand years ago?
The Rabbis of that time said that the grass must not be
walked upon lest it might be bruised, which would be a sort
of "thrashing," and that a flea must not be caught while it
hops about, since that would obviously be a kind of "hunting;" and seeing that both thrashing and hunting were
contrary to the Sabbath rest, all acts falling under these categories must be contrary to the Divine rule !

The more commonly known "direct method" of the
Unions—or as the Royal Commissioners say, "what is
termed 'strike,' or a simultaneous cessation from work on
the part of the workmen"—is familiar enough in its public
outlines, and the only necessary observation at this place
seems to be that the power of strike, which breaks out in
large events of which all can judge, is also a latent power
exercised with constant practical effect, and with little public
manifestation, in the bureaucracy of the Unions. Strikes,
lock-outs, and trade outrages therewith connected, are important enough for a separate chapter.

INDIRECT METHODS.

The "indirect methods" of the Unions, the general
spirit of which, as expressed by the Royal Commissioners,
is "to limit the number of workmen to be employed in any
"branch of industry, and to repress competition among the
"workmen themselves," branch out into a great variety of
minute rules and regulations that may not be exhaustively
enumerated, but the effect of all of them is certainly enough,
as the Royal Commissioners have reported, "to create"
what is termed "a monopoly of labour, with its attendant
power to command a higher rate of wages," as well as
shorter hours, and other main objects of the Unions. The
Union leaders, on the other hand, in their evidence, associate
these minute regulations with great moral and social ends,
such as the development of a fair amount of work as a

standard to which both the weaker and stronger workmen should conform and earn the same wages; the independence of workmen as a body; the improved health, comfort, and moral habits accruing from this independence. Though it is difficult to discern what connexion there may be between these results and the regulations in question, yet in regard to some of the regulations at least, if not all, one can see that they deal with matters in which working men as a body, and individually, are entitled to concern themselves and to have a voice, but scarcely in the form of absolute rules of labour, or as one section bearing down by force another section of the working body.

Some of these labour-limiting and anti-competing regulations are common to nearly all the Unions. Others are born of particular trades, and reproduce the general purpose in amusing varieties, such as the "anti-chasing rule" among the masons, and the "anti-laying-bricks-with-two-hands" among the bricklayers. It is absolutely necessary to abridge and generalise remarks on this jungle of Trade-Union regulations, and let us begin by dismissing what is the most common regulation of all, and one sufficiently ascertained, viz., excluding non-Unionists and dismembered Unionists from employment in their trades, so far as they can be excluded, in order to come to such peculiar features of the Trade-Union code as the following:—

I. LIMITING THE NUMBER OF APPRENTICES.

The Unions have taken up strong ground on this point, and yet ground that is never quite definite or intelligible. Mr. Allan, of the Amalgamated Engineers, said before the Royal Commission, that "his society set its face against the "employment of apprentices beyond a certain proportion, "to prevent an overplus of labour and to keep wages up."[1] But on being asked what the limit was, he said "the num- "ber of apprentices was not fixed by any rule, was regulated "by trade custom, and depended on the class of work."[2] On being further interrogated, Mr. Allan let out a secret

[1] Q. 879-84, 925-9.   [2] 905-8.

importing more the spirit of a close corporation than the
spirit of a wholesome philanthropic interest in the cause of
labour. He said, "Workmen seek to control the appren-
" tice system, because in many establishments they find it
" difficult to introduce their own sons to the trade as they
" would wish."[1] This line of hereditary succession is mo-
delled so closely on that of the Peerage, that it is liable,
when carried down into all the trades of the country, to
infinite complications, and, if it should ever obtain legal
force, to suits in Chancery of which there would be neither
limit nor solution. Mr. Allan, on being asked whether his
society would go so far as certain workmen of Sheffield in
not allowing a nephew as an apprentice because his father
had not been in the trade, gave a frank negative, and, as his
own opinion, thought "such conduct very absurd."[2] Apprentices failing in the direct line from father to son, Mr.
Allan was of opinion that collateral heirs ought to be admitted, as in the case of the Crown or the Peerage. Other
Union leaders waive any principle of limitation of apprentices, while admitting that it is a constant method of Trade-
Union action. Mr. Richard Harnott, for example, of the
Operative Masons, said, that "what is a reasonable number
" is left entirely to the discretion of the workmen in each
" shop, who complain to the lodge, and the lodge then com-
" municates with the employer."[3] Mr. Macdonald, of the
Manchester House-Painters' Alliance, said, "an old agree-
" ment between employers and workmen was to have one
" apprentice to five journeymen, but *in fact the number*
" *is now rather below than above the mark.*"[4] Mr. John
Macdonald, a master brick-builder of Glasgow, said that the
action of the workmen's Union with respect to apprentices
was a great grievance. "In June, 1865, the workmen re-
" solved that no master should employ more than five ap-
" prentices, whatever the number of workmen he might
" employ. After remonstrance the limit was extended to
" seven, to which the masters have unwillingly submitted."[5]
Yet Mr. Houseley, general secretary of Operative Brick-

[1] Q. 926.   [2] 928-34.   [3] 1087.
[4] 2313-2316.   [5] 3468, 3493-8.

layers, could say that "the society does not limit the number
of apprentices; a few lodges do, but it is not the rule."[1]
A singular chaos thus exists on a matter of the greatest possible interest between the head and tail, the central understanding and local self-will and action of the Unions. Mr.
Proudfoot, secretary of the Trades' Council of Glasgow,
suggests a further idea on the question of apprentices. He
says, "it is the journeymen who teach the boys. A master
" may have as many apprentices as he likes, but if he wants
" them taught he ought to pay for it; he pays a man wages
" for his work, not for teaching apprentices."[2] This remark
is valid to show some relation undiscovered by the Unions
between the number of journeymen and the number of apprentices, but it is quite invalid for Mr. Proudfoot's intention
that if a master pays a man for his hour or day's work, he
should also pay him over and above for any help or teaching
he gives to an apprentice; because it is quite clear that in
so far as a journeyman aids or teaches an apprentice he is
detracting so much from the other work for which his employer pays him. Besides, the boy helps him, if he
helps the boy. The difficulty is to see how, under views
which seem derived from the law of heritable succession on
the one hand and from the region of metaphysics on the
other, and yet are left wholly indefinite by the Unions themselves, any boy may be trained to a trade at all. Mr.
Macdonald, the master brick-builder of Glasgow, says, "an
" apprentice works among men but not under men, who
" may, however, direct (and ought, he thinks, to direct) a
" boy as to what he should do," at the same time avowing
the duty of the master or his foreman as regards the instruction of apprentices, where duty is plainly only another word
for interest.[3] But the harmony and co-operation of the
journeymen with masters and foremen would seem essential
to a comfortable and successful apprenticeship in any trade.

One naturally turns on a grave point of this kind to what
Mr. George Potter said. Mr. Potter, from his leading position in the Unionistic body, was repeatedly called, or voluntarily came before the Commission as an interpreter of

[1] Q. 2009.   [2] 8049-8058.   [3] 3670-7.

the policy of Trade Unions in its most perfect and cultivated form. But it was a little drawback on anything he said, that Mr. Potter always appeared on these occasions in two characters—as President of the London Working Men's Association, and as an humble member of the London Carpenters and Joiners' Society—and that to most questions put to him by the Commissioners he had two voices, one or other of which he selected at his own pleasure. On this question of apprenticeship, Mr. Potter spoke only as the humble London carpenter and joiner, and on that footing his reply was that his society " had no rule limiting the number of apprentices." Mr. Applegarth, a much more authentic representative of the carpenters and joiners of the kingdom, gave the same reply to question 247, but on being asked (248), " Is any " such rule observed in practice ? " his reply was, " If there " is any in practice, it is not in the *general* rules ; but in the " *working* rules the men put whatever they like into them, " and it rests between them and their employers as to " whether they are adopted." The utmost interference of local unions of workmen with the number of apprentices would thus appear to be provided for without any general direction on the subject from the higher sanhedrims. Yet, if this is to be matter of arbitrary regulation at all. the regulation would require above most others to proceed on some definite principle. It is clear that every trade, to avert its rapid decline, must bring up apprentices in proportion to the men who emigrate, die, or fall away from it ; and that if the trade be a thriving and extending trade, the number of apprentices must be increased in the same ratio, in order to sustain its means of extension. It is enough, however, to have thus pointed out from the evidence that to limit the number of apprentices is one of the " methods " of the Trade Unions, and that the effect, as the intent, of it must be to keep down the supply of qualified labour to the trades.

The question of apprenticeship, whether as regards the number of apprentices to be admitted to a trade, or the proportion of apprentices to the number of journeymen in a particular shop or work, may not easily be reduced to any fixed arithmetical rule beyond that practically determined by two

facts : (1), that employers who over-supply their works with
apprentices under any circumstances cannot find their interest in that course of procedure; and (2), that in a trade
where wages are rising, and the demand for more labour is
steadily increasing, the number of boys seeking to enter
such a trade will reasonably be increased, and that it is not
the interest of the journeymen in the trade, or of working-
class parents, whether of one trade or another, to place any
arbitrary arrest on this natural movement. The question,
moreover, especially as regards the demand of Union workmen to be paid extra for teaching or allowing apprentices,
differs materially in one trade as compared with another, and
depends much on the conditions under which work is practically conducted. Where piecework, for example, is the
rule, or workmen take out work from employers and are
their own masters in the details of its execution, the question
of apprenticeship passes under different conditions from
those which prevail when men are paid by the hour or
the day. Mr. Nasmyth who, like other chiefs of our great
engineering establishments, where talent and faculty are of
the greatest consequence, was a resolute advocate of piecework before the Royal Commission, put the question of
apprenticeship in the following light :—" When a man," he
said, " takes a piece of work on piece-pay, he often stipu-
" lates that he shall have two or three boys. The cleverest
" boys in the works are picked out, and the men pay these
" boys 2s. 6d. a week extra of themselves. It is not the
" boy paying the man, but the man paying the boy, and the
" effect of that has been to make every boy emulous of
" being picked out." [1] This is the more remarkable since
it relates to establishments wholly under the control of employers and their foremen, and does not embrace many
examples in the textile, hardware, and other manufactures,
where the employer gives out materials of work, and has no
direct control over apprentices or the number of apprentices.
The Trade Unions may be excused for not having arrived
at any definite conclusion on so complex a subject; but
that a " limitation of apprentices" should be sent forth with

[1] Q. 19,319.

the full authority of the Unions over all the trades of the country, must be admitted to be objectionable, and at variance in essential respects with any general improvement of the condition of the working classes.

2. PIECEWORK.

To the question, " Has your society any rule against piece-work ?" the Union witnesses gave almost unanimously an affirmative reply. It was evidently a point on which they had fully deliberated, and on which they were prepared to make strong argument. Fines are imposed in some Unions upon members who take piecework, and in many cases piecework has been banished from the shops. Mr. George Howell (Bricklayers) said, "it leads to scamping of work, and ultimately tends to break down wages"[1] Mr. Coulson, secretary of the same society, thought "the abolition of " piecework would put an end to dishonourable practices in " executing work."[2] Mr. Proudfoot said : " Scotch Unions, " as a general rule, discourage piecework by asking men " who take it whether they do not think that if many did " so the price of labour would fall." [3] There was a general testimony on the Union side as to the tendency of piece-work to end in inferior workmanship, and to encourage men to work long or irregular hours, and to fall into bad habits. Mr. Allan (Amalgamated Engineers), after a long cross-examination in which he admitted the excellence of the work in the Government and many private piecework estab-lishments, still adhered to his opinion that "as a general " rule the work done on piecework is inferior."[4] " The " almost total abolition of piecework in certain districts " has certainly not had the effect of making the work " worse." [5] But this opinion was not borne out from other sources. Mr. Alfred Mault, secretary of the General Builders' Association, while admitting the natural tendency of piece, as of contract work, to depreciate the quality of the work, observed "that this tendency may be guarded against in the selection of men to whom piecework is given," and condemned the interference of the Unions in this matter.[6]

[1] Q. 1680-5.　[2] 1552.　[3] 7999.　[4] 674.　[5] 733.　[6] 3182-9.

Mr. Robinson, of the renowned Atlas Works at Manchester, could say, "The plan of doing piecework in establishments "like ours has given us such a reputation that we get a "higher price than other firms. It is much easier to check "the *quality* than the *amount* of work." Mr. Abram S. Hewitt, an American ironmaster, said that "among the "larger number of mechanics in the United States there is "a preference for piecework; and in almost all works in "which it is possible to pay by piecework, the rule is to do "so. Had never heard of any objection to piecework from "the Trade Unions."[1] Our Unions are thus either in advance or rear of their American brethren on this point for one; and it may immediately be a grave question whether our Trade-Union democracy, in falling back on a communistic practice, or the American democracy, in following out its instinct of individual liberty, is more or less in the path of destined progress than the other. Mr. George Potter put the Union argument against piecework in this elevated point of view:—"Piecework should be discountenanced "because it is desirable for the health and vigour of mind "and body to limit the extent of labour to that to which the "human frame is ordinarily adapted;"[2] and there can be little doubt, to adopt somewhat plainer language, that the Unions are hostile to piecework, mainly because it does not comport with their general system of inducing a limited amount of work to which workmen of all capacities shall conform, the strong or energetic reining back their powers so as to meet the weak or the less willing at some half-way term, that may generally pass as "a fair average amount of work," though the former class should somewhat exceed and the latter fall somewhat short of it. But when a shop or band of workmen are watching each other to see how little they can all do, it is not likely that they will arrive at any great average performance. This, in reality, is a branch of Union action that falls under the category defined by the Royal Commissioners as "repressing competition among the Union workmen themselves," to which end, as shall presently be seen, various other forms of action are pursued.

[1] Q. 3889-90.   [2] 320.

3. " CHASING.

This term, though now, perhaps, more or less obsolete, may be conveniently used for various processes of the Unions to limit the amount of work done by a given number of men, after the given number of men available has itself been limited by the other processes already adverted to. It appears to have had its origin among the masons, where employers were believed to put strong and skilful men at the head of the scaffold lines as a stimulus to the rest ; in much the same way, it may be supposed, as the best and strongest reapers take the "head rig" in a harvest-field. It was not said that the men who could not keep pace with these lively stonemasons lost any wages, but it was averred that the latter had some extra pay for their " chasing," and that as they were merely breaking the health or the hearts of the other men, they ought to be put down. This object was well-nigh accomplished even in 1867. Mr. Connolly (stonemason) said that " the society's rule as to ' chasing' " was introduced to put a stop to the practice, which is not so " much in vogue at the present time."[1] " Fines are imposed " on members transgressing the rule."[2] " A member would " refuse to work with a non-society man transgressing the " rule."[3] In point of fact, the same rule is common to many Trade Unions. The members are counselled against doing an amount of work which others may not be able to do, or which may be in excess of the more or less indefinite quantity known as " the fair average " ; and this counsel is enforced by discipline and penalties.   Mr. Alfred Mault said " the labourers' Unions have also ' chasing' rules," and quoted, as specimens, rules of the Bradford and Leeds Labourers' Unions, the one cautioning members against doing " double the amount of work " required by the Union, and the other limiting to eight the number of bricks to be carried by a labourer.[4] The same witness said there were the most various estimates of a fair day's work among the men themselves—" has known bricklayers varying from 300 to 900 bricks."[5] The general facts thus stated being

[1] Q. 1327.   [2] 1340-1.   [3] 1350-3.   [4] 3120-6   [5] 3190.

characteristic, under modified forms, of many of the trades, the only difficulty is to discover a justifiable reason of such repression of any man's natural power of work, even supposing him working in company with others at a common wage. Mr. George Potter was silent on this subject, but Mr. Richard Harnott (Operative Masons) entered upon it in a philosophical spirit, and his statement was: "The society considers that it knows what amount of work "a man ought to do. A man should not be free to over-"exert himself."[1] This contains a considerable amount of thought, but unfortunately does not in any way satisfy the equity of the case, because the employers, on the enforced terms and principles of the Unions themselves, are paying an average wage, and for this wage are entitled to have all that the men can severally do, what the strong man can do without over-exerting himself, and what the weak man can do without over-exerting himself;—and this contract made, and the average wage arranged, if the Unions proceed to enjoin on all their stronger men to lessen down their work to what the weaker men can do, it is clear that the employers lose one-half their bargain, and for an average wage are in danger of getting only a minimum of work.[2]

4. RESTRICTION OF WORKMEN TO PARTICULAR WORK.

This is another form of the "interior repression" which appears from the Inquiry to have a prevailing play in the rules and practice of the Unions. A stonemason may not

[1] Q. 1215-1289.

[2] "Chasing" among the masons has been incidentally compared in this passage to the "head-rigging" in a harvest field. Trade-Unionists, enamoured of the "anti-chasing" rule, may turn with an agreeable divertisement of their ideas to a description by Allan Cunningham (Life, by Rev. D. Hogg, p. 179) of the last day of a harvest-cutting in which he was himself a leading performer. There was not only the "head-rig" man, but a Highland clan in the centre of the line, who had a pair of bag-pipes blowing to cheer them forward in the work! Such "Derby-days" of labour must be rare now. The scene of Cunningham's account was in the valley of the A,E on the Scottish borders. The name of the place is neither difficult to spell nor to pronounce; but the episode itself has a deep meaning.

set a brick, or a bricklayer a stone, or either do any portion
of the work that belongs to a plasterer, the plasterers themselves being divided into orders who must not encroach on
each other. The labourers attending on Union workmen
are for the most part in an extremely bad case, being
dragged on smaller pay through all the internecine quarrels
of their superiors, and often left desolate through no fault
of their own. The labourers find a questionable relief in
organizing a war among themselves in imitation of their
superiors. All bricks must be carried in a hod, and no
bricks carried in a wheelbarrow, and the number of bricks
in a hod must not exceed a limited number. This is the
most forbidding aspect in these Trade Union records, because it shows that while the Unionists are at war with
employers, with non-Unionists, and with the public, they
are no less at war among themselves, and recognise in each
other, the nearer they work together, only enemies.

All this form of Trade-Union action seems in the conception of the Unionists themselves to be what may be
called a "market-question." That is to say, having fenced
off our general market against supply on all sides by such
rules as we can, let us now divide our general market into a
great number of minute subdivisional markets, fencing off
each by rules in the same way, the one against the other.
If lobsters happen to be plentiful, as they sometimes are in
Billingsgate, they must not be allowed to do service for
crabs, which happen to be scarce ; no one who comes for
salmon must be allowed to take turbot ; and as for herrings
and sprats, they must have no intercommunication whatever
in supplying the demand. The same policy has occasionally exemplifications in the Stock Exchange ; but it is the
device of men who, with little heed of the natural laws and
forces in operation around them, are pursuing blindly the
spirit of monopoly and "cornering" to its last dregs ; and
a similar course applied to the broad field of trade and
industry, as the Trade Unions really do and may apply it,
can have no good consequences. Nay, but must have the
most dismally bad consequences to the working-class
interest.

The general results of this review of the "methods" by which the Trade Unions propose to attain their cardinal object of always higher wages earned in always shorter time, are these : (1) by a series of elaborate rules to limit the external supply of labour to each trade, and to repress in this interior and guarded circle all competition of labour, and freedom of labour to pass from one branch of the trade or trades to another; (2) by force of organisation, with collected funds, to declare a strike for higher wages or shorter hours, or both, in the supposably favourable circumstances thus produced ; and (3) to keep this power of "strike" well in hand for the daily and systematic enforcement, under active bureaucratic agency, of "the rules" at all points over the whole sphere.

IV.

THE "strike," or resolution of a society of workmen to cease from labour until their demands be conceded, embodies in its most palpable and developed form the "direct action" of the Unions; and though there is a subtle form of this action, as has been seen, much more constantly operative, yet it is desirable to learn from the evidence before the Royal Commission how the public events called "strikes" arise, by what formalities they are decreed, how they are sustained and enforced, and with what results they are usually attended.

HOW STRIKES ARE RESOLVED UPON.

Mr. Richard Harnott, secretary of the Friendly Operative Masons, probably gave the most explicit account of the process of the larger Unions in decreeing or authorising a strike. "When any body of members," he said, "wish the "existing arrangements with their employers to be altered, "either by an advance of wages or by a reduction of the "hours of labour, the matter is laid before a branch com- "mittee, then before the central committee, and lastly be- "fore the whole society by means of printed reports, each "member having a right to vote upon the proposition. "When the consent of the society has been obtained in this "way, a notice is given to the employers concerned that "within a given time the desired change will take place; "and at the end of the specified time, if no arrangement "has been come to, the workmen concerned go out on "strike."[1] In this process ample means would seem to be

[1] Q. 1047-53, 1121.

provided for careful deliberation, for collecting all the facts bearing on the policy of so serious a step, and for passing the question through various channels of judgment before final decision. The ultimate appeal to the votes of all the members of a Union is not so distinctly put by any of the other witnesses as by Mr. Harnott. Mr. Allan, for example, speaking for the Amalgamated Engineers, said : " Before a " strike can take place the grievance must be brought before " a branch committee, or a district committee if one exist, " and then before the executive council, and the consent of " each body obtained." There is no mention by Mr. Allan of the final appeal to universal suffrage which obtains in Mr. Harnott's Friendly Society of Operative Masons. Mr. Applegarth (Amalgamated Carpenters and Joiners) said his " council have power to withhold support from members " on strike who have struck against the decision of the " council."[1] Mr. Williams, general secretary of Operative Plasterers, said : " The rules of the association do not " allow a man or any number of men to cease work unless " 'the authorities' have investigated the affair thoroughly."[2] Mr. Coulson, secretary of the Operative Bricklayers, not only covered the whole ground of final appeal to universal suffrage, indicated by Mr. Harnott, before any strike could take place, but made this condition much more strict in its application, though the literal accuracy in this respect of Mr. Coulson's definition may be doubted. The substance of his evidence was that no single member in any district could strike " without the consent of the members of the " whole society, before whom the executive council, after " receiving an application, lay the matter through the " several lodges."[3]

It follows from the whole evidence, that in the larger Unions there is a process of deliberation before a strike can be decreed, and the unanimity with which the Trade Union witnesses before the Royal Commission claimed the honour of having discountenanced and prevented many strikes encourages the idea that there is a growing sense of responsibility among the active and managing members of

[1] Q. 96-9.   [2] 1805.   [3] 1418-21.

the Unions as to precipitating events which inflict so much misery on the working classes. But nearly the whole value of this deliberative and conservative force in the Unions is lost when one comes to consider what the same witnesses say immediately after they have given these assurances. Take Mr. Harnott, for example, already adduced as having given the most explicit account of the deliberative action of the Unions, and who yet immediately to questions asked, answered that "in cases where attempts are made by em- " ployers to reduce wages or increase the hours of labour, to " introduce piecework, or to employ non-society men, mem- " bers are allowed to strike *without obtaining permission from* " *the society*, provided a majority of the members of their " branch consent."[1] The same laxity crops out in Mr. Allan's evidence. "A strike," he said, "without the sanc- " tion of the 'authorities' would be held good by them if " the circumstances of the case required immediate action."[2] The account of Mr. Proudfoot, secretary of the Trades' Council of Glasgow, was that "the whole association must " approve of the strike in some cases ; in others a particular " branch may strike with a majority of the votes of the " members of the branch."[3] As far as can be made out from the evidence, the process of the Unions in decreeing strikes would seem to be this, viz., that where a decided advance in wages or reduction of hours is proposed, the question of " strike " in enforcement of the proposition has to undergo more or less deliberation, and to pass through various ordeals, as the organisation of the several Unions may have provided ; but where any reduction of wages, or any extension of hours, or any breach of the rules of the Union as to piecework, employment of non-society men, and other innumerable details embraced in the rules, is concerned, there is a free power of strike in every branch or shop, and that such strikes will be sanctioned, or cannot easily avoid being sanctioned, by what are called "the authorities" of the Union. The effect of Trade Unionism is thus to overcharge the whole atmosphere of employment with an electric force of strike ; and the presiding geniuses

[1] Q. 1117-21.　　　　[2] 708-13.　　　　[3] 8098-9.

who told the Royal Commission how admirably they had
kept this electricity under their direction and guidance, may
have in reality little more control over it than over the physical electricity of the heavens. The general condition
produced is well described, in its essence, by Mr. Robert
Last, general secretary of House Carpenters and Joiners.
" Minor strikes occur daily, and the strikers, one or more,
" against an encroachment on the part of the employer, are
" entitled to strike pay."[1]

MR. A. MACDONALD ON THE ORIGIN OF STRIKES.

Mr. Alex. Macdonald, in giving evidence as to a colliers'
strike in the Wigan district, that had issued in serious outrages and calamities while he was under examination, said
the strike was proceeding against his advice, and the advice
of Mr. Pickard, the local mining agent, and that "the local
" leaders had no more power in the matter than the gentle-
" men sitting round the table."[2] The general testimony of
Mr. Macdonald on this question was that the evil in such
cases came of universal suffrage, and of the men not yielding at once to the order of their leaders. The rule of the
Miners' Associations in the matter of strikes would appear
to be democracy tempered by leaderism, and differs somewhat from the republican order of other great Unions, in
which there is a certain hierarchy of committees and councils, with deliberation on the part both of the "authorities"
and the members. Yet no Trade Union witness more emphatically asserted the value of strikes to the working classes
than Mr. Alex. Macdonald. He came a second time before
the Commission only to state that in the whole course of
his life he had never known more than one instance in
which an advance of wages was not the result of " pressure
by combination," and that of all the strikes he had known,
nine out of ten had been successful for the workmen—the
few exceptions being strikes "resisting a fall of wages occa-
sioned by over-production."[3] This line of statement did

---

[1] Q. 248-9.   [2] 15,644.   [3] 16,332.

not sustain well the test of cross-examination, nor would it
stand in the light of any close experience before or since.
The only fact is that Mr. Macdonald was fully conscious of
much improvement in the condition of the miners in his
time, and expressed himself, a little careless of any exact
analysis of cause and effect, with due warmth on the whole
subject. The important query suggested, not alone by what
Mr. Macdonald said, but by the general account given to
the Commissioners of the origin of strike decrees, is
whether it be rational or expedient to confide to the brain
of one man, or two or three favoured leaders of multitudes
of men who do not always follow their advice, or even to
an executive council or hierarchy, a dictatorship of strikes
in any branch of industry? The impression conveyed by
the evidence on this vital point is that of an often fatal
resolution or impulse breaking forth among the Unionists
without check or regulation, or any due estimate of the probable consequences.

If the Trade Union "authorities" have thus by their own
process a too limited control over the declaration of strikes,
it follows that they can have little opportunity of judging
deliberately beforehand whether the circumstances of the
trade be favourable to the demands made in a great majority of "strikes," of guarding their funds against the heavy
drains which these struggles so often entail, or of securing
that the strike will be conducted, prolonged or ended, and
ruled throughout by the prudence and legality which they
invariably claim in the evidence for their proceedings. Yet
all these conditions as regards strikes are of the last importance, both to the interests of the Unions and the interests
of the public.

INFORMATION OF THE UNIONS.

The Union witnesses before the Royal Commission nearly
all asserted the exercise of careful deliberation as regards the
favourable or unfavourable circumstances of trade in cases
of strike. Mr. Coulson, for example, said, "before an ap-
"plication can be considered, particulars as to the precise

"state of trade, &c., are obtained from the lodge."[1] The information on which the council deliberates would thus appear to be derived from the parties who are applying for sanction to strike, and for strike pay. All the larger Unions, indeed, keep records of rates of wages, hours, and numbers employed and unemployed, and in their correspondence with the branches must be in possession of much information that might be utilised to very beneficial ends. The Society of Amalgamated Engineers professes to have full records of this kind. "It has complete cognisance," said Mr. Allan, "of the rates of wages in different parts of England and Scotland;"[2] and the witness showed that this knowledge was employed in various useful ways. But as regards its application to strikes Mr. Allan became somewhat hazy. The society does not take into account the question of competition between employers; the fact of some firms being prosperous while others are in difficulty does not weigh; but if there is reason to believe that there is a falling off in general demand, the society would probably refuse to sanction a strike. Mr. Allan, however, declined to explain in detail how the information as to a falling off in demand was obtained, and said "it was generally got from officials in the establishments."[3] Any information the employers could give as to demand or the general state of trade would seem to be eschewed. The disregard of employers is put in the strongest form by Mr. Connolly, of the Operative Stonemasons. "We do not take masters into account at all in our arrangements."[4] Making every allowance for the care with which the Union "authorities" use such information as they possess where an advance of wages or a reduction of hours is contemplated on any determined scale, there is no evidence of such a diagnosis of the state of the trade, and of the general commercial and monetary conditions by which it is affected, being before them in any case, though in all cases accessible if they sought to obtain it, as would justify the conclusions to which they may come. And even were this otherwise, the sphere over which strikes are allowed to occur through individual or local

[1] Q. 1418-20.   [2] 946.   [3] 948-50.   [4] 1349.

impulses, dragging the Union "authorities" along with them *nolens volens*, would render any safeguard thus provided of so much less value against the universal strike epidemic.

PROFIT AND LOSS OF STRIKES.

The evidence from other sources than the Unions as to the failure, loss of wages and funds, and manifold evils of strikes, would form a volume in itself. But to enter on that side of the question is beside our main purpose, which is to elicit from the Unions themselves what they admit, what the members of the Unions have experienced, and what the true interest of the Union workmen in the case may be.

The strike pay allowed to Union members falls to the merest weekly pittance, or to nothing, according to the funds available. The highest strike allowance appears to be from 10s. to 15s. a week. There is a loss to this amount to the funds of the Union for every member on strike, and there is the much heavier loss to the incomes of the men themselves who are on strike. There is thus a double loss—a loss to the funds of the Union, with a corresponding sacrifice of the beneficial purposes for which the funds have been ostensibly collected; and there is a loss of the wages of the men during the period of the strike. In short, the men on strike not only lose their whole wages while the strike continues, but the general body also lose the weekly allowance promised them by the Union, which is their own common fund to rely upon in circumstances of real and unavoidable need. To carry this double loss through all the strikes of the Unions would obviously lead to startling results. But, for illustration, take two leading examples from the Minutes of Evidence. The Society of Amalgamated Engineers in six months of 1852, according to the testimony of Mr. Allan, spent 40,000*l.*, or indeed the whole of its funds, in a general struggle with the employers. There were 12,000 members, and taking the wages at the moderate average of 30s. a week, and the whole period of idleness per man at only three months, the Amalgamated Engineers lost on that occasion to themselves alone more than a quarter of a million

of money. The pretext of this waste of resources was the
enforcement of two rules, which the Amalgamated Engineers
expunged at the end of the strike, though they were in no
sense illegal rules, but were simply untenable and impracticable at the time. Then there is the memorable struggle of
the building trades of London in 1859 for shorter hours, of
which Mr. George Potter was a prime mover, and according
to whose account to the Royal Commissioners the results
were an expenditure of funds, 24,000*l.*, and 30,000 men idle
for twenty-six weeks, say at a sacrifice of 30*s.* per week—
total loss to the workmen themselves, 1,194,000*l.*[1] This
enormous waste in money alone, and the infinitely more
pitiful results to families if they could be collected or even
imagined, were endured without even gaining the few hours
less per week, and this too at a time when warehousemen,
clerks, and factory and other workers were obtaining
easily by a more reasonable process the Saturday half-
holiday. These, though prominent, are after all but feeble
examples of the loss of strikes; for it is not unusual to
find miners' funds of more than a hundred thousand pounds
disappearing in a few months, and yet the men left wholly
disorganized, many of them unemployed, houseless, and
penniless, at the close of the insensate procedure.

In all cases there are two considerations by which the
profit and loss of strikes may be pretty accurately gauged,
viz., (1), that the object contended for is either a few hours
less work in the week for the same wages, or a halfpenny
an hour more of wages per day; and (2), that even in the
instances in which a protracted strike ends in the full object
being gained, the advantage thus apparently established in
favour of labour is all too inadequate to indemnify the self-
inflicted loss of the workmen in the strike-interim during the
future working period of their lives. To these considerations
has only to be added that any advantage gained by a strike
has no real permanence, but may be reduced, and is often
reduced in a few months by an adverse turn in the state of the
trade, in order to prove with sufficient conclusiveness that the
loss of strikes must greatly exceed the profit to the workmen.

[1] Q. 500-15.

Mr. Applegarth said that in his Society of Amalgamated Carpenters and Joiners, "the number of strikes involving a large number of men are about twelve in a year"[1]—one a month ; and in his account of the fund nearly a third of the whole expenditure of a year arose under one out of three or four rules of strike pay, this one rule being applicable and highly favourable to "officers" on strike. Mr. Allen, Chief-Secretary of the Boilermakers' and Iron Shipbuilders' Society, testified that during the previous four years strikes had cost the Society 5,803l., though they had been all unsuccessful ; and that this absorption of the funds had prevented the stipulated payments being made to members of the Union for travelling expenses.[2]

This is a financial question that ought to be chiefly interesting to members of Unions themselves. A thorough balance of profit and loss on strikes would be an extremely valuable document. But unless the Unionists are at the pains to arrive at this result for themselves, it is not likely that any one shall have the means or will to work out the sum for them, though there can be no doubt of the side of the account on which the balance would be found largely to preponderate.

CONDUCT OF STRIKES.

As regards the conduct of strikes when they have been duly declared or simply precipitated, there are three general means available to secure their success, viz., (1) that all the members of the Union in the strike district will loyally cease from labour, which in the usual case can be safely calculated upon ; (2) that other workmen will not go in and take their place, which is not so reliable, and has landed the Unions in a course of tactics forming the *questio vexata* of the whole strike procedure ; and (3) as circumstances may determine, and workmen and employers may alike feel themselves in an awkward dilemma, an appeal to arbitration, which, if effective in any sense at the middle or the end of a struggle, might have been equally effective at the beginning. Mr.

[1] Q. 54.   [2] 17542-97.

E

Rupert Kettle, in his evidence before the Royal Commission, divided dealing with strikes by arbitration into three
groups. First, cases of disagreement on the terms of a
future contract, which are difficult of solution ; second, disagreements as to subsisting contracts, which are more easy
and may be readily adjusted by this process ; and, third,
" disagreement on matters of sentiment, which are much more
frequent than those not actually engaged in trade would expect. A foreman differs with a workman, or there is some
ebullition of temper on one side or the other ; and this leads
to a strike, before the matter calms down." [1]   Mr. Edmund
Ashworth, Chairman of the Building Committee of Manchester Assize Courts, who had been acquainted with strikes
for forty years. said "he had no faith in any strike resulting
satisfactorily by arbitration, the men being governed exclusively by their committee." [2]   Of course, if strikes
frequently occur on disagreements of mere sentiment and
petty ebullitions of temper, it may be supposed that the committee or council of the Union, which has had no act or part
in the origin of the strike, are as helpless as anybody else
in bringing it to a close, and that it remains a matter of
sentiment, temper, and sheer physical endurance and sacrifice to the end.

PICKETING.

The chief element of success in strikes, however, to the
Unions, apart from the loyal adherence and endurance of
their own members, is to warn off and prevent other labour,
and to debar employers from doing anything they could
hope to do with all the Union forces fairly and wholly
withdrawn from the field of labour. The mode of Trade
Union action to this end varies much in character and
degree. There is the comical mode ; in which the Unionists surround a body of voluntary workmen coming in by
train, give them meat, money, and drink, and get up a jolly
fraternal sort of spirit, under which the incoming workmen
are packed off by train next morning to where they came
from. There is also the tragic mode ; in which a body of

[1] Q. 6989.   [2] 4326.

colliers on strike surround the pit mouths armed with staves, and are ready to belabour any one who ventures to go down to the work they have deserted. But the official rule of the Unions is to place "pickets" round the works struck against, whose duty is to inform all comers that the works are under strike, and that it would be unbrotherly and indiscreet, if not dangerous, to violate the laws of war thus established. It will be observed that "picketing" is a term of purely military origin, and that there can be no doubt of the belligerency in which it has been coined. The execution of this rule lies on the borderland of a somewhat free *esprit de corps* to which the Unionists profess a desire to confine it, and of the grossest violence, which the law cannot permit, and which no "Union authority" in many cases is powerful enough to avert.

The subject of picketing had much attention in the Inquiry of 1867-9, because it happened that while the Commission was sitting several unfortunate tailors in London who had carried their operations of this kind much beyond the bounds of moral or social suasion, were convicted of conspiracy and sentenced to severe penalties. Yet "picketing" was generally approved and strongly advocated by the Trade-Union witnesses. Mr. George Potter, who can always be trusted to give the most plausible interpretation of Trade-Union policy, said "the means we adopt, of course, " is placing what we call pickets on the job where the men " have struck. We do not object to that because we con- " sider it a legitimate piece of business. The pickets are " selected from the work where the strike is, to *suggest* to " any man applying for a job there the *advisability* of re- " fraining."[1] It is obvious, from what Mr. Potter says, that close picketing is extended to "a work," and even to "a job" in a work, where there can hardly be any general question of value of labour to vindicate, and where the ruin of an employer may be treated with equal unconcern. There is also much delicacy in Mr. Potter's alleged instruction to the pickets, simply to "suggest" to any one applying for work the "advisability of refraining;" but, at the same time,

[1] Q. 491.

E 2

one cannot conceal that under all this delicacy of expression the " advisability of refraining " may imply to the applicant for work every degree of fate, from whether he is to starve, to be hooted out of society, to be cudgelled, to be shot, or otherwise have his live endangered. Mr. Potter's evidence does not in the least help one through the problem of reconciling the Unionists' sense of freedom not to work, and the freedom of other equally respectable men to work in their stead. Mr. Abram S. Hewitt, of the United States, told the Royal Commission that "picketing would not be tolerated in his country in the form in which it is practised here ;" [1] and of recent date the armed forces of the United States have been frequently employed in suppressing what appears to the American Republicans to be so gross an infraction of the right of the citizen and the right of labour. The difficulty is to see how this rule of " picketing," contended for by Trade Unions, can be brought in practice within such bounds of moral and all manner of free suasion as to place it under the protection of any principle of law that would hold good in reason and in necessary social equity. The Royal Commission, in its Report, conceded freely the right of workmen to combine, and to resolve to work or not to work, and to give or withhold their labour on whatever terms they pleased, provided the combination should be voluntary, and that "*full liberty* be left to all other workmen to under- " take the work which the parties combining have refused, "and that *no obstruction* be placed in the way of the em- " ployer resorting elsewhere in search of a supply of labour." But the " picketing " of the Unions stands as an irreconcilable jar between these two points reached in the Inquiry of 1867-9, and in practice is constantly passing into overt forms of coercion and outrage.

LOCKOUTS.

" Lock-outs " are attending shadows of " strikes," but shadows that sometimes prove terribly baleful. They are the Unionist power of the employers coming in rear of the

[1] Q. 3952.

more developed Unionism of the workmen. The Unions strike against individual employers in the hope of taking them in detail, and drawing resources from some in the interim to accomplish the overthrow of one or two selected victims. The employers, in order to avert this injustice and common danger, have said, "No; when a partial strike is "threatened, let us decree a lock-out, so that the general "interests may be more equitably adjusted." It is an altogether unhappy state of affairs; and this retaliatory war of employers and employed is strongly to be deprecated. There is no free play in it either for the good feeling that ought to subsist between employers and employed, or for the natural laws that will have their own way in the end, let employers or employed do what they please. But it may be observed that the finding of the Royal Commission was that "associations of employers were frequently of a tempo-"rary character, and dissolved as soon as the contest with "the workmen, which had given rise to them, came to an "end."

TENDENCY OF TRADE-UNION ACTION TO VIOLENCE.

The ordinary methods by which the Trade Unions pursue their trade objects cannot be dismissed without observing the extremely narrow and practically undefined line between many of these modes of action and what is simply lawless and unjustifiable personal violence. The Unionists are always hovering between the assertion of their own combination rights and dire encroachment on the rights of others; and there is no law among themselves strong enough to keep them on the safe and only tenable side of the boundary. This is not a question of political economy. The "dismal science" may here be set wholly aside with all the gratification which this dismissal of an important branch of study can give to the Unionists. The effort of associated bodies of workmen, however numerous and well organised, to rise superior in their own advantage to fundamental principles of trade, production, consumption, money, finance, and foreign exchange, which are not of any man's

making, and over which neither capitalists nor workmen have
the slightest control, is an effort as worthy of common pity
as it is a cause of common suffering ; but it does not meet us
at this part of the case. The question here is simply one of
individual and social right, and whether the Trade Unions,
with the most complete freedom of doing with their labour
and with themselves whatever they please, can be allowed to
hinder or directly injure any but themselves, save in so far
as these consequences may be involved in their own full and
proper liberty of action—a large margin on which they hinder
and hurt others, by the way, for which there is no remedy of
any kind, and which the community must helplessly suffer in
proportion as this liberty of action on the part of the Unions
may be more or less prudently exercised ? Now, taking the
evidence of the Trade-Union witnesses themselves as to the
official action of the Unions, it is quite obvious that this
action much exceeds what can be accorded to associated
bodies, however extensive, with any reasonable or equitable
respect to the rights of others not included in their own
voluntary membership. It breathes coercion throughout,
and this breath passes naturally, and hitherto uncontrollably,
into acts of which the law must take cognisance, and must
restrain. Hence the history of Trade Unionism has been
marked by an ineffaceable trail of outrage, which all have
reason to deplore.

THE BOUNDARY BETWEEN RIGHT AND VIOLENCE.

To show the exact point where the lawful ends and the
lawless begins, let us quote a few sentences from the Report
of the Royal Commissioners :—

"With regard to the general question of the right of workmen to
combine together for determining and stipulating with their employer
the terms on which only they will consent to work for him, we think
that, *provided the combination be perfectly voluntary, and that full
liberty be left to all other workmen to undertake the work which the parties
combining have refused, and that no obstruction be placed in the way of
the employer resorting elsewhere in search of a supply of labour*, there is
no ground of justice or of policy for withholding such a right from the
workmen."

The Royal Commissioners thus allowed for the disadvantage in which individual workmen, or small bodies of workmen, might be placed in treating with their employer, and held that they were entitled to all the weight which union and numbers could give in their stipulations as to the terms and conditions of their labour. To the extent of this right of association, and its power in the labour market, they could recognise no limit, and advised none, save that the association should be voluntary. " But upon the same principle," their Report goes on to say—

" We think, whilst conceding to such workmen as desire to exercise it an extended right to combine against their employers, especial care should be taken that an equal right be secured to those workmen who desire to keep aloof from the combination, to dispose of their labour with perfect freedom as they severally think fit. The workmen who combine are no more justified in constraining any other workman to combine with them,—to bring his labour into common stock, as it were, with theirs,—than an association of capitalists would be in constraining an individual capitalist to bring his capital into common stock with theirs ; and it is the more important that the law should protect the non-Unionist workman in his right freely to dispose of his labour as he thinks fit, because, standing alone, he is the less able to protect himself."

The same principle which, in the judgment of the Royal Commission, entitled workmen to combine to any extent in order to get rid of the weakness of treating individually, or in an isolated way, with an employer or employers, entitled any workman outside the combination to the secure protection of the law in disposing of his labour as he thought fit, just in the sense that he was an individual, and was weak and helpless against the combination as an individual workman would be against the real or imaginary power of an employer. The Royal Commission sought to give to workmen, in disposing of their labour, the fullest power of combining that may exist in any other market—money, capital, stocks, or goods—and probably exceeded this measure, because however markets may be "ringed," "beset," "forestalled," or monopolised, it is doubtful whether combination in any market on the scale accorded to associated workmen would be tolerated. But outside this great power of combi-

nation, the Royal Commission left the small fringe of liberty,
viz., that the combination should not obstruct any one out
of its own voluntary membership, who came to buy or sell
in the market, to employ or be employed, and that the
public force should be exerted to protect all who thus came
in the exercise of a natural right. This is understood to be
the basis of our law as regards Trade Unions, and it is a
basis of law to which our Trade Unions are supposed loyally to conform. But after the review already taken of the
most refined interpretation of the action of the Unions from
the mouths of their own leading witnesses, there can be no
doubt, on this evidence alone, that the Trade Unions do
not conform to their legal foundation in any true sense. It
would be scarcely too strong, indeed, to say that the Trade
Unions are habitually transgressing the right of non-Unionists, without a full admission and observance of which, in
the deliberate judgment of the Royal Commission, the
Unions have no right to exist at all. Putting aside the
coercion among the Unionists in their own circles, there
remains enough in the ordinary process of a " strike," sometimes occurring for no greater purpose than to expel a non-
Unionist from employment—with its " picketing," mobbing,
and animosity of the " strikers," fermenting to the point of
rage against any one crossing their design—to prove that
the system pursued by the Unions is a direct infraction of
the saving clause, without which the Royal Commission
could not see that the Unions had any ground in reason or
equity on which to stand. Mr. George Potter, in his philo-
sophic view of the question, professed before the Commission
that the action of the Unions over other than their own
members was confined to " moral suasion," and that all the
Union agents and " picketers " were carefully instructed not
to exceed " moral suasion." But can the picketers be expected to know, and may they be the sole judges, where
" moral suasion " ends and an intimidating and compulsory
action over the will of others begins? The recurring trials
in the courts not only prove how fallacious it would be to
rest the equal rights of her Majesty's subjects on any instruction of the Unions to their agents and picketers, or any

discipline they are capable of exerting over a mass of men on strike, but they are also constantly rendering more clear wherein all the misunderstanding consists. Unionists, in a strike, assume that they have of right a monopoly of labour in the trade or workshops to which the strike is applied, and in the means adopted to enforce this untenable assumption there is an inherent coercive quality, which is a severe temptation to the individuals who place themselves through over-zeal, or are placed by pay, in the front of such a battle, and forms in reality a kind of hotbed unavoidably prolific of all the more flagrant outrages that have brought so much disgrace on the Unions, and not on the Unions only, but on the intelligence and *morale* of the working classes of the kingdom.

V.

THE SHEFFIELD AND MANCHESTER OUTRAGES.

A SERIES of outrages of the most flagrant character in the town of Sheffield, extending over a period of ten years, had greatly excited public feeling at various dates prior to the appointment of the Royal Commission. The outrages were so abominable and so horrible that the Trade Unions hastened to disavow and repudiate them *in toto* as being wholly outside their line of policy. But these avowals did not slacken the tide of outrage in any degree. Within three months after the issue of the Royal Commission it was found necessary to issue a Special Commission to inquire "on oath" (with extraordinary powers of securing witnesses against liability for their own criminal conduct, in so far as they might be found to give true evidence) into acts of intimidation, outrage, or wrong by Trade Unions in Sheffield ; and within three months more the Trade Union outrages in the Manchester district were found to be so formidable that they could only be dealt with by a Special Commission of the same kind. These special investigations form part and parcel of the Trade Union Inquiry of 1867-9.

THE SHEFFIELD OUTRAGES.

In the Sheffield case the history divulged was briefly this— viz., that the Unions in the exercise of their ordinary discipline of enforcing contributions to their funds, limiting the number of apprentices, and authorising workmen for employment, were in the practice of carrying away the "bands" or "nuts" of the grinding-wheels and other working tools supplied by the employers, stealing the goods in the hands

of workmen, blowing up shops and houses with gunpowder,
and shooting with pistol and ball obnoxious persons in the
streets ; that the Sawgrinders' Union, of which one William
Broadhead was secretary, took a leading part in organising
these crimes, in which other Unions participated ; that the
grinders were always ready to stop working in any case
where one or two forgers were in arrears to the Union, or
under its ban. and were paid by the Forgers' Union while
on strike, and *vice versâ :* that the minor employers in the
special industries of Sheffield, men who were workmen
themselves and employed or gave out jobs to other workmen, were required to contribute to the funds of the Unions,
though denied all benefit or relief from the funds given to
other members, or, failing such contributions, had to take
the consequence of the outrage discipline ; that a large body
of men were kept constantly on " strike pay" out of the
contributions thus enforced, and that from among the men
thus " on the scale," as it was called, were selected the
ruffians employed to perpetrate the annoyances, the abstrac-
tion of working gear and tools, thefts, and other deeds of
violence against life and property, all essential parts of the
discipline ; that for every outrage a distinct hire was stipulated, and that this hire was paid *pro rata* out of the funds
of the Unions interested in the perpetration of the outrage.
There is little need to dilate on these Sheffield outrages. the
horrors of which can never be obliterated. The only purpose is by simple analysis to get down to the root of an evil
which is far from being extirpated. The notorious Broadhead, in a letter to the Trades Defence Committee of Sheffield, before the Special Commission had come on the field,
has left a little record of what seemed to him of the nature
of mere floating outrage in the innocent atmosphere around
him, which it may be well to quote :—

"James Linley was once blown up, and twice shot at. He died
seven months after this last time, but whether those outrages on Linley
were done by Union men or others has never been ascertained. Henry
Jackson and Joseph Helliwell were burnt by an explosion of powder at
two separate times at Tower Wheel. Mr. Joseph Wilson's house was
also blown up, and there was also the outrage at Russell works, and

the threatening letters to Messrs. Smith and Wheatman. There is also the Hereford Street outrage, which I was nearly forgetting (if it is to be attributed to our trade)."

To the further query of the Trades Defence Committee, Broadhead replied in the same letter, "We are prepared to give evidence upon what we know, but *that is very little.*"

"Non mi ricordo" was thus the style of Broadhead at this pleasant juncture, but it is difficult to believe that the Trades Defence Committee of Sheffield required on any part of the subject a refresher from so lagging a memory.

Of the process of inquiry pursued in Sheffield a few notes from the examinations will be enough. George or "Putty" Shaw swore :—

"I saw Mr. Broadhead at the meeting of the society. He was known by the name of 'Smite 'em.' One night in his house Clarke came to me and asked if we would blow 'Old Topsey' up. 'Old Topsey' was Helliwell. Clarke said we could have 3*l.* for it. I said 'Yes.' He went up stairs to see 'Smite 'em,' and brought down three kegs of powder. I took them to my mother's, and put them between my bed and the mattress. We did not use them all. We put smithy slack into part, and sold two of the kegs to a man named Simmonite, and drank the proceeds at the 'Green Man' and the 'Corner Pin.' We put the remainder of the powder with the smithy slack into Helliwell's trough, above which he worked, and when glazing scattered sparks."

Poor Helliwell, though not killed by this exploit, was subjected to many weeks of severe suffering. But Clarke and Shaw got their 3*l.* for an imperfect job from Broadhead. This man himself, when placed at bay as to the repeated attempts on the life of Linley, thus replied :—

"Am I to understand from you, then, that you did hire Crooks to shoot at Linley in the first instance?—I regret to say that I did.

"And did you pay him 20*l.* for it?—My impression is that it was 15*l.*, but I will not be certain about it.

"Did you hire Crooks and Hallam to shoot at Linley a second time?—Yes.

"Did you pay to Crooks and Hallam 20*l.* for the second shooting?—My impression is that it was 15*l.* on both occasions, but I will not be certain as to the exact amount."

With respect to the Hereford Street outrage, of which Broadhead had only the most distant and forgetful recollec-

tion when writing in answer to queries of the Trades
Defence Committee of Sheffield, and in which outrage a
man, Farnehough, and his whole family, were blown up all
but fatally, by an explosion of gunpowder placed in the
cellar of their dwelling-house, the Royal Commission had
under examination a Mr. Robert S. Danter, who was sent
down along with Mr. George Odger under the authority of
no less a body than the Amalgamated Society of Engineers,
to inquire into this great scandal on the whole Trade-Union
system.   Odger did not appear before the Royal Commission, but the evidence of Danter was that he and Odger
reported to the Amalgamated Engineers that Broadhead
had no hand at all in the Hereford Street outrage.[1]   Broadhead himself, when brought to book, made a much more
honest statement ; and the Sheffield Commissioners have
recorded in their report, that " Samuel Crooks was hired
by Broadhead to commit this outrage," and that the Saw-
makers' Society and the Saw-Handle-makers' Society between them found the " blood-money."

It would be idle to declaim on a code of Unionism that
revolted the moral feeling of the civilized world quite as
much as the revelation of the murders of Burke and Hare
in Edinburgh, or of the secret assassination societies in
Ireland, or of " Thuggee " in India, in bygone ages.   The
substantial question is how great bodies like the Trade
Unions, enjoying under the sanction of the law the right of
association in its largest form, on the condition that the
association shall be voluntary among the members themselves, and that the association shall not exercise any violence
upon any one outside its pale, could happen to be com-
promised by acts so immoral and so disgusting, and should
remain so insensible to their own interests as that to this
day acts of the same kind, though perhaps not so flagrant in
organised inveteracy, should be the constant result of Trade
Union procedure ?   The atmosphere of opinion evolved in
the Sheffield examinations is perfectly freezing as regards all
sense of right and wrong as between workman and workman,
and between workmen and their employers.   The policy

[1] Q. 7608.

leading up to "the outrages" was said by witness after witness to be customary, to have existed even before the Unions in their modern highly developed form existed, to be common to all trades—"the tailors would take away the goose and the sleeve-boards" just as the grinders took away "the bands" and "the nuts"—and that the "outrages," though not desirable, were a natural sort of thing in all the circumstances, as if the harmless gaffery of a village shopboard were to be the prelude and justification of a nationally organised system of Trade-Union crime.

Broadhead himself put the idea in its most perfect practical form. "If the law would only give the Unions some power to recover contributions without having recourse to such measures, there would be no more heard of them."[1] He had just said a little before that "rattening" might occur in 150 minor questions between the Unions, and not their own members only, but employers and non-Union workmen.[2] It was in default of the law not coming with all its force in execution of the decrees of the Unions that the Unions had to execute their decrees by force in this way for themselves! Could any confession be more ludicrous if it were not at the same time so horrible? But the question in its most tragic involutions always reverts to its original and simple form, viz., What conceivable right can Trade-Unions, or any other associations, have to exercise a coercive force, either through the law or without and against the law, save in so far as some coercion of Unions over their own members may be legally exploited by rules voluntarily adopted among themselves? What right in reason, or under any civilized law, can the Trade Unions, after withdrawing their labour *en masse* from an employer, have to obstruct, interfere, or meddle with any measure of the employer in the dilemma in which by their free right of association they have thus placed him? Still more, what right can they have to obstruct or injure non-Union workmen who are not in their membership at all? Until the Trade Unions have the common sense to perceive in their own interest that this assertion of coercive power is untenable, and until, indeed,

---

[1] Q. 13,241.   [2] 12,157.

the laws of the country pin them down firmly to a strict observance of this boundary line, whether they have the common sense to perceive it to be in their own interest or not, outrage will continue to be, as it has been, the constant and inevitable outcome of the modern Trade-Union action.

THE MANCHESTER OUTRAGES.

The Manchester outrages differ in little from those of Sheffield. They only bring us among different branches of trade, in which the same common principles of violence are found to prevail. They are quite as bad as the Sheffield outrages in every sense ; fully more destructive, indeed, of life and property than the Sheffield outrages ; and they have a special feature of their own to the effect that the Union monopoly was asserted within given lineal bounds, that one Union came into violent collision with another Union on their respective frontiers, that fathers, sons, and nephews were engaged in destroying each other's property and lives, and that it was a war to the death in a great measure between Unionists themselves and one class of working men and another—the most miserable of all results to which any working-class policy can fall. The outrages in the Manchester district had chiefly arisen among the building trades. Brickmakers and bricklayers were deeply implicated. But the brickmakers' and bricklayers' Unions burnt their books and all accounts of their expenditure as soon as they heard that a Commission of Inquiry was coming down. Brickyards were found to have been nightly invaded, tens of thousands of bricks in many cases destroyed, needles stuck into the clay to render it unworkable, all the buildings and timber inflamed with torch and liberal libations of naphtha, many horses hamstrung for no other reason than that they had been employed in hauling timber out of one fenced Union district into another, masters and foremen blown up by gunpowder-flasks with fusees thrown through their windows, several policemen and watchmen murdered, and many employers, who were but hard-working men themselves, ruined and driven away. The Commissioners, in their Report, say—

> "That no act of intimidation or outrage was traceable to any association of employers,—that all such acts were instigated and sanctioned by the several Unions,—that they were all deliberately planned and executed in furtherance of a system which had for its object the subjection of both masters and men to the rules of the Union,—and that the largest sum we have found to have been paid for an outrage was 20*l.*"

In short, all the abomination of the Sheffield outrages in another sphere.

With what feelings Trade Unionists contemplate such facts as these is a question that must be left to their own consciences. But there are a few points on which their minds may dwell a little. To restrain such frightful outrages Parliament framed the Criminal Law Amendment Act, against which the Unions have protested ever since. Broadhead required that the law should step in and enforce whatever decree any Union committee, assembled in any back-parlour of any public-house in the kingdom, might pass, in order to save him and others from the irresistible temptation to which they were exposed of hiring men to commit outrage and murder. It is improbable that this monstrous claim will soon be revived. Yet it has to be borne in mind, as an unavoidable corollary of these Sheffield and Manchester disclosures, how easily a body of associated workmen, imbued with the idea that their trade belongs to them alone, in a peculiar and emphatic sense, and nursing this idea till it becomes a warm and vital part of their being, may fall into a course of action aggressing upon the rights of others, and, under the keen feelings and all but desperate passions which seem inseparable from such movements, carrying them ever farther away from the only reasonable and the only legal constitution of a Trade Union. The Minutes of Evidence and Report of the Royal Commission on the "Labour Laws," to which we shall have to refer, give more light as to what the Unionists require the law to do for them, and what they forbid the law to do against them. But that there is an impassable limit to legislative concessions in this direction must be universally admitted. There

can scarce be any Unionist in his sober senses so ill
informed as to imagine that this country will be content
to be ruled by a Trade Union *imperium in imperio*, or that
there is not a boundary where the law must say, in the
clearest reason, peremptorily to all such associations—
" Thus far and no farther ! "   The law of the community
—the law which regulates and protects the secular rights
and interests of all classes, and each person of all classes—
must be superior to the law of self-constituted bodies within
the community, if there is to be any community at all.

VI

CUI BONO?

The "objects" which Trade Unions propose to accomplish, and the "methods" by which they endeavour to accomplish these objects being thus ascertained, the subject has arrived at a definite stage, and now passes upon more critical ground. Both the "objects" and the "methods" of the Unions have been taken from the evidence of their own authorities, and but little heed has been given in this expository part of the question to the testimony of witnesses on the other side, many of whom were persons of great experience. For the rest, reference has been made to the Report of the Royal Commission itself, to which there were three dissentients—practically, indeed, only two, Mr. Thomas Hughes and Mr. Frederic Harrison, to whose separate report consideration shall have to be given at a subsequent stage. Thus far, exception can scarce be taken to anything that has gone before. The preceding chapters give a full and correct outline of the aims, the policy, and the administrative action of the Unions as professed by themselves, with only so much argument and illustration as might serve to suggest to the reader the points at which the Union system may be found to impinge on justice between man and man, on the public and common-weal, on social order and social progress, on interests which the law in the highest conception of equity is bound to preserve, or may even pass into crimes which the law is bound to repress. There now arise, therefore, questions of the gravest importance, such as the effect of all this organised combination and activity, as hitherto directed, on trade, on the well-being of the working classes, on the interests of the Unionists themselves, and the extent to which the law can sanction the systematic procedure of the Unions, and conform by continuous concessions of legal principle to all the demands of the Union leaders. Supposing the result of these and such questions should be adverse to the Unions, there will remain the question by what transformation they may hope under law to carry out their objects more beneficially than hitherto to themselves, and less injuriously than hitherto to other people.

RÉSUMÉ.

Before proceeding to this severer ground it may be useful briefly to resume what has already been established, viz. :—

1. The objects of the Trade Unions are divided between " benefit objects " and " trade objects."

2. The " benefit objects " are the only constitutionally declared objects of nearly all the Unions, and are the real and chief objects of many Unions that seldom come before the public.

3. The " trade objects " are the real, though not the constitutionally declared, objects of all the more publicly active Unions, their " benefit objects " being subordinate to these, and adopted chiefly for the purpose of raising funds in promotion of the " trade objects."

4. The " trade objects " of the Unions are " to resist " reductions of wages, to enforce advances of wages, and to " shorten the hours of labour."

5. The " methods " by which the Unions propose to accomplish the " trade objects " are—First, the power of strike, or cessation from labour until the trade demand be conceded, with weekly pay from the funds subscribed for " benefit objects " to the men on strike; and—Second, within this general method, elaborate codes of working rules, such as to limit and exclude apprentices, to authorise adult workmen to be allowed to work, to repress among authorised workmen any excess of labour in the working hours, so that the strongest may not do more than the weakest, to drive away non-authorised or non-unionist workmen by unsocial

treatment, &c., in enforcement of all which petty rules the general method of strike may be brought into operation in any place or at any moment. Among other "methods" claimed by the Unionists is that of "picketing" the district, the shop, or the job struck against, and warning off all labour from the prohibited ground.

6. The "benefit objects" of the Unions are friendly insurance and mutual help in case of sickness, loss of tools by fire, death, or old age and infirmity. Some of the Unions only insure two or more of these benefits to their members, and the rate of payment, by which they are supposed to be insured, is various; but in the larger Unions, such as the Amalgamated Engineers and the Amalgamated Carpenters and Joiners, the "benefit objects" embrace all this scale, and in these cases the contributions of the members, besides some entry-money and fines, are 1s. per week. The payments, though thus made to insure the benefits to the members, are expended freely on management and trade purposes.

These are the Union laws both of aim and action, obtained from the highest Trade-Union evidence, leaving out everything of a disputable or unaccredited quality. They are the features of Trade Unionism as painted by its chief artists, and there is no reason to doubt the design and ability with which they have laboured to make the features as regular and beautiful as possible. Indeed, no one can follow the details of the system without being impressed by the cleverness with which the Trade-Union policy has been constructed towards given ends, by the great amount of energy and money expended in its administration, and the power as thus elaborated the Unions have, or may have for a time over the trade and well-being of the country. Moles or beavers could not possibly be more active, ingenious, and constructive of their own way of living than the Trade Unionists have been for the last twenty years. The only fault of the process seems to be that it wants atmosphere, eyes, comprehensive understanding, and observation of general causes and effects, that may be at variance with, and at any moment destructive of, the "house at home,"

built and rebuilt with such marvellous steadiness of instinct.
The beavers, by no end of labour, gather together their
houses in the waters, but the poor creatures cannot be supposed to know anything of climatic laws, rainfalls, frost,
thaws, floods, and droughts in the river, and so find themselves from time to time seriously disturbed in their operations; and when their houses are swept clean away, or are
left high and dry, they proceed to build again; and all
admire the instinct, the constructive capacity, and the un-
wearied industry of the beavers. The same admiration
must be fully accorded to Trade Unionists. They have
been busily constructing and reconstructing, for twenty
years, an interior system of their own; they have spent
enormous labour and huge amounts of money in their
architecture; great parts of the edifice have fallen down
time after time into the floods, but they have proceeded
slowly and by still heavier sacrifices to build up again; and
yet their policy throughout, and as it now stands, appears to
be not only in antagonism to common law, statute law, and
law of common equity among themselves, but, what is still
more remarkable, there is not a particle of evidence to the
present hour that this beaver-like activity has had the smallest appreciable effect in accomplishing any of their prime
objects, either of advancing wages or shortening the hours of
labour.

FAILURE OF "THE OBJECTS" OF THE UNIONS.

Nothing is more difficult than to discover in the volumi-
nous evidence of 1867-9 or later facts, any advantage gained
to the men by the costly proceedings of their Unions. The
failures of strikes, with all their heavy loss of wages and
funds, are much more numerous than the partial successes
and compromises by which these disastrous events have
sometimes been terminated. Thus, Mr. Robinson of the
Atlas Works, Manchester, on being asked,[1] "Whether the
Unions have substantially altered the rate of wages?" replied, "I think not." This witness laid before the Commission a table of rates of wages paid to all classes of skilled

[1] Q. 18,988.

workmen in his branch of trade from 1851 to 1866 [1] ; from which it appeared that the advances during that lengthened period were immaterial in all classes save one, the boiler-makers—*i.e.* "platers," "riveters," and "holders-up"—to whom there had been a rise of 6s. upon 24s. a week; and this advance Mr. Robinson traced to the rapid extension of iron-, shipbuilding and the making of girder-bridges for railways, by which these classes of workmen were enabled to obtain substantial advances of wages from the easy and natural action of demand, without any Union formality, procedure, or expense.

Nor must it be supposed that great efforts by strikes, both on a large and small scale, were not made by the Society of Engineers during this period. There was not only the six months' struggle in 1852, in which Mr. Allen confessed that the Society lost 40,000*l.* of its funds, and the men had finally to work on the old conditions, but other strikes were con-stantly cropping up the whole time, and placing the skilled labour in the United Kingdom under permanent disad-vantages. Mr. Robinson records the strike of iron-workers in the West Riding of Yorkshire in 1864, one result of which

[1] *Abridged Table of Average Wages at the Atlas Works to Skilled Workmen.*

	1851.	1861.	1866.
Fitters, Erectors, Turners, and Borers . . .	30·18s.	... 30·44s. ...	30·56s.
Grinders . . .	29·40	... 30·	... 30·
Joiners . . .	26·36	... 27·22 ...	28·72
Patternmakers . .	30·50	... 30·38 ...	30·50
Painters	23·25	.. 26·91 ...	28·91
Coppersmiths . .	—	... 29·75 ...	32·40
Planers, Slotters, and Shapers . . .	19·87	21·86	21·5
Brass-moulders . .	Piecework.	... 31·50	31·42
Iron-moulders . .	Ditto.	... 34·12	Piecework.
Angle Ironsmiths . .	36·	... 35·50	38·
Platers	29·66	... 33·77	36·
Riveters . . .	26·06	... 30·	32·13
Holders-up . . .	23·	... 26·	29·
Helpers	19·50	... 18·15	18·12
Smiths	30·27	... 31·33	32·30
Strikers	18·45	... 18·96	19·75

was that his own firm were driven to import boiler plates from France, as other firms were driven to do from Sweden ; and this importation had continued ever since, the foreign plates of some sizes being much cheaper than the English plates, while the quality was quite equal. A strike broke out in the Gorton Foundry at Manchester (Messrs. Beyer, Peacock, and Co.), employing 1,800 men, in 1866, under one of the most unreasonable pretences ever heard of. It was an umbrage of a small portion of the men—the black-smiths—against a foreman, who was a superior judge of work. The appearance of a "head-centre" from London on the scene did not improve this silly disturbance. The whole works were dragged into a protracted and inveterate strike, and the labour wholly stopped till the employers were beaten, the foreman sent away, and the new men who had come forward were dismissed. In this case of successful strike there was no advance of wages in question, and none was gained ; but can it be supposed that great public works may be thus suspended without lessening the demand for labour, and retarding such advances of wages as might otherwise arise ?

In 1865 occurred the Brierley Hill strike, embracing the whole iron trade of North and South Staffordshire. The ironmasters of England had given notice, in consequence of the low price of iron, of a reduction of 1s. a ton in puddlers' and of 10 per cent. in millmens' wages. The Puddlers' Unions at first gave their assent to the reduction, but the result was a general strike, lasting from four to six months, and it was soon discovered that the general Union body were supporting the men on strike. The number of men thrown out of work was more than four times the number of puddlers, who were the only principals in the strike, and the loss to the district was not less than a quarter of a million sterling. Each man on strike was the cause of depriving four other persons of employment.[1] Mr. Bates, owner of one of the largest works in Staffordshire, was compelled to close them finally, and abandon the field. The men, or as many of them at least as could be employed, returned to work at the terms as

[1] Q. 10,567.

originally arranged and originally agreed to. But the loss to
the trade was deep and permanent. "Having stopped our
work for six months," said Mr. W. S. Roden to the Commission, "we lost a great deal of the trade, which of course
"went elsewhere, and which we have never recovered. My
"works at present" [Nov. 1867—two years after the great
folly] "are working only three days a week, and have been
"working only three or four days a week for months. Had
"it not been for the North Staffordshire strike we should
"have been practically in full work up to the present time." [1]
Is there a working man of any intelligence who may not see
the insanity of such a mode of advancing wages?

The strike and lockout in South Wales last spring is too
recent and too deeply impressed on the public mind to require any remark. The total direct loss inflicted was com-
puted by Lord Aberdare to be 3,500,000l., whereof the chief
share fell on the working people ; and other estimates have
placed it even much higher, at four and even five millions
sterling. But a million or two of money less or more appears to be of little consequence in these lamentable esca-
pades. The struggle in South Wales was followed by a resump-
tion of work not only at 2½ per cent. more of a reduction of
wages than was offered by the employers, but by a greatly
diminished amount of available employment ; and the wick-
edness of bringing about by evil counsels such a hideous
catastrophe was only aggravated by the hypocritical levity with
which the misguided and injured working people were assured
that they had come off with a great victory because the employers had been forced to agree that wages in future shall
be regulated by some form of arbitration or conciliation. It
might no doubt be urged, in similar rhodomontade of miners'
agents, that great advances of colliers' wages were obtained
in 1872-3 by strikes and by pressure of Union methods.
But to balance that account it would be necessary to relate
how these advances have been followed by equal reductions
in 1874-5. What the Miners' Unions really did in these
years was to waste much golden time to themselves and to
the country in forcing advances of wages, which in so far as

[1] Q. 10,572-630.

they rested on any sustainable basis would have come without any wasteful efforts ; and further to waste many more
golden hours to themselves and the country a second time
in vainly resisting inevitable reductions of all the previous
advances.

But while it is thus clear the Unions cannot permanently
advance wages, it might have been supposed that they would
have had some success in making wages more uniform in
their respective trades over all parts of the kingdom where
they exerted any influence.   Even this moderate effect, however, cannot be traced to their action in any perceptible
degree ; and this is the more striking since the more intelligent representatives of the Unions, with what seems a
dim foresight of a sphere in which Trade Unions might
really have a useful and practicable office, dwell on the records
they keep of rates of wages in the various districts, and the
large amount of attention they give and expense they incur
in conveying workmen to places where their work is in
large demand, and, it may be presumed, at rising wages. Mr.
Alfred Mault, representing on the employers' side the most
thoroughly unionised trades probably in the kingdom—the
general building trades—gives the Royal Commission the
following variations of wages at their extremes in England,
taking only populous places and centres of active industry :—

Masons	8d. to 3¾d. per hour.
Bricklayers	8d. to 4½d. ,,
Carpenters and Joiners . .	8d. to 4⅝d. ,,
Plasterers	8d. to 4¼d. ,,
Slaters	8d. to 4¾d. ,,
Bricklayers' Labourers . .	5¾d. to 2¾d. ,,

" Wages of Plumbers, Painters, and Glaziers vary just as much as in
     the other trades."[1]

When one reflects on this anomaly it must be perceived
to be hardly within the scope or nature of Trade-Unionism,
as now constituted and conducted, to equalise wages, or to
promote a common well-being of its respective fraternities.
The first point, as we have it from the Unionists themselves,
is to maintain wages at the highest rate wherever it may be

[1] Q. 3010-5.

established ; and it is most improbable that the local unions
where this highest rate exists would permit the general
officers to introduce a multitude of workmen from the lower-
paying districts, by which means the highest rate would be
reduced. The second point is to try to raise the lower rates
of wages by keeping a large number of men on strike, and
feeding them out of the common " benefit funds," to which
the members of the Union on the lowest scale of wages pay
as much as those on the highest.   It is thus clear that until
the Trade Union policy be completely remodelled, there will
not only be no tendency from that source to any greater uniformity of wages in any particular trade throughout the
kingdom, but that the members of the trade working on the
lowest scale of wages will always be the most severely
fleeced in their contributions to the funds as well as in their
actual wages income.

One of the most marked advances of wages among the
older established trades was adduced by Mr. James Wilson,
of the General Builders' Association, in the case of the
tanners of Leeds, whose wages had risen 10 to 15 per cent.
within two or three years, but there were no Unions among
the tanners of Leeds.[1]   The rise of wages of domestic
servants and of farm labourers in the North of England and
Scotland, as well as many other classes of work-people
among whom there has not been any trace of organised combination, greatly exceeds anything that can be shown among
the most closely defended Union trades. As for the shortening of hours of labour, this amelioration neither began
among the Unions nor has it had among the Unions its
most successful results.   If nine hours has been enforced by
a strike in some cases, as by the building trades of London,
it is seen in others, as in Sheffield, that the regulation passes
away when found inconsistent with the profitable existence
of trade, and that the Unions have as little power by arbitrary process to shorten hours as to advance wages.

There is here an important question, deserving the most
careful examination by the Unionists themselves. They
know the cost of the Unions, they know to what extent the

<hr />

[1] Q. 4693-4.

wages they do earn are curtailed by the Union procedure and expenditure; and it is surely the part of prudent men to inquire what return in advance of wages, or shorter hours, the Unions, in the ample experience of twenty years, has made to them for this cost, and for accumulating liabilities for "benefit objects" which must either break down or be secured by "extra levies."

THE HIGHER CONSIDERATIONS.

There is one sure enough conclusion, viz., that the Unions, as hitherto conducted, cannot possibly succeed in accomplishing both their "trade" and their "benefit" objects. If the too inadequate payments for friendly insurance purposes are to be freely appropriated as they have been to management expenses and out-of-work pay in the pursuance of "trade objects," the "benefit objects" can never by any chance or by any "extra levies" conceivable be fulfilled, and there is no financial insurance of these objects whatever that will bear investigation. In so far as the payments are really made for these "benefit objects," the money might as well be cast into the sea. On the other hand, if the payments of the members are to be put into the bank at interest. and reserved for the discharge of the "benefit objects" separate funds must be formed by another scale of contributions for the "trade objects," or the "trade objects" must cease to command the activity and expenditure hitherto so lavishly bestowed upon them with no discernible avail. Of course, if during the last ten or twenty years of activity, expenditure, and turmoil, as appears, the Unions have not advanced their "trade objects" in any compensatory degree, the latter alternative could be adopted with advantage to the members of the Unions; while, at the same time, the formation of separate funds, by additional contributions, for "trade objects" would simply be adding to the cost of what has hitherto had no profitable return. The plain result is that the Trade Unions have not been attaining either of their two classes of "objects;" the "benefit objects" have been sacrificed to the "trade objects;" and the visible

produce of the "trade objects" has been *nil*. If this be so,
and if on an honest investigation of this subject it must be
found that the members of the Trade Unions have so far been
simply wronging and heaping up future disappointment to
themselves, then all that class of essentially superior considerations, viz., the extent to which they have been injuring
others, restraining trade, and narrowing employment for
themselves and for other working people, and robbing the
community by incessant interruptions of labour, when labour
has been most in request and most necessary to the general
weal and equity, pass into a very clear atmosphere, and are
entitled to the highest weight.

The legal *status* of the Unions is another part of the
subject requiring more radical study than it has yet obtained.
The Unionists are not satisfied with their legal position as
it stands, and, on the other hand, there are grave reasons to
be dissatisfied with the practical lapse of common principles
of the law, to the end of covering or winking at all the ex-
ploits and tactics of the Unionists. There must be some
understanding, for example, of the principle laid down in the
Report of the Royal Commissioners that, while conceding
in the fullest sense the right of any combination of working
men to withdraw their labour, and do with their labour
whatever they please, this right of the combination must
not be held to interfere with the right of other working men
to supply their labour if they should so please ; and that
this right is all the more necessary to be protected by the
law, inasmuch as it is the natural right of every man, and in
the face of a combination must be weak, and requires all the
strength the law can give to it. It should be generally
understood what this means, and if the meaning be right, it
should have potency not only in the councils of the Unions,
but in the law itself, and in its practical and efficient administration. Again, it is difficult to conceive the law of this
country falling into such degradation as that in the case of
an employer of labour, himself under contract, and entering
into contract with his workmen, the latter should be at liberty
to throw down their tools at any moment under any of the
numerous petty disputes that arise under the "working

rules" of the Unions, sanctioned only by themselves, without some check upon such conduct, or some effective financial redress to the employer where such conduct is indulged without semblance of excuse. The law of contract, the obligation which an employer owes to his workman and a workman owes to his employer, must be upheld, if the trade of the country is not to fall into general ruin. As for the claims of the Unions to have protection for their funds like insurance societies, these are capable of the most simple and obvious settlement. The Unions have only to adopt a scale of payments fairly adequate to the "benefit objects" insured, and to place the payments under secure reserve at interest for these purposes as they arise. But there is a great difficulty in the law sanctioning and protecting funds paid in for certain purposes and spent for quite other purposes—or, in other words, sanctioning and protecting what, on its face, is a transparent fraud. These and other legal questions involved in the procedure of the Unions, and in their growing demands for higher privileges and special exemptions from common legal responsibility, are worthy of the most careful consideration ; nor is there any reason to conclude that Parliament, in its oozy and jumbling process of conceding whatever the Unionists demand, has yet arrived at any solution of these questions that will solidify into law, or be the source of anything but future evil.

And, in fine, it appears necessary that all these Trade-Union matters should be brought to the test of impartial reason, and that some account should be taken of the views of the masters of economic science who have devoted their lives and their genius to the elucidation of this question of labour and the reward of labour ; so that partial clubs and associations of working men, however numerous or however animated, may not be for ever butting and wasting themselves against a blind wall, but may see more clearly the course wherein the interest of the whole working body is most likely to be found.

VII.

BENEFIT FUNDS AND THEIR APPLICATION.

THE Trade Unions profess to be friendly societies for the insurance of certain benefits to their members on a given scale of weekly payments. They place this part of their business in the forefront of their constitution and rules, and often in the titles they assume, and they make it the foundation of claims for legal protection of their funds, as if they were friendly or benefit insurance societies only, and levied and expended their funds wholly to that end. There is no purpose of trade societies more legitimate than this, or by which, faithfully fulfilled, they could hope to exercise a more wholesome influence over the general value of labour, or the well-being of their own members. But it was soon discovered in the Inquiry of 1867-9 that while this was the professed object of Trade Unions, it was in many cases a profession and little more ; that the "trade objects," already discussed, were the prime objects of the Union, and that the "benefit objects" were simply a decoy to attract members and funds, and that the funds thus obtained were freely and unlimitedly expended on altogether other purposes than those for which they were nominally paid. In other words, the "benefit" part of the system is what, in any other case than that of the Trade Unions, would be pronounced a swindle.

OPINIONS OF THE ACTUARIES.

The Royal Commission put into the hands of Mr. Finlaison, actuary to the National Debt Office, the rules and reports of the Amalgamated Society of Engineers ; and Mr.

Allan, late secretary of that Society, afforded Mr. Finlaison all information he could give towards the solution which the Royal Commission sought of Mr. Finlaison, viz., whether the payments of the members of the Society were sufficient to implement the purposes for which they were made. The Amalgamated Engineers are pre-eminent among Trade Unions, and there can be no doubt that Mr. Finlaison had before him one of the best examples of Trade Union finance that could be produced. Of the Memorandum written by Mr. Finlaison, so fully exhaustive of the subject, it is unnecessary to say more (though its conclusions may have to be reverted to) than that it must be a wonder to any one reading it now in 1876, that so numerous and intelligent a body as the engineers should have gone on, for six years, since that weighty and irrefutable document of science and figures was published, without changing their whole system both of revenue and expenditure.

It is fairer, on the whole to the Unions to take the case of the Amalgamated Carpenters and Joiners, on which Mr. Tucker, actuary to the Pelican Insurance Company, reported; because, first, it was on that case the examination before the Royal Commission chiefly turned, and the Union leaders brought their utmost defensive evidence; and, second, because the Amalgamated Carpenters and Joiners have adopted precisely the same finance rules as the Engineers, and being a younger society its funds necessarily present a more favourable temporary aspect. The older a benefit society is, if there is a radical falsity in its finance, it is only so much nearer its inevitable doom. The chief, but yet not all, the purely "benefit" reliefs which the Amalgamated Society of Carpenters and Joiners promises to its members for a weekly payment of one shilling, are—

1. An allowance of 12s. per week in sickness.
2. A superannuation allowance of from 8s. to 5s. per week according to the duration of membership.
3. A funeral benefit at death, or divided between death of wife and member, of 12l.

In order to gauge the sufficiency of one shilling a week for these three purposes alone, some age must be fixed at

which the superannuation allowance is to begin. There is
no limit of age in the rules of the Carpenters and Joiners,
only a member must have been twelve years continuously
in membership before he be entitled to the minimum superannuation of 5s. a week. Mr. Tucker, in this extraordinary
vagueness of the tables of a society proposing to secure life
benefits of any kind, assumed the liberal limit of 60 years
of age at which any superannuation allowance could be due,
and on this assumption he found that to secure these three
benefits, members entering at various ages would have to
pay up to 60 years of age the following sums :—

At 25 years	.	.	.	.	£3	4	0 per annum.
,, 30 ,, .	.	.	.	.	4	1	6 ,,
,, 35 ,, .	.	.	.	.	5	6	0 ,,
,, 40 ,, .	.	.	.	.	6	10	6 ,,
,, 45 ,, .	.	.	.	.	7	14	6 ,,

Any number of young men, of 25 years of age, and forming themselves into a society, and taking only new members
at the same age, could not possibly secure these three
benefits alone by a payment of 1s. a week, or 2l. 12s. a
year. The whole compact would break down before a
majority of them were either dead or superannuated. But
if older men, up to any working age, were brought in at the
same rate of payment—as the rule of the Engineers', Carpenters and Joiners', and other Trade Unions is—the collapse would be all the more rapid. The data of the results
thus applied to the Amalgamated Carpenters and Joiners by
Mr. Tucker, require further that every penny of the money
paid in and not disbursed for the three benefit purposes
named, as they arise, shall be invested and reserved at 3l. 5s.
per cent. per annum in compound interest; but what did
he discover as to the actual employment of the funds of
this Society? He had the accounts of 1865 before him,
and out of a total income of 10,487l. there had been dissolved in expenses of management and various disbursements, 6,733l. Of these disbursements only 1,634l. were
paid for sickness, funeral benefits, and superannuations, so
that not more than 50 per cent. of the whole income of the

Society from the contributions of the members were paid
and reserved from the annual expenditure for these three
important benefits, though to secure them fully the whole
income would, in the opinion of the actuaries, be all too
inadequate. The accounts of 1866 showed similar results.
Out of an expenditure in that year of 11,809*l*., 2,669*l*. were
appropriated for sick allowances and payments at death,
and out of a total income of 16,539*l*. a surplus of only
4,731*l*. was carried to the fund. Fifty-five per cent. of the
whole contributions of the members were consumed on
other purposes than those for which they were levied.

The three benefits named, moreover, though the most
important, are not the only benefits of a friendly character
professedly assured by the Amalgamated Society of Carpenters and Joiners. There are promised payments in cases
of accident, loss of tools, benevolent grants in cases of distress, and towards emigration, of which Mr. Tucker reported
that "no provision for them whatever exists in the present
contribution of its members." But greatest of all, there is
an item of expenditure very obscurely entered in the rules
as "donations to members out of work from causes other
than sickness," which, when inquired into, is found to be no
other than the "strike allowance" distributed freely in the
case both of individual workmen and of masses of workmen,
and forming the real purpose to which the funds are held at
all times to be subservient. To show the fearless dissipation of the contributions of the Amalgamated Carpenters and
Joiners for sick, funeral, and superannuation benefits on
quite other purposes, it is only necessary to present the
following analysis of what became of the large income,
16,539*l*. of 1866 :—

Trade expenses ("members on strike, &c.")				30	per cent.
Management expenses	.	.	.	. 25	,,
Benefit paid·and reserved	.	.	.	. 45	,,

These facts from the accounts of a model Union dispose
conclusively of any claim of such societies to be considered
insurers of benefits turning upon sickness, death, or superannuation, for the money they receive. What appears is

G

simply that certain contributions are levied on false pretences of insurance, and that the greater part of the money
thus raised is spent on "trade objects," and on "strikes,"
"donations to members out of work," and other methods of
loss and expense by which these objects are attempted to
be accomplished. There is nothing to be made out of the
reports of the actuaries but this, and one is glad, therefore,
to turn from so lamentable a disclosure to what the Union
representatives said in defence or palliation of what is *primâ
facie* a gross fraud on the working men betrayed into such
heavy contributions from their earnings.

APOLOGIES OF THE UNIONISTS.

Mr. Applegarth, secretary of the Amalgamated Carpenters
and Joiners, on being recalled, frankly admitted that he was
"altogether unprepared for this," [1] and begged the Royal
Commissioners to understand, in contradiction, as already
noted, of what he had stated in his first examination, that
his society was "pure and simple a trade society," and that
it principally existed for so-called trade purposes, though
there were "excellent benefits" in connection with it. This
was putting the cart and the horse at least in their proper
places, but it was a distinct repudiation of the insurance
character and obligation of the Trade Unions ; and nothing
more was left to Mr. Applegarth than to adduce any special
or general resources on which his Union and others relied
as a matter simply of confidence and understanding among
their members to keep themselves afloat.   Mr. Applegarth
and the other Trade Union witnesses said very ably all that
could be said on this head.   There are three main apologies
in their evidence for the perversion disclosed by the actuaries
in the expenditure of their benefit funds.

(1.) It was alleged that the funds of the Unions gain
much by the large number of their members who are annually cut off for non-payment or some other offence, and who
leave in the Union all they have previously contributed.
"We excluded last year." said Mr. Applegarth, from the

[1] Q. 6539.

Amalgamated Carpenters and Joiners, "1,000 and some odd members. Now we should have a profit from those members of 2,000l., or perhaps more even than that." A full sixth of the members would appear to be cut off every year. This failure or secession of members is a source of some profit in all friendly and insurance societies ; and in the hands of the Trade Unions, with absolute powers of "exclusion." profit from this source may be greater than in other societies ; but this profit cannot improve substantially, on insurance principles, the funds of the Unions, for the obvious reason that the excluded members can rejoin, after a lapse of years, under the same or nearly same rate of contribution as when they were much younger men. Mr. Applegarth said it was customary for members of his society to be excluded and readmitted three or four times. But there is no gain, as he seemed to think, to the permanent funds of the Union from this source, save in a fictitious grabbing, from year to year, of money contributed by excluded members, more than lost already by the fact that these excluded members have ceased in the interim to pay their weekly contributions, and may rejoin the society at any future period of their lives on much the same scale of contributions as at the first. The only sure inference from this apology is, that a large proportion of Trade Union members are wasting, in the heyday of their years, large sums of money without in reality assuring themselves of any benefit whatever ; and that the Union "authorities" are under a most dangerous temptation, as members advance in years, to set aside their counsels and their interests, and to exclude them on arbitrary pretences from the society in order to relieve the fund, in which they have the largest stake.

(2.) It was apologised by Mr. Applegarth that there are various sources of income to Trade Unions which the actuaries had not taken into account. There are some entrance fees, and there are threepenny and sixpenny fines on members for being six or eight weeks in arrear ; and there are, no doubt, many other small fiscal exactions which weigh on the wages of working members of the Union, and which might go to lessen in some small degree the burden

of "management expenses." These in the Amalgamated
Society of Carpenters and Joiners appear from above-given
figures to be 25 per cent. of the whole gross income. Mr.
Applegarth said, in respect to this dead weight of management expense, that there was really a direct profit to his
Society from some parts of it, of which he instanced printing and publications. For every copy of rules, for example,
the members paid threepence each, and for monthly reports
a penny each, and on all this there was a large profit to the
Union. This adds a new burden to the members that is
not in the contract, and surely Mr. Applegarth is intelligent
enough to see that the whole profit from these printing
operations goes, or ought to go, into the gross annual income
of his Society, and that as 55 per cent. of this gross income
is squandered in purposes wholly different from the sick,
funeral, and superannuation benefits for which the members
pay their ordinary one shilling a week, any overcharges for
entrance fees, fines, and prices for printed documents, only
prove how much more dearly to the members the whole
financial base of his Society is being consumed.

(3.) It was contended by the Trade-Union witnesses that
they had a resource in extraordinary levies on their members, which was sufficient to cover any deficiency that
could arise in their funds. The general idea of the Union
secretaries examined was, that if they had only a few thousand pounds in the bank, and the sum was not deemed
sufficient to carry them over the year, they had only to
announce an extra levy, and it would be paid; and that
what the total liabilities of a society to its members might
be was a matter of little or no concern! Mr. Applegarth
put this resource of extra levies in the strongest possible
point of view. His Union was not only ready to pay at
once whatever extra levies might be necessary to fulfil its
obligations to its own members, but was ready cheerfully to
pay any extra levy necessary to help other Unions in the
same direction. Talk of this kind, of course, is rather
wild, and has broken into froth a hundred times over in the
history of Trade Unions. But the actual state of the case
will be best seen from what Mr. Finlaison and Mr. Tucker

found the deficiency of the funds of the Amalgamated Engineers and the Amalgamated Carpenters and Joiners to be in 1867, and which the intervening years, on the system pursued, can only have increased.

DEFICIT OF FUNDS IN 1866.

Mr. Finlaison, valuing the three great benefit insurances of the Amalgamated Engineers in the ordinary way applied to Friendly Societies, found these liabilities of the Union to be 2,553,715*l*. ; and valuing in the same way the whole assets of the Union—the contributions of its 33,000 members until 60 years of age, the reserved money in hand 138,113*l*., and all the arrears due—he found the total value of assets to be 1,367,042*l*., and the deficiency of the funds in 1867 to be thus no less than 1,186,673*l*. By a further analysis, in which he took into account, in the most patient and skilful spirit, the effect of secession or " excluded members," and other exceptional elements in the case of Trade Unions insisted upon by Mr. Allan, Mr. Applegarth, and others, Mr. Finlaison finally reduced the deficiency of the assets of the Amalgamated Engineers on the three benefit insurances alone to 453,930*l*.,—to which had to be added on the principles of expenditure proceeding in the Union a liability for "donations to members out of employ" of 547,042*l*.—making a total uncovered liability of 1,000,972*l*., for which there was no provision save by extraordinary levies. The amount of extraordinary levy due by the Amalgamated Engineers to carry out their expenditure and assure their promised "benefits" was thus, in point of fact, 30*l*. 10*s*. per member as far back even as 1867. Mr. Finlaison's most reduced estimate of the deficiency of the Amalgamated Carpenters and Joiners on the three benefits was 46,414*l*., and on "donations to members out of employ" a future charge in present amount of 155,094*l*.—a total visible deficiency of 201,508*l*., requiring an extraordinary levy of 33*l*. 9*s*. per member.

Mr. Tucker, by a less exhaustive process than that of Mr. Finlaison, found the deficiency liability of the Carpenters '

and Joiners to be 85,408*l.*, for which there was only a fund
in hand of 13,052*l.* ; but in seven past years 9,840*l.* had
been spent for other purposes than the insurance, and, without reckoning interest, the fund in hand might have been
22,892*l.* Mr. Tucker's estimate of the deficiency liability of
the Engineers, making large assumptions in favour of the
Society, as in the case of the Carpenters and Joiners, was
679,734*l.*, against which there was a fund in hand of
138,113*l.* But the Society, he found, had spent in sixteen
years, for extraneous purposes, 334,648*l.* ; so that again,
without reckoning interest, the funds in hand might have
been 472,761*l.*, which is about exactly the same sum as Mr.
Finlaison found that the Amalgamated Engineers by an extraordinary and specially reserved levy could have proceeded in 1867 to place the " three benefits " in an assured
form. That extra levies of this heavy amount can be made
on the members of Trade Unions must be set aside as
wholly impracticable. There is nothing in the rules of the
Unions that could be construed in a court of equity as an
obligation to pay such levies even if the members had the
means ; and no extra levy can be declared within the Union
itself until carried by a majority of votes. The only extra
payment likely to be submitted to is one designed to tide
over some emergency of a few months or a year ; and as such
levies increase, as they must increase in the most powerful
and most business-like Unions from the pressure of their
" benefit " engagements, there is a point when the extra
levies will be so heavy that everyone, save the older men
clinging to the provision which they had fondly laid up
against infirmity and the workhouse, will find that it is
better to be out of the Union than in it, and when the
system must fall.

Examples of the breaking-up of Unions from this cause
are by no means rare. The large accumulated funds that
have been dissipated time after time by the Amalgamated
Miners and other fighting Unions, leaving the patient con-
tributors bare of any means of support in their extremity,
only to be harangued and urged by their leaders to begin
anew the self-denying task of weekly contributions, destined

to go the same bad road as all preceding contributions, would form an enormous *per contra* to any advantages realised by the men, and exhibit an appalling waste of one of the most sacred of all funds—the working man's savings and capital.   On the other hand, there are humbler and quieter Unions that succeed by a more regulated action, and a better system of accounts, in distributing a tolerably secure amount of relief among their members.   In one case that came prominently before the Royal Commission of 1867-9 —the " Friendly Society of Operative Stonemasons," represented by Mr. Richard Harnott, secretary—the Union had adopted the rule of separating their payments for "trade" and "benefit" purposes.   One portion of the members paid 4*d*. a week for trade benefits only, and another portion paid 7½*d*. a week for sick and other friendly allowances superadded to the trade benefits.   This separation of funds for totally distinct purposes marks a degree of good sense very rare among the Unions that figure actively on the public stage ; and yet it was almost wholly vitiated in this case by the fact that the trade and benefit funds were after all not kept separate in the expenditure, but formed a common fund.[1]   The haphazard course of the large fighting Unions has a tendency to beguile the smaller and ordinarily less bellicose Unions into an unsound system of finance.   But the Amalgamated Engineers and the Amalgamated Carpenters and Joiners stand in some measure apart.   They are among the largest and the most consolidated Unions in the kingdom : they have not, for a few years at least, been involved in the unceasing warfare of strikes and lock-outs on a heroic scale which appears to be the lot of the various amalgamations of miners ; and there is probably a growing sense of financial responsibility, both among their members and their officers, which preserves them from being swayed by balloon experiments from their own centre of gravity.   At any rate, there can be no more favourable test of Trade Union finance, or of the degree of wisdom with which pounds, shillings, and pence are managed in Trade-Union affairs, than is afforded by the accounts of these two great Societies.

[1] Q. 1032-1133.

Now, the general fact to be observed of the funds of the Amalgamated Engineers and the Amalgamated Carpenters and Joiners is that from 50 to 55 per cent. of the contribution of one shilling per week from the members was being consumed every year on other purposes than those for which the contributions were paid.   In this annually-expended moiety of the contributions of the members there was a small modicum that went to the sick, funeral and superannuation allowances for which the contributions were made.   In the case of the Carpenters and Joiners this modicum was 1,634*l*. in 1865, and it was 2,669*l*. in 1866 ; and in the natural course this demand of the members on the fund for the benefit allowances for which they stipulated must on an average of years constantly increase.   Supposing even the " trade " and " management " expenses not to increase, though they are by far the most lively parts of the expenditure, this annually increasing demand of the members for benefit allowances must produce a pressure on the funds which they will be eventually unable to sustain.   Let it be kept in mind that the estimate of the actuaries is that the whole contribution of the members, though reserved from year to year at interest, and drawn upon only for the benefit stipulations, with all trade objects and management expenses eliminated, would be barely adequate.   The apologies offered do not meet this financial exigency in any degree.   There is no doubt a great *esprit de corps* among Trade Unionists that makes them somewhat regardless of expense.   They may not care much for the " benefit objects " to which they subscribe, and may be happy in thinking that meanwhile they are throwing vigour into the great struggle with their employers.   But as they grow older, and fall into sickness, and have children and wives to bury, and become old and infirm, they will reasonably enough look for the reliefs for which they have paid, and shall certainly have been grievously wronged, and miserably disappointed, if they do not receive them.

VIII.

EFFECTS OF THE TRADE UNIONS ON TRADE.

It might be safely inferred from the rules and action of the Unions, as these have been given from their chief interpreters and apologists, that they could have no good effect upon trade, but the contrary.

Set aside all unlawful violence, all acts of outrage, already fully or half discarded by the Unionists, and there remain certain permanent features of the Union policy. The systematic interference administered with compulsory power of strike, not only over employers in the conduct of their business, but over working men in the disposal of their labour—the frequent interruptions and withdrawals of labour, whether on a large or small scale equally arbitrary—and the constant effort to limit the supply of labour in each trade and each division of a trade, and to limit it most in the prosperous and expanding times that revisit nearly all trades, when, in order to secure the new ground, the supply of labour should be most amply increased—are equally acknowledged official Union operations, of which no one, accustomed to think and reason, can doubt the bad effects in impeding trade, in spreading social injustice, and in narrowing the sphere of employment and wages, from the enlargement of which all the prosperity of the working classes must come. They reproduce, indeed, in these enlightened and civilized days, a new form of the old feudal abuses and predatory obstructions against which our ancestors fought so stoutly under the name of "restraint of trade," and for which they found a remedy in the resources of the common law. A free course had to be made for trade in England from the earliest periods of our history—free passage on our highways, free and open markets for goods and staples, no monopolising, no obstruction to the common freedom necessary to each and all—even free light, air, and water to all and each; and no one, whatever his mastery or possession, to obstruct or injure another in what was a common and natural right of everybody. Much of this ancient difficulty has been removed, and the principle of law elicited in the long struggle has been too well established to be wholly lost. But now appear on the scene the Trade Unions, under whose self-made codes almost every section of the highly organised industry and trade of this country is found to be barred and hindered in its free and legitimate course to an extent of which there is probably no parallel in the most barbarous times. It is thus the old fight on the same ground, but under new circumstances; and no rational person can doubt that in this intricate policy of the Unions, in so far as it is policy in action, there is an exquisite but yet rude revival of the old contention in this country that there must be no obstruction, under whatever cloud of authority veiled, to common right.

CONCLUSIONS OF THE ROYAL COMMISSION.

This important question, however, may not be dismissed on a general inference, however certain and apparent. The Report of the Royal Commission dealt somewhat gingerly with the "effects of Trade Unions on trade," not that there was any want of evidence before the Commission on this point, but probably in 1867-9, when stocks and values of goods, and the markets for them, were all in a regular and progressive form, it did not appear to be of urgent moment, and the Commission may have declined to report more than was enough for the occasion. The moving cause of the inquiry was the terrible outbreak of Trade Union outrages in Sheffield. It was necessary to call the Unions to account, and to see what *raison d'être* they could establish under the law. The Trade Unions demanded this inquest; and so the apologetic strain of the Unions bulked largely in the evidence throughout, and was the main burden of the Commission.

The Report simply concluded, therefore, on this substantial part of the case :—(1) That in respect of industries in which foreign competition does not enter, "the operations "of Trade Unions may have tended to enhance, of late "years, the cost of production," and that "there is nothing, "à priori, to prevent the operation of Trade Unions from "raising the cost of commodities until the rise is checked "by the diminution of consumption." And (2) that, in respect of industries in which foreign competition does enter, "we have been unable to arrive at any very definite solution "of the problem whether or not Trade Unions have had, of "late years, a mischievous operation in this direction ; . . . "and taking the returns of our export trade during the last "few years, we cannot state that we have traced any distinct "connection between its fluctuations in particular employ- "ments, and the prevalence of Trade Unions in those em- "ployments."

Of course, this is a feeble and inadequate deliverance. But we, who have had six years' more experience, must not complain that the Royal Commissioners did not know as much as may be known to us all now. Yet before proceeding to what may be considered a demonstration of the effects of Union action on trade, it may be useful to glance at some of the evidence that was before the Commission on this part of the question.

EVIDENCE ON THE BUILDING TRADES.

The building trades are probably as fair a sample of trade exempt from foreign competition as can be chosen. Though there have been some instances of importing foreign doors and windows, yet the erection of houses is an essentially domestic industry. Let all reference to the disgraceful proceedings of the bricklayers' and brickmakers' Unions at Manchester, involving district monopolies, exclusion of machine-made bricks, and war to the knife in night burnings and assassinations, more like the state of life among Red Indians than civilized beings, be here wholly excluded from view, and let attention be confined to the effect of the most ordinary and approved rules of the Trade Societies.

Mr. G. F. Trollope, of Messrs. George Trollope and Sons, builders, said :—

> " With regard to the amount of work men will do within a given time, things have been getting worse and worse. The men have a theory that, if there is work for three men to be done, they are doing their cause a service if they can somehow scheme it that four men shall be employed, and hold that it does not concern the employer, who has only to put a profit on what he pays to his men, whether the work is done quickly or not. This is a most unrighteous state of things." [1]

It will be observed that there is no question here of raising the rate of wages. The permanent tendency of the state of things described by Mr. Trollope, indeed, must be to lower wages, man by man, mediately and immediately, in the building trade. The smaller amount of work done for the larger amount of wages being the ruling consideration, and the employers being expected by the Unionists to put their profit on to whatever sum the wages amount to, the whole burden of this Union policy must fall on the community, on the owners and occupiers of houses, and, in other words, on the working classes chiefly, who of all classes most need a supply of better and cheaper houses.

Evidence of this kind before the Royal Commissioners was so abundant that they entered this sentence in their Report :—

> " We are disposed to think that the operation of Trade Unions may have tended to enhance in these trades of late years the cost of production, and that houses and other buildings might have been somewhat better and cheaper at the present time had not Trade Unions interfered so extensively and so vexatiously with the proceedings of the employers. It does not necessarily follow that they have raised wages in those trades, and improved thereby the condition of the workman ; the contrary, in the long run, is more probab'e."

This being the result of Trade Union action in the building trades, it is only necessary to imagine the same action in

---

[1] Q. 2920-3.

other domestic industries in order to perceive that the general effect of thus making necessaries of life costlier than they otherwise would be, in pursuit of a wholly elusory advantage to the clubbists, falls from circle to circle *in cumulo* on the working classes, both as consumers and producers, and that the final result is a diminution of the volume of practicable trade, and a corresponding diminution of the amount of employment and wages, with all the straits which these results carry to the working man.

With respect to industries in which foreign competition enters closely, and in which there is every reason to think that it will be more operative in future than it has been in past times, the evidence before the Royal Commission was not so full as it may have since become, but the following testimonies in 1867-9 are worthy of note.

Mr. Samuda, shipbuilder on the Thames, for example, said :—

"My greatest customers used to be, five years ago, France, Russia, Prussia, Egypt, and Turkey. I have had as much as 700,000*l.* worth of orders from those different Governments in my yard at one time ; but at the present moment France is competing with me, and taking away my Prussian orders ; she is also taking away from me my Egyptian orders, and at this time there is in France no less than 380,000*l.* of work going on for two of those Governments who have been my own customers for fifteen years." [1]

Mr. Samuda, at that time, employed only 200 workmen, where he used to employ 1,200 to 2,000.

Mr. Robinson, of the Atlas Works, Manchester, putting in a table of the delivery of locomotive engines by his firm and their destinations from 1834 to 1866, said :—

"It will be plainly seen that where at one time we had the control of certain markets, we have lost it ; and that Prussia and Würtemberg, and France and Austria, to which we formerly sent locomotive engines, have now become manufacturers themselves for their own countries, and very important competitors with us for neutral markets, such as Russia, Spain, Portugal, Italy, and so forth. The proportion of engines supplied for abroad since the years 1855-6 has been constantly diminishing as compared with the number supplied for England. I believe

---

[1] Q. 16,757.

Mr. Schneider, of Creuzot, is able to make his engines quite as satisfactorily as English firms ; and I know to my cost that last year when
negotiating a contract for forty engines for Russia, when I thought I had
the thing in my own hand, Mr. Schneider walks in and takes it off. It
has just arrived at this point : supposing that we can make an engine
for 2,000*l.*, and the foreigners can make it for 1,980*l.*, in all probability
they would get the order. Now, everything that contributes to the fact
that ours costs us 20*l.* per engine more, of course gives them a facility in
competition. . . . . At Creuzot the average wages of all the men in
their engine factory only comes to 2*s.* 11*d.* per day of eleven hours ;
whereas, in our works it reaches 3*s.* 10¾*d.* for the same number of hours
— with us they work ten hours, but I have calculated it for eleven hours
to make it proportionate—and including the piecework balances we pay,
it actually reaches 4*s.* 5¾*l.* as compared with their 2*s.* 11*d.*" [1]

Mr. Beyer, of Beyer, Peacock, and Co., Gorton Foundry,
Manchester, said :—

" In some branches of manufacture the Germans have outstripped
us. In iron and steel it is very clear they are in advance of us ; and I
will give you one instance. At one of the largest establishments on the
Continent, that of Borsig, at Berlin, they could not make a crooked,
that is, a crank axle, and they began to make their locomotive engines
with a straight axle. That was probably in 1837 or 1838. Now things
have quite changed. When we want a really good axle we are obliged
to send to Germany, they make it of such a superior material." [2]

To which Mr. Robinson added : "We have paid the
highest price for German axles."

Mr. Roden, managing partner of Earl Granville's coal
and iron works in North Staffordshire, detailing the circumstances of a strike in 1865, which lasted twenty weeks,
threw out of employment four times the number of men
responsibly concerned in it, and caused a direct loss to the
North Stafford district of a quarter of a million of money,
said :—

"The operations of the Unions in North Staffordshire closed Mr.
Bates's large works finally. It became a question with us whether we
should give way to the men and be ruined, or not. If we did not get
our work done at the same price as other people [South Staffordshire
and North of England districts] we should be ruined, and we determined to close our works for ever rather than proceed on the terms

[1] Q. 19-019-39.   [2] 18,935-8.

demanded. It was entirely in consequence of the strike in North Stafford-shire that Belgium had such a lead of us. The Belgians went in immediately, and took orders for enormous quantities in Russia, France, and Germany, far more than they could execute, and we have not yet succeeded in getting that back. Indeed, my works have been working only three days or four days a week for months. I have no hesitation in saying that, had it not been for the North Staffordshire strike, we should have been practically in full work up to the present time."[1]

Mr. Mundella said :—

"I have known strikes to drive away trade, and I have known strikes to introduce trade in other localities abroad. In regard to our competition with France and Germany, I can recollect that only twelve years ago there was scarcely a steam-power hosiery machine in France ; now they are making as good as we are."[2]

Dr. George Lloyd, of Lloyd and Co., glass trade, in which there has been an active and over-meddling Unionism, said :—

"Foreign competition is increasing almost daily. There are many articles now introduced from the Continent in flint glass which formerly were inadmissible, partly because they were of inferior quality, and partly because they were inapplicable to the English market, and were too expensive. Now the quality is improving, and the cost of production and labour in England is greater than abroad."[3]

These opinions, delivered to the Royal Commissioners six years ago, are enough, both from the high authority of the persons from whom they emanate, and the great amount of our exportable commodities which they cover. to prove the closeness and keenness of foreign competition with the manufacturing industry of this country—the only purpose, indeed, for which they are here adduced. It would be as absurd to think that the great nations of the Continent are to be always asleep while we are always awake, and to take from us contentedly at our own prices whatever we manufacture for them, as it would be to think with the late Mr. Allan, of the Amalgamated Engineers. that the fact of Trade Unions being in course of rapid formation on the Continent, and that Union rules, strikes, and all the rest of the obstructive Union policy. will soon be going on all over the world as they are doing here, affords any solution whatever

[1] Q. 10,586-610-649.   [2] 19,423-434.   [3] 18,346

of this economical incident of foreign competition. To apply a blister through the International Association or any other medium to one part of the industrial body in order to counteract the effects of a blister already applied to another, partakes too much of surgical quackery to be accepted in a complicated subject of this kind. Still less may it be thought, on the other hand, that a remedy against foreign competition is to be found in a reduction of British wages to the foreign level. This is a remedy which has never been in question, and it is only due to observe that the employers, chief managers, and chief engineers of works above quoted, as well as others who might be quoted, were most unwilling —save in cases of great strikes extending over months or half a year on some dispute of wages as between one district of the United Kingdom and another, and involving a great lapse of production and impossibility of fulfilling orders —to say that the action of the Trade Unions had favoured foreign competition against British industry; because when brought to account by the Commissioners they were unable to aver that the Unions had really had any effect for the last twenty years in raising wages in any appreciable degree, though by strikes and other obstructive methods they had caused much trade to pass away from the hands of their employers and from themselves into foreign channels. This is a striking disclosure in itself, seeing that to "advance wages and resist reduction of wages" is the chief and avowed object for which all this Trade-Union organisation and activity, waste of funds, and loss of trade and labour, are expended. The purport of the evidence before the Royal Commission, from other witnesses than Trade Unionists, was simply to the effect that foreign competition is a permanent fact which the manufacturing industry of this country has to encounter in any case; that our foreign customers in the course of a few years are found first to leave us, then to become our competitors; and that it devolves on the energies of British capital and commerce, and on the skill and superiority of British artisanship, to recover in new forms the ground thus periodically lost through the proper, regular, and indeed congratulatory advance of other nations. But it is surely indiscreet, or even suicidal, for any portion of the working men of this country by any Union action utterly profitless to themselves, to hasten this process more than enough.

In the natural course, supposing our industrial energies to stagnate as the Union policy would seem to compel them to do, it would follow that in proportion as foreign nations thus ceased to be customers, and became competitors against us in our own and neutral markets, wages would rise in foreign nations and fall here to a degree in which British industry might perchance raise up its head again, though doubtfully and under much greater difficulty than it should have had in maintaining its original superiority. But so far the question of wages would appear, from the evidence of 1867-9, to have had little or no place in the actual problem. The British workman, in branches of trade exposed to foreign competition, earns much more than the foreign workman ; and the condition on which this prosperity may be sustained or improved is, that both employers and employed be energetic, inventive, resourceful in their mutual spheres, and that the capital and labour of the country be not sat upon in any way by the Trade Unions, as if there were no such fact as foreign competition in the case.

RATE OF WAGES NOT THE CHIEF QUESTION.

The extent to which the action of Trade Unions arrests trade, and lessens the demand for labour and the average rate of wages, cannot be estimated from considerations alone of temporary advances of wages obtained by particular Unions, or of whether in branches of trade under other Unions there has been any advance of wages at all, to which class of considerations the Royal Commission appears to have confined its inquiry, or at least restricted the scope of its conclusions. The Unions seldom obtain advances of wages that are not impending without any action of theirs, and that might not be obtained by another course than theirs ; when they do force an advance, it is usually a provisional advance to be followed by a reduction under given circum-

II

stances ; when this necessary reduction comes, they either
submit to it with good grace, or in bad temper after a long
and costly struggle, or they succeed in their resistance, in
which case they find they can only be employed in diminished
numbers; and the law to which capital and wages are alike
subject asserts its power under all these futile and incessant
efforts, that never rise after all above a merely temporary and
provisional arrangement, itself the source of new strifes and
misunderstandings.   Nothing can be inferred from such
spasmodic movements as to the general value of labour, or the
substantial reward and prosperity of the working classes.   It
is not only necessary to take into account the heavy loss
sustained by the men, first, in forcing the advance, and,
second, in resisting its reduction ; but also that in the inti-
mate relation of supply and demand by which the one through
prices practically measures the other, the diminished production arising from the Union action gives an inflated range
to prices, and forces a limitation of demand by which any
advantage apparently gained is not only imperilled, but often
for a long period of time completely overthrown.   The
evidence that the Unions, beyond acting as a mere disturbing force, have had any direct effect in raising wages in
their own province was so slight that the Royal Commission
waived any formal decision as to the effect which the action
of the Unions had, or was calculated to have, in depressing
and diminishing the productive industry of the country—the
question on which the attainable wages, and every other
interest, of the working classes absolutely turn.

EFFECT OF DIMINISHED PRODUCTION CAUSED BY THE UNIONS.

It is manifest, however, that, apart from nominal wages,
there are elements in the action of the Unions that have a
direct and powerful effect in narrowing the sphere of trade,
in raising the prices of commodities, and in producing an
inflation of values and a disturbance of relations between
one branch of trade and another, under which all classes,
Unionists themselves not the least, find themselves incom-

moded, until the general tension becomes so great that the course of trade collapses, and falls into more or less protracted periods of depression and common loss. The rate of production, when trade is expanded and has fair opportunity of making a permanent advance, is of infinitely more account to the workman than any question of wages that a Trade Union has ever raised with employers; and time in this sense is more valuable even than money. The time lost in "strikes" alone, of which for ten years there has scarce been a week or even a day without many examples, often on a gigantic scale, throughout the kingdom, must, when summed up, be an immense subtraction from the productive power of the country—its power, that is to say, to produce commodities when they are in full or increasing demand, and when it is supremely necessary that the production should be so adequate to the demand as to keep it in force, in order that there may be more workmen employed and more wages for them all to receive. It is important that the Unionists should be brought to see that, in making labour dear by the utmost ingenuity of contrivance and action to employers, the employers, in so far as this elaborate process has any effect, can only sustain themselves by making the products of the labour dearer to the consumers, and that the consumers will not and cannot move one iota in this direction beyond what suits themselves, though the Unionists and their employers should alike be reduced to distress or ruin.

We have only to fancy, therefore, what is indeed the sober reality—viz., all the principal trades of the country organised in this close Union formation, and all bent on making labour dear in nominal wages to the employers, not only by strikes for higher wages and for shorter hours at the same wages as the longer hours, but also by strikes and cessations from labour breaking out sporadically in the various industries of the kingdom in enforcement of innumerable minor rules and matters of sentiment tending to the same end, in order to perceive what must be the result. There must be an enormous loss of productive power in all these trades; and, if the demand upon them be either equable or on the increase, what the several trades produce must be always scarcer, more difficult to supply, and commanding for the time a higher price, whether the Unionists have obtained higher wages or any of their minor objects or not. But, in either case, the results immediately appear in the weekly expenditure of the Unionists themselves. House-rents are higher, coal is much dearer, boots and shoes and clothing are rising in value,—every kind of ware thus acted upon by the Union artisans can only be bought with more money ; till it is found that the current wages are not so adequate as they were, and some general advance appears necessary not only in the Union circles but among the whole wage-earning population. It is precisely at this stage, however, that the Union action becomes most excited, that strikes are most frequent and on the largest scale, and that production is restrained and diminished more than ever, leading inevitably to still higher prices, with the consequent greater difficulty and poverty among consumers. This cycle might go on for ever but for a Nemesis that has been working unseen in its folds from the beginning. Every successive advance in the price of commodities has been steadily limiting the demand for them, and preparing a catastrophe in which it is found that the movement has been proceeding on a hollow basis—not on the increase but on the restraint and stoppage of productive labour—and that both profits and wages must fall for a time under diminished trade to a lower level.

The action of the Trade Unions has effects on prices and on the course of trade somewhat analogous to those of suc-cessive issues of convertible paper currency or frenzies of speculative over-trading, the only difference being that these act on demand, and the Unions on supply. But the economic law violated in both cases is the same : the ultimate results are the same ; and it is a rather hard trial of patience, after so much has been done successfully to correct these evils in financial and commercial circles, to find the old demon of derangement rising in a new form of strength and blindness among the working classes.

What is thus described has been so abundantly and

painfully illustrated since the Royal Commission closed its inquiry in 1869, that some facts must here be adduced, that have since transpired, and of which there can be no interpretation but one.

ILLUSTRATIVE CASE OF THE SCOTCH PIG-IRON TRADE.

Let us take first, for example, the statistics of the Scotch pig-iron trade. They are more regular and complete than any accessible statistics of the whole pig-iron trade of the kingdom ; but what is true of the Scotch pig-iron trade, on the points to be referred to, is true also of the pig-iron trade of England. The following are the production of each year, the average price in each year, and the stocks at the close of each year, of Scotch pig-iron, in the five years from 1869 to 1873 inclusive :—

	Production.	Average Price.	Stocks.
1861	.. 1,150,000 tons.	... 53s. 3d. per ton....	620,000 tons.
1870	... 1,206,000 ,,	... 54s. 4d. ,,	... 665,000 ,,
1871	... 1,160,000 ,,	... 58s. 11d. .,	... 490,000 ,,
1872	... 1,090,000 ,,	... 102s. 0d. ,,	... 194,000 ,,
1873	... 993,000 ,,	... 117s. 3d. ,,	... 120,000 ,,

These figures must present a greater puzzle to the political economist than he often meets with, for they are in direct disharmony with the most assured principles of his science. That increased demand and higher prices will elicit increased production is as sure a law of trade as any law can be in a sphere where the natural course is always liable to be disturbed and circumvented by perverse human action. Yet it appears from this five years' record of the Scotch pig-iron trade that the production is greatest when the demand is weakest and the price lowest, and that the production is smallest when the demand is strongest and the price highest. In 1869 there could be produced with ease 1,150,000 tons, when the price was 53s. 3d. per ton, and when demand had pressed so little on supply that there was a stock at the end of the year of 620,000 tons ; but in 1873 no more could be produced than 993,000 tons, when

the average price of the year was 117s. 3d., and the increasing demand had reduced the stock to 120,000 tons, or practically, in so great a market as Glasgow, no stock at all.   It
must not be pretended that there was any decay or want of
productive force during the manifestation of these extraordinary results.   In the years of greatest pressure of demand
there were always from 20 to 30 available furnaces out of
blast ; there was no end of capital on the spot to build new
furnaces and extend the working staffs of the furnaces ; nor
was there any falling-off in labour, the labour and the men
of 1869 being all there ; but the fact was that the men,
though rewarded by higher wages, could not be got to do
the same amount of work as when demand was slack, and
prices and wages low.   The result of annually diminished
production of pig-iron, in face of annually increased demand
and higher prices and wages, is referable mainly to the
" Union action " of the coal and ironstone miners.   The
furnacemen had no chance of improving their condition
either in numbers employed or rate of wages, because there
was really less work for them to do in the brisk times of
1872-3 than in the slack times of 1869-70.   They were
directly injured, as well as all other classes of workmen in
the iron trades, by the conduct of the miners, who, after
having caused by their frequent strikes and unsteady labour
the stocks both of coal and pig-iron to be exhausted, fell
into the unhappy blunder of entering into a new series of
strikes for more wages on every rise of price when the
market had become a monopoly, and the price was anything the holder chose to ask, or the " bulls " on the exchange to speculate upon.   The prices of coal and iron in
1872 and 1873, when the stocks had gone, might be hugely
profitable to some few people at the expense of the consumers, but they were indicative of the value neither of
coal, iron, nor labour, and to masters and men alike were
simply the signal of a speedy downfall of the trade.   Yet in
1872 and 1873 mining strikes in thousands and tens of
thousands of men at a time were frequent over the whole
country, aggravating to the last hour all the mischief that
had already been done.

The interdependence of many branches of trade, so that what may seem prosperity to one is only loss and difficulty to the others, is thus an important fact in the general economy. It often happens that Trade Unions, in fighting, as they think, only against employers, are fighting still more madly against each other.

THE COAL TRADE.

The course of coal in production, rapid disappearance of stocks, and prices, in those five years, was the same in all respects as that of pig-iron. The question was the subject of inquiry by a Select Committee of the House of Commons in 1873, from whose Report our facts will be drawn, while taking occasion to correct some of its lame conclusions. Nothing has been more perverted to conceal the true facts of the case, and not only to justify but to carry off in triumph, the action of the Unions, than the report of this Select Committee on Coal. But let us see.

The following are the quantities of coal raised in Great Britain in the five years ending 1872, and the increase of each year on the year preceding :—

	Raised.		Increase.	
1868	103,014,207	tons.	1,312,765	tons.
1869	107,299,634	,,	4,325,902	,,
1870	110,289,722	,,	1,862,654	,.
1871	117,186,278	,,	5,826,290	,,
1872	123,386,758	,,	5,717,794.	,.

Increase in five years...... 19,045,405 tons.

The Select Committee doubts, in its Report, whether the amount of coal raised in 1872 was more than 120,000,000 tons. There was no account of stocks of coal, nor was the Committee able to determine the extent to which the accumulating heaps of small coal without a market till the Coal Famine came, may have entered into these returns of coal " raised " in the years 1871 and 1872. The Draft Report said that the small coal lost because unmarketable until the

Famine years "would be measured by millions of tons each year," so that there is but a florid account of the labour applied in the collieries in these estimates of increased production, more especially in the two last of the years. But in any case, if weight is to be given to the statement of the Select Committee that the production of 1872 was probably not more than 120,000,000 tons, the increase in the five years must be reduced to 15,658,647 tons.

Compare with this the annual increased production in the five years at the head of the Select Committee's table, when there was no such increasing demand for coal, and when no such high wages were earned :—

1859	.	.	.	6,786,665 tons.
1860		.	.	7,733,262 ,,
1861	.		.	5,066,614 ,,
1862	.		.	3,447,147 ,,
1863	.		.	5,692,800 ,,

Increase in five years . 28,726,488 tons.

To what cause can this disastrous lapse of productive power when it was most needed, and most highly paid for, be attributed but to the incessant strikes, suspensions of labour, and general slackening of labour, by the miners' associations? The Select Committee say, from the evidence before them, that "there has been considerable disturbance " in the minds of the workmen employed in and about the " mines respecting the number of hours per day or per week " during which they deemed it their interest to work, and " that the general tendency had been to reduce the hours " of labour. It has also been stated that the Mines Regu- " lation Act, passed last Session, has tended to the same " result, and that the consequence has been that the mines " have not produced the quantity of coal which would " otherwise have been obtained from them." On a fair consideration of the evidence the Select Committee might have affirmed much more. But it is singular that in this Report not one word is said as to the effect of the numerous great strikes extending over long periods, and the innumerable bye-motions by which the mining Unions, after having obtained from a kindly but unguarded Parliament a severe limitation of hours per day, resolved to work only four or five days in the week, when coal was most scarce and dear.

No attempt whatever was made by the Select Committee on Coal to estimate the loss of production from these causes, or how far the production save for these causes would have been adequate to avert the Coal Famine with all its disastrous consequences. But the Committee could emit the general aphorism, since become famous in Union circles, that " the real order of events had been (1) the rise in the " price of iron ; (2) the rise in the price of coal ; and (3) the " rise in the rate of wages ;"—which, however true to facts as contemplated from a balloon two or three miles above the actual world, becomes through the elimination of necessary elements of inquiry the most transparent of fallacies. An increased demand for iron brought an increased price, and an increased demand and price of coal followed by necessary consequence. No power of capitalist or master could have averted a rise of wages in these circumstances, because the coal and iron trades were being rapidly extended, employers were increasing the number of their workmen, and the workmen were making, and might have continued in larger numbers than had ever before been known in this country to make, higher earnings for a lengthened period. But what arrested this prosperous movement was that the policy of the mining associations did not permit this extension of the trade to take place ; the higher their wages, and the larger the number employed, they produced less, and not more ; and supply thus checked and broken down in its efforts to keep pace with demand, coal and iron rose to the "famine prices," when every one but the miners themselves saw· that the game was up, because they were prices which consumers neither would nor could pay, nor the general trade of the world support. The result was the sudden and great collapse under which both employers and employed in the coal and iron trades may probably suffer severely for some years.

That there was no want of men on the books of the mining Unions when the pressure of demand came, and that the only want was that the men would not put their shoulders to the wheel in order to save their general interest from a calamitous fall, would seem to be fully proved by the following figures from the Select Committee's Report :—

	Number of Men Employed.	Quantity of Coal raised per Man.
1870	. . 350,894	. . . 321 tons.
1871	. . 370.881	. . . 317 ,,
1872	. . 413,334	. . . 299 ,,

The Mining Inspectors, in their reports embracing 1873, bring this reductive process of coal-raising to the following results :—

	Annual Product per Man.	Daily Product over 313 Working Days.
1864	. . . 327½ tons.	. . 27½ cwt.
1868	. . . 317 ,,	. . 20 ,,
1873	. . . 271 ,,	. . 17½ ,,

The price of coal was more than doubled within two years. The average wholesale price in London was 18s. 6d. per ton in 1870, and in the first five months of 1873 was 32s. 6d. The price to the consumer in London is five shillings above the wholesale price when the rate is low, and seven shillings when the rate is high. "In London," say the Select Committee on Coal, "the wholesale price on the Coal Exchange reached 45s. for two days in February last." The wages of colliers within the same period were doubled and more than doubled. "The earnings of the working miners," the Select Committee report, "have enormously increased," and they add that, according to much evidence, the greatly increased earnings "have been improvidently spent."

It can scarce be necessary to pursue this subject farther. The colliers are paid, not by the hour or a day of hours, but by their output of coal; so that in this respect they have every stimulus to increase their output when wages are high, and nothing remains to account for the anomalous results of those years but the erroneous ideas instilled into their Unions that to limit production is in all circumstances the way to advance wages; that the less we all do the more we shall all get for what we do ; that even when the commodity we produce has passed out of stock and out of all real market value, and is only kicked about between "bulls" and "bears" in the exchanges on a gambling basis of speculation, every rise of price, even in these circumstances, is a new ground for our working still less, and demanding wages in proportion to the prices struck between the "bulls" and the "bears!" Such are the ideas that have guided the Miners' Associations, and which they have done their best to translate into action. The drama has been wrought out on a splendid arena, covering, indeed, nearly the whole civilised world, for what really brought the increased demand for iron and coal was the liberality of the British capitalist in lending his money to make railways in North and South America, and nearly every quarter of the globe, in the hope that while cheering and helping the British workman in the meanwhile he might perchance reap some profit to himself in the end. The whole of this arena has since been strewn with wrecks—confiding capitalists and deluded workmen plunged in the same common loss and grief.

This is no doubt a flagrant example of Union action, of which we do not often see the like, and of which, it is to be hoped, we may not soon see the like again. But it must nevertheless be held true that the policy of the Unions, in suspending labour, withdrawing labour, forbidding labour, under the hope of advancing wages, in so far as it is active, must in all cases have precisely similar results, and that the whole system, as hitherto informed and organised, is destructive of trade, of the demand for and the rewards of labour, and of the true interests of the working classes.

IX

LEGALITY OF THE TRADE UNIONS.

THE position of the Unions under the law has been not the least vexed question in their recent agitated career. It has been found difficult,if not impossible,to recast the general laws of the kingdom—laws of civil right and wrong, laws of public right and wrong, and laws of mere crime as regards both public and private interests—into a mould that would satisfy the jurisprudence, and cover and legalise the action ' of hundreds of self-constituted clubs of workmen, whose notions of jurisprudence are confined to the promotion of what is not only a small, but an economically impracticable club interest. Hard as this task may be, however, Parliament has lent itself to it not unwillingly of late years ; and, forgetful of all the beneficent legislation since 1832, the principles on which it proceeded, and the solid but splendid opportunities it opened to the working classes, has by the multiplicity of its Acts— Workshop, Mining, Factory, and Trade Union Acts—helped on the more violent of the Unionists, while precipitating the most serious and calamitous industrial crises.

There is a widespread conviction that this legislation has already much exceeded the bounds of reason, and that little but evil, or evil at least in enormous disproportion to any good, has come from it. Yet the trade Unions are by no means satisfied with the legislative triumphs they have accomplished, but are pressing forward keenly for more, till their position substantially has come to be that if the common law of England cannot, in view of the multitude of interests which it touches and regulates, be swiftly enough reformed and adapted to their purposes, it shall at least be wholly suspended in so far as their acts and interests are concerned. This is an aspiration n which there can be no doubt they are doomed to be eventually disappointed.

Nothing could be simpler than for the Trade Unions to put their constitutions, rules, and action in conformity with the law as it stands after all recent concessions in their favour, and to acquire all the advantages of being lawful companies or societies, the complaint of want of which on their part has hitherto been either a puling or a merely sinister cry. This position, if adopted, need not interfere in the least with their legislative activity. While conforming to the law, and thereby gaining legal advantages, they might be as active reformers of the law, in the constitutional way, as ever. But this is the one course the Trade Unions so far have shown no disposition to take. What they want is to have all the advantages of being lawful bodies, and at the same time to be above and defiant of law in their own action and methods of precedure.

SIR WILLIAM ERLE'S MEMORANDUM.

The legal position of the Unions obtained much con-sideration in the Inquiry of 1867-9, and Sir William Erle, Chairman of the Commission, with the consummate legal knowledge and acumen of which he is master, drew up a memorandum of the law relating to Trade Unions as it stood at the period of the Inquiry. Every point where Trade Unions or similar bodies could be reached at Common Law by legal action or indictment was stated by this eminent authority with a lucidity that left nothing to be desired ; and the memorandum has the great advantage to plain, un-learned people, wishing only to know the truth, of showing how the Common Law arose ; how it proceeded from the people themselves in the adjustment of rights and duties in all the various affairs and relations of life ; how the rules thus adopted in the concrete passed under the changes and progress of society into the form of principles of lasting value and application ; and how the principles of Common Law, thus winnowed and generalised from age to age, stand co-related in practical administration, not to one section of human interests, but to all.

The principles of the Common Law may be innovated upon by Statute Law. But a statute to have any vitality must embody a principle; and it is because statutes so seldom do embody a principle that, while created in shoals by the Legislature, they pass away in almost equal numbers through the slowly receding path of desuetude, or fall dead-born as soon as enacted, because inapplicable to the actual course of life, or in so far as attempted to be applied are found to make all the conditions of life worse than they were before.

BEARING OF THE COMMON LAW ON TRADE UNIONS.

The Common Law, against which the Trade Unions have been in practical rebellion for some years, must be acquitted of intent to oppress them in any exceptional or invidious fashion. It is the law under which all men, and all societies of men, live in this country. It is the product of ages of experience and social changes, and of stores of judicial wisdom and equity which no one age or three ages could supply; and it is a law which has come to us from times when there were no such bodies as the Trade Unions in existence. But the respect in which the Common Law does appear to have confronted the Trade Unions somewhat awkwardly is that it bears record that from the earliest times in our history there was an evil which all generations of our ancestors could not endure, whether in the light of the liberty of the subject or of the common weal, and which came to be known and judicially interpreted as " restraint of trade." This evil presented itself in a great variety of forms from one age to another, and in forms, indeed, in which the present generation requires some historical lore in order to comprehend their true meaning; such as, for example, the regulation as far back as the days of Ethelstan and William the Conqueror, forbidding traffic in produce or commodities beyond a certain value outside an open market "unless with a witness." In these old times there was great faith in free markets ; great distrust of "forestalling," "engrossing," or any kind of monopoly that might help the richer dealers against the poorer, or injure both rich and poor in their common right of a free supply of commodities ; and hence a determination to maintain "a free course of trade."

One of the aptest illustrations of the general idea is probably the common law of highways. The highways must not be obstructed against the passage of goods, or of the humblest wayfarer, by the feudal baron and his retainers, or by King Mob, or any other faction, at their peril. If the highway was closed for repairs by due public authority, that was a different matter, and the traffic had to stop, and private people to go about a little, till the object conceived in the general interest was accomplished. But the free passage of the highways must not be obstructed by any number of people on the pretext, say, of hunting rabbits. If any number of people do not choose to deal at a certain shop, they must not gather round the door, and prevent either the shopkeeper from getting out or other customers from getting in, and other people from passing to and fro.

A great many acts and forms of action thus came to be recognised by Common Law as in "restraint of trade," and on the ground of being both subversive of individual right and inimical to the common good, requiring themselves to be restrained and corrected by law.

But it would be a crude mistake to suppose that acts which may have been deemed in restraint of trade in one age remained stereotyped as Common Law offences in all subsequent ages, or that the Common Law has not been administered with reference to its essential principles in the light and experience of all the circumstances of the case and the time. Sir William Erle, in an action so recent as the time of George III.—" R. v. Waddington "—adduces a remarkable example of the elasticity of the Common Law without any infraction of its principle. The defendant was convicted and punished for "engrossing" hops—that is, buying them wholesale with intent to sell them again wholesale—and though the judgment, in all the circumstances and opinions of the time, was deemed to have been righteously given, yet it was traversed and overthrown by subsequent judgments on the ground that the act in question, "engrossing," or buying on wholesale with intent to sell again on wholesale, has an opposite tendency from that which was believed to be its tendency in the reign of George III. A free present of this instance may be given to the Trade Unions, because it conveys to them the useful lesson that, with such abundant confidence as they profess in their economics, there is no need to force an overthrow of the law, which, if an obstacle in their path to-day, may be a safeguard to-morrow. On the other hand, there are niceties of equity in the Common Law which would appear to be wholly lost sight of in the present *furore* of Trade-Union legislation and Trade-Union demands for legislation. For example, Sir William Erle says that while there is nothing at Common Law against a man or any number of men stopping their labour, free of contract, an action would clearly lie for "causing loss of service by enticing away servants from their hiring," and that if two or more combined for this purpose to injure an employer, using money for the purpose, it would become a crime, as in the case of paying witnesses to conceal themselves before an approaching trial, or voters to be out of the way at polling time. In this there is nothing but what appears rational and equitable, and in consonance with what the law conveys in other spheres than employment of labour.

But what does "restraint of trade" under the Common Law, in its application more especially to Trade Unionists, on the whole and in its essence import? Sir William Erle gives this answer:—

"The unlawfulness depends on the degree of restraint resulting from the circumstances. Questions of degree cannot be defined without a standard of measure; unlawful restraint of trade, therefore cannot be defined, but it may be described; and the best description I can offer is this, that at common law every person has individually, and the public also have collectively, a right to require that the course of trade should be kept free from unreasonable obstruction. Under the general principle, the law relating to freedom in disposing of either capital or labour, or both, is included. Every person has a right under the law, as between him and his fellow-subjects, to full freedom in disposing of his own labour or his own capital according to his own will. It follows that every other person is subject to the correlative duty arising therefrom, and is prohibited from any obstruction to the fullest exercise of this right, which can be made compatible with the exercise of similar rights by others."

The principles of the Common Law are thus both reason and equity in an almost perfect form. They are principles entitled to be received with respect, and to be encroached upon by new laws only with the greatest care and judgment, more especially so long as no new or superior principle has been discovered, or until it be seen how any new principle can be co-related and harmonised with the principles of the Common Law throughout the general sphere of relations to which they apply. It would certainly be a wild absurdity to suppose that a few men heading the Trade Unions are so much wiser than all who have lived before them in this country for a thousand years, and all who now live with them, as to be prepared to say that what the Common Law has founded with respect to the rights of every person in the disposal of his goods, capital, or labour, and with respect to the rights of the community to remove obstructions to a free course of trade, may be overridden or swept away.

THE STATUTE LAW ON TRADE UNIONS.

It is obvious, however, that under the action of the Trade Unions of modern days, involving direct and more than *quasi*-coercive interference with the liberty both of employers and workmen, serious difficulties were sure to occur between them and the Common Law; and so there arose another class of laws, applicable to Unionists, known as "the Combination Acts"—statutes passed sometimes to fortify the principles of the Common Law, and sometimes to modify the law so as to give greater scope of action to the Unions. It is a striking proof of the ephemeral character of legislation of this kind that it is only necessary now to mention two statutes, one that was repealed, and another that came in its place.

The Act 5 Geo. IV. c. 95 repealed all previous Trade

I

Combination statutes, and enacted that no combination, with some specified exceptions, was to be indictable in itself, and that recourse by workmen in such combinations to "violence, threats, or intimidation," was to be a misdemeanour subject to not more than two months' imprisonment. This Act was a great concession to the Unions, not only removing previous statutes deemed more severe than there was any necessity for, and recognising as free from offence permanent and consolidated Unions of working men subject to the general principles of the Common Law, but reducing, where workmen in such Unions resorted to "violence, threats, and intimidation" in enforcement of their purposes, the class of offence and the related penalties. It was immediately found, however, that this was an amount of liberty which the Unionists could not carry. Acts of violence rapidly increased, and assumed more subtle and varied forms. Hence the Act 6 Geo. IV. c. 129 was passed the following year, repealing the previous Act, yet not only confirming but actually extending in important respects the right of combination recognised under the repealed Act, and differing from it only in defining that offences by Unionists should not only be acts of "violence, threats, and intimidation," but also "molesting" and "in any way obstructing" others in the exercise of their rights, and that the punishment for such offences should be "not more than three" instead of "two months." The extension given by the 6 George IV. to the right of combination was that combinations and strikes in the matter of wages or hours of labour should be exempt from all liability to penal consequences, whether under Common or Statute Law. Of course, the Legislature of that period could not foresee the innumerable peccadilloes to which, under the development of Unionism, "strikes" would be applied in the workshops of the kingdom, such as a foreman acceptable enough to the employer, but unacceptable to the strikers, an apprentice more or less, a man employed on piecework, the employer choosing to give one man a somewhat lower or higher wage than another, &c., &c.; and how much more bitter and injuriously in "restraint of trade" Unionism was destined to become than in that or any previous age. But nothing could more clearly prove than this Act that there was no hostility in the Legislature, as far back as the reign of George IV., to the right of combination among any number of working people as to the terms on which they would dispose of their labour in the matter either of wages or hours, and that the legal difficulty of the Unions then, as it remains now, was that in the exercise of this full and perfect right, to be asserted as often, as effectually, or ineffectually, and on as many pretexts as they pleased, they must not directly aggress upon and violate the equally well-established rights of other people.

Yet this is what neither Common Law nor Statute Law, nor Parliament nor Press, nor any power of reason whatever, has hitherto been able to cause the Unions to comprehend, or even to approach to see the magnitude of interests it involves, among which the interests of labour itself have the chief place.

LAW OF CONSPIRACY.

The Law of Conspiracy is a common law, and applies to offences against trade as to all other offences, from the simplest private wrongs, in the suppression of which the public has an interest, to acts of treason or sedition against the State. It does not appear that any indictment for conspiracy could lie against Trade Unionists unless they agreed and combined to carry out the coercive and violent acts specifically prohibited in the statutes. But if there be a coercive and violent intention, and an exchange of consent to carry out this intention, there is conspiracy even though the intention be not effected. Murder, for example, is a crime ; but a conspiracy of two or more persons to commit murder, even if the murder be not committed, is also a crime. Certain acts also, when committed by a number of persons with mutual agreement and determination, are criminal, which if committed by an individual would be much less criminal, or scarce bear in the eye of the law the mark of crime at all. These features of the Law of Conspiracy have been greatly ridiculed and much opposed by

I 2

the Trade Unions; but they are valuable and essential parts of every system of jurisprudence; and though Sir William Harcourt, and latterly Mr. Cross, have professed to see how the law may be modified, yet it may be safely remarked of all attempts of this kind, that they can only have one of two results: they will either produce a re-laxation of the Law of Conspiracy that will be generally and soundly applicable, or they will give greater liberty to conspire criminally to Trade Unionists than to any other class of people.

Such was the state of the law relating to Trade Unions at the period of the Inquiry, and it is only necessary at this stage to look at "The Trade Union Act, 1871," following on the Report of the Commissioners.[1]

TRADE UNION ACT, 1871.

The first clause of the Act of 1871 annuls the ancient common law doctrine of "restraint of trade" to the extent that it shall have no force against any member of a Trade Union liable to criminal prosecution, and, as may conse-quently be inferred, that the Law of Conspiracy cannot be brought to bear against Trade Unionists save in connexion with overt acts of violence, threatenings, intimidations, moles-tations, and obstructions, described in the 6 George IV. c. 129, and more precisely defined in the Criminal Law Amend-ment Act. Then follow clauses which, on the same ground —viz., "that the purposes of any Trade Union shall not, *by reason merely that they are in restraint of trade*, be unlawful," —proceed to enact some of the most curious contradictions

---

[1] The "Criminal Law Amendment Act," on which so much has been said of late, also followed upon the Inquiry of 1867-9, and was simply a definition of the terms of the Act 6 George IV., of the vague-ness of which there had been complaints on the part of some of the Unions. This Act imported no new severity or restriction into the law whatever. On the contrary, it contained a clear delineation of the boundary lines where trade action on the part either of masters or work-men passes into unlawful coercion, violence, and, in short, crime. But this Act will come under consideration in connexion with the late Royal Commission on the Labour Laws.

that have probably ever been seen in the statute-book. The twofold effect attempted to be produced is that the Trade Unions are to be perfectly competent for all civil purposes, such as purchasing or leasing land, selling, exchanging, mortgaging, and transacting with the outside public, and that all agreements or trusts into which they enter in this way shall not be rendered void or voidable; but that as regards all agreements or bonds *inter ses*, between one Trade Union and another, or between a Union and its own members—in. any agreement, for example, as to the application of its funds to "provide benefits," to "furnish contributions whether to employers or workmen," or to "discharge fines," &c.,—in all this line of obligation, in short, between the Unionists themselves, the Trade Unions shall be held at law to be "Free Lances," and that any agreements or trusts they have in this form shall be void at law, "though not unlawful," and shall not be enforceable in any of her Majesty's courts.

There can be no doubt that the *Fagin* of Mr. Dickens, under a statute of this kind, could have carried on a very flourishing business to the end of time, as he did for a long while, and may be doing still, without such a statute. There was little objectionable in the exterior transactions of *Fagin*. He knew the value of money, goods, land, and mortgages as well as anybody else, and his transactions and investments of this kind were generally of a law-abiding and valid character. It was only in the interior working of his system, how he got his goods and money, and the wrongs he inflicted on persons and on the interests of the community in his interior process, that any great iniquity was found. The task assumed by the Legislature of making the Trade Unions all legal outside while all is to be void at law inside, is one that cannot be easily achieved, or easily reconciled with any fixed principles of polity or justice, if Trade Unions are to be corporations enjoying any legal recognition or confirmation whatever. It would be a relief, indeed, to think that any party to this Act of 1871 had the remotest perception how such legislation could be carried through, or brought ultimately into any form that would stand.

The only other clauses of the Act of 1871 – a very short Act

—requiring notice are those providing facilities for the official registration of Trade Unions, to the end of protecting the funds of the Unions from embezzling or runaway officers and the like, to which there has been no manner of objection on public grounds, and to which the Unions have always had such free access by simply conforming their rules and action to the law, that any complaint on this score cannot be denied more than a little outbreak of Trade Union *jeu d'esprit.* But it is worthy of being observed that, in providing for the registration of Trade Unions, the Act of 1871 set aside the recommendations of the Royal Commission, and adopted a wholly different course. The conclusion of the Commission was that Trade Unions might be registered through the Registrar of Friendly Societies, on his seeing that their rules and by-laws were not intended to secure the following purposes:—

" 1. To prevent the employment, or to limit the number, of apprentices in any trade.

" 2. To prevent the introduction, or to limit the use of, machinery in any trade or manufacture.

" 3. To prevent any workman from taking a sub-contract, or working by the piece, or working in common with men not members of the Union.

" 4. To authorise interference in the way of support from the funds of the Union, by the council or governing body of the Union, with the workmen of any other Union when out on strike, or when otherwise engaged in any dispute with their employers, in any case in which such Union is an unconnected Union."

The Royal Commission of 1867-9 threw into these qualifications the sum of their evidence and inquiry as to what was necessary for the Trade Unions to pass into a legal position. There was a clear and perfect logic in the Report of the Commission, connected on one side with the law as it stood and on the other with the law as it might with all consistency and equity become. The conclusion of the Commission was that there was no limit to the action of voluntary combinations of workmen as to the disposal of their labour but one, and this was that the combination in the exercise of its full right should not attempt to override the equal right of other workmen, or to obstruct and injure employers more than was necessarily involved in the exhausted exercise of their own full right—or, in other words, the refusal of their labour. On this basis the law could give all legal rights to Trade Unions as corporations. On the other hand, the law could not without stultifying itself, lend its powers to bodies in whose avowed rules and constitutions this principle was contravened. The Commission also made a strong recommendation in favour of such Trade Unions as separated their benefit from their trade funds, and suggested for consideration whether such Unions might not be placed without other limitation under the Friendly Societies Act. But the Imperial Parliament in 1871 made these conclusions of little account, and enacted a much more facile method, whereby Trade Unions might be registered, and become legal bodies, with great legal rights on the exterior, and no legal obligations on the interior side. It conveys but a poor idea of the value of such inquiries to find that they have so little effect on the course of legislation. Yet how many Trade Unions have been registered, or what progress has been made in bringing Trade Unions into a position more conformable to law, under the Act of 1871? The Registrar for England reports that, to the end of 1874, 173 Trade Unions had been registered under the Act of 1871, of which twenty-nine had been dissolved, and that in many cases, notwithstanding his repeated remonstrances, the rules are still contrary to law, self-contradictory, or do not express the real intention of the framers.[1]

There was one good thing which the Act of 1871 did. It cut off the Trade Unions from registration under the Friendly Societies and the Industrial and Provident Societies Acts; but this was a result which, after the opinion of the actuaries as to the prevailing practice of levying contributions for benefit purposes and spending them on totally different purposes, could hardly in any case have been avoided.

---

[1] See Report for 1874, in which the Registrar has some important remarks on this subject.

X.

It was of much advantage to this Inquiry that Mr. Hughes and Mr. Harrison were members of the Commission. They took a strong pro-Union view of the whole subject from the beginning, and were always helpful in putting questions to the leading Union witnesses, when in a dilemma, that had the effect of eliciting a fuller explanation of Union policy and resource in the interior conception than might otherwise have been obtained. When Union secretaries were non-plussed, for example, by the evidence of the actuaries on the alarming deficiency of the benefit funds, Mr. Hughes and Mr. Harrison were always glad to interpose, " Yet in case of any " actual deficiency, of course you would make a special " levy ? " and were always delighted to be told that special levies to any amount would be cheerfully paid. In this way they unfolded much of the *rationale* on which one cannot but believe the affairs of societies, under the direction of so many active and intelligent men as the Trade Unions, to be conducted, that might possibly have remained hidden. Mr. Hughes and Mr. Harrison, however, had after all to record their dissent from the Report of the Commission, and they appended a " Detailed Statement" of their own, which embodied their " conclusions from the evidence," and their solution of the whole question—moral, social, economical, and legal.

This " Statement " is masterly in its command of every item of the evidence that could be adduced to support its conclusions, but it is too deeply imbued with the art of special pleading, lightly explaining away much that was certain, and leaving undetermined nearly everything that was capable of determination, to be of any logical value. But, as a special pleading in favour of the Unions, it is almost exhaustive, and in that sense has considerable value. It is improbable that the case of the Unions can be presented again in any more attractive and specious form.

"GREAT EXTENT AND INCREASE OF UNIONISM."

The conclusions of Mr. Hughes and Mr. Harrison were—

(1.) "The great extent and increase of Unionism"—a proposition which no one can have any motive to dispute, though the evidence, by admission of the two Commissioners themselves, has afforded only contradictory statements on the subject.   In the largest and most consolidated Unions the number of members annually cut off for non-payment of contributions or other offences is so large in proportion to the total membership that the ranks can only be recruited by an annual rush of new members somewhat incredible, or by a return of old members who on paying past arrears and resuming the weekly contributions are readmitted, but who have in most cases to take a lower place in the scale of benefit, and at every readmission are losing members of the Union.   Many must thus join and rejoin the Unions not from any freewill, or from any profit, but because they find this course under Union action the only _modus vivendi_ open to them.   There is no evidence or knowledge to what extent the councils and action of the Unions represent the opinion and purpose even of their own members ; and when the Unions are assumed to be a type of the will of the working classes in general, their representative quality becomes imperceptible.   The only thing certain on this head is that in 1867-9 there was a lively sense of "the great extent and increase of Unionism" ; and that now in 1875-6 this sense is as lively as ever under painful occurrences in all parts of the country.

"IMPROVED CHARACTER OF UNIONISM."

(2.) "The improved character of Unionism."   This conclusion was reached by a parenthesis excluding the Sheffield and Manchester outrages, which in 1867-9 were events of yesterday, and in incendiarism, machine-breaking, assassination, and every form of ignorant violence on life, property, and trade had not before been equalled. These outrages were not only the main reason why the Royal Commission of Inquiry was issued, but the special investigations of which they were the subject formed the most substantial and inseparable part of the Inquiry. Yet Messrs. Hughes and Harrison, in reaching their second conclusion, thought that all this part of the evidence might be reasonably set aside. It was only a passing cloud in the air, with no root or sequence in the natural soil of Unionism. "Outside the area of the Sheffield and Manchester districts," they say, "there has happily been no vitriol-throwing of late by Unionists!"

"HIGH CHARACTER OF THE PRINCIPAL UNIONS."

From "Improved Character of Unionism" the advance was easy to (3) "High Character of the Principal Unions" —Amalgamated Engineers, Amalgamated Carpenters, Manchester House-painters, Miners, Glassworkers, and others specially named. It is so little our design to disparage Unions conducting useful business in a business-like way, and the two Dissentient Commissioners have betrayed so grave a misapprehension of the procedure of these "high-character" Unions, as will immediately appear, that this conclusion may be passed over with every possible credit it may reflect on the Unions, in order to make an observation more germane to the essential matter.

There was much questioning in the Inquiry as to the effect of the Unions on the character of workmen, and on the tone of feeling between workmen and employers, which counts a good deal in the successful negotiation and adjustment of the various differences that may arise between parties so closely related. The question was so important that it obtained a place in the Report of the Commission. On one hand it had been contended that the Unions had destroyed the cordial and friendly feeling which used to be common between the two classes. On the other hand, it was asserted that all this cordial and friendly feeling was hollow sentiment, and implied only "mistaken notions of inferiority on the one side and patronage on the other." The Commission could not decide authoritatively between such conflicting assertions, but reported as "the apparent result of the inquiries" that any habitual code of sentiment implying patronage on the part of employers could not now be revived, and that "a substitute had to be found for it in the "feelings of equity, enlightened self-interest, and mutual "forbearance, which should exist between contracting "parties, who can best promote their several chances of "advantage by aiding and accommodating each other." To find this substitute for worn-out sentiments, and to find it, indeed, on the basis of the Unions themselves, viz., that the two classes meet and contract henceforth on terms of equal independence of each other, a good feeling between employers and employed, such as exists between a trades-man and his customers, between the man who has the raw material in his hand and the man who can manufacture it into something useful and valuable, between the man who wants a loan and the banker who can lend, in short, be-tween all contracting parties, must still be deemed of the last importance to the end in view. That the action of the Unions so far has not tended to produce this good feeling, but, on the contrary, the more active it has been has engendered only bad feeling between employers and em-ployed, is a proposition which no rational person, on the evidence of 1867-69, or on the evidence of the daily events of Unionism, can be bold enough to dispute.

With respect to the effect of the Unions on the character of workmen there was the same conflict of evidence. On one hand it was testified that the best workmen were losing in skill, in self-reliance, and in desire to excel in their work, and that the general body were falling into indulgence and dissipation under the influence of their Unions. On the other hand, it was replied that the real effect of the Unions was to raise, not to depress, the character of the workman, and that work was as well or better done under the Union

rules than it could be without them. Mr. George Potter
gave his full assurance that men under the Unions became
soberer, more intelligent, and more respectable every way;
and there was much testimony to the contrary. A question
of this breadth is not to be determined offhand. There
must be a certain amount of truth on both sides. It is
difficult to believe in any rapid deterioration either of the
skill or character of our working men, but one should like
to make this profession of faith without lessening in any
degree the obligation of the Unions to scan very keenly the
tendency of their procedure, because when the deterioration
has come, neither the power of the Unions nor any other
power may be able to arrest or amend it.

"INFLUENCE OF THE UNIONS ON STRIKES AND WAGES."

(4.) The conclusion of Mr. Hughes and Mr. Harrison on
this head is remarkable in its complete antithesis to the
common belief not only of the public, but of the Unionists
themselves. The Dissentient Commissioners conclude from
the evidence that the effect of the Unions is not to increase,
but to diminish the number of strikes, and that the Unions
have had little or no influence in raising wages. Of course,
a statement of this kind betrays a strong bias, but nevertheless it conveys some truth, though it may not be safely
averred that either Mr. Hughes or Mr. Harrison had any
clear comprehension of what the truth of it was. It is true
that, taking the Trade Unions overhead, they have had
little or no influence, by strikes or other action, in raising
wages. It is also true that in various great trades under
Union organisation—the engineers, the shipwrights, the
ironfounders, the compositors and printers, and others—
there have been not only comparatively small advances of
wages for a dozen years, but very rarely any great open-air
strikes, while at the same time all these Unions have been
carrying on quiet underground strikes in enforcement of
their rules. Still, this leaves the endless multitude of strikes
with which the public are familiar unaccounted for. Whence
and how do they arise?

The verdict of Messrs. Hughes and Harrison was that " strikes were shown to be most frequent, and certainly the " least orderly, where the Unions have acquired no real " command over the workmen, or are struggling into " existence." But this verdict places these disastrous events, the frequency and magnitude of which cannot be disputed, almost wholly outside the circle of Union action and responsibility, which every one must perceive to be contrary to common sense. Some Unions are more notorious than others for organising great strikes. In a review confined to four or five years, one could probably always count on one's five fingers all the great Unions that have been figuring most prominently in this way during that period. But the *mêlée* has a wonderful power of circling round and maintaining a high fighting level. When one Union falls back, either contented or exhausted, there is always another to take its place in the ranks ; and, indeed, there is scarce one of the model Unions referred to by Messrs. Hughes and Harrison that has not had great struggles on the broadest scale of strike with the employers. There is also a considerable number of Unions that seldom or never strike on their own part, but are always glad to be bottle-holders, and to go in with money and cheers to a miners', builders', or any other strike, as if it were a genuine amusement, as well as with the most chivalrous unconcern as to whether the direct effect of the strike may not be to rob themselves, and to cripple and injure their own trades. But it would be idle to believe with Mr. Hughes and Mr. Harrison, that when any of " our strongest, richest, and most extended Unions " cease for a time to organise strikes on the grand scale, they cease in any degree to administer strikes in another form. The enforcement of their unaccepted rules in all the various shops and districts is a constant source of strikes, and there is always a large number of their members, who have struck or have been required by them to strike, on their " donation " rolls.

The error of the two learned gentlemen consists in having picked up from the evidence an idea, as regards strikes, generally true of a great majority of the Unions over a

period of three or four years, without any insight into the
inner working of the Unions, and the means by which the
strike movement is propagated and sustained in undimi-
nished volume and disaster from period to period. Their
conclusion that the Unions have had little or no perceptible
influence in raising wages must be accepted as the fact,
though it is liable to temporary exceptions, as in the case,
for example, of the miners in 1872 and 1873. It is only a
pity that two members of the Commission, taking so prominent a part in the Inquiry, had not the courage to infer
from this fact that the elaborate action and expenditure of
the Unions to raise wages fails in its main purpose, since it
is impossible to see what other inference can be made.

"PRACTICES OF THE TRADE UNIONS."

The conclusion in the "Statement" with respect to (5)
"The Practices of Trade Unions" carries us into matters
of business of great interest both to Unionists and employers, and a reasonable consideration of which would
seem more necessary than almost anything else to a better
understanding and more amicable relations between the two
parties. The "practices" to which Mr. Hughes and
Mr. Harrison refer are "piecework, equalisation of wages,
" limit of production, apprentices, resistance to machinery,
" and hostility to non-Unionists;" and their conclusion is
that, "with respect to all the customs and rules complained
" of, no sensible public injury has been shown to result from
" them," and that they must be left in perfect neutrality and
indifference, on the part of the law or the public, to the
solution of "a standing struggle between conflicting
interests." Mr. Hughes and Mr. Harrison may possibly
be more enamoured of "standing struggles" than is at all
common either among workmen or employers. The ordinary dictate of prudence in the case of a "standing
struggle" is to get it to sit down under some rational and
equitable settlement as soon as possible. The disposal of
these practical matters in the "Detailed Statement" is
loose and unsatisfactory beyond toleration. Acknowledged

injustices of the gravest character and magnitude arising
from the " practices of the Unions "—acknowledged, indeed,
in the same breath by the Statementers themselves—are put
aside with stolid *nonchalance;* vague inferences are made
on precise questions, in regard to which there can be no
pretence for any vagueness, that are directly contrary to the
evidence ; and while the general apology throughout is
that, whatever the grievances may be under Trade Union
practices, they are grievances in which there can be no
State or Legislative interference—a question, by the way,
that was not on the carpet—the " Statement " itself does
not end without invoking the aid both of State and Legislature to enforce "the practices." The result is a medley
of unreason that has seldom been adventured.

On " piecework," for example, with respect to which
many employers and many workmen have certain opinions,
and many Unions directly contrary opinions, the simple
argument of Mr. Hughes and Mr. Harrison is that "it
" would be impolitic for the State to step in on either side
" of the controversy." Who out of Trade Union circles is
likely to question this as a general proposition ? The real
difficulty is that many of the Unions insist on forcing their
prohibition of piecework on employers and workmen against
their will ; and that in this and similar attempts the
strikes, disturbances, and coercion of the will of others by
the Unions in shops occur, which it is desirable in some
reasonable way to avert.   One reasonable way would seem
to be that if a Union man does not like piecework, he not
only need not take it, but may rely on the number of his
fellow-Unionists that a free course will always be open to
him to obtain his favourite daywork ; and that, on the
other hand, employers wanting piecework and workmen
desiring to have piecework should have the same liberty.
But this does not suit the Unions ; they must enforce their
rules not only on their own members, but on everybody
else in the trade, employers included ; and it is they, and
they only, who have presumed to demand that their
" working rules " should be ratified and enforced by Act of
Parliament.   It was the excuse of Broadhead, in the

Sheffield outrages, that under the absence of law enforcing the rules of his Union, he was strongly tempted, much against all his moral instincts, to hire explosionists and assassins to supply the unfortunate omissions of the law! It is lamentable—in this craving of the Unions for force of their own, and legal force in addition, to coerce others on a matter like this of piecework, on which there must be some room for liberty of opinion on the most strictly technical grounds—to find Mr. Hughes and Mr. Harrison, after having rested their whole argument on a deprecation of State interference on one side or the other, dropping complacently into the conclusion (p. 50 of "Detailed Statement") that having found "all the customs or rules" of the Unions so free of any public injury, it would be wise in their opinion to have them generally enforced, and that this was an object in which the Legislature might co-operate!

Then, in the much vexed matter of "equalisation of wages"—or what appears to be the determination of many of the greatest Unions to bring wages to a uniform level, irrespective of the skill or amount of work done—the two Dissentient Commissioners deny that there is the least trace of anything of this kind in the practice of the Unions. "The Unions endeavour to establish a minimum " standard of wages, but they make no attempt to fix a " maximum." This question is one that could not be disposed of by such *ex cathedrâ* announcements, and it is only necessary to refer to the reply on this and cognate points of the London Journeymen Curriers' Society—one of the oldest Trade Unions in the country, and one that in respect of wages has not for at least a hundred years lowered its flag to any other branch of handicraft—in order to show how little Mr. Hughes and Mr. Harrison may have studied the evidence of which they professed to give the whole philosophical results. The Journeymen Curriers say, in answer to the queries of the Royal Commission, "The evils most " apparent in Unions are opposition to piecework, enforce- " ment of maximum rates for weekwork, and the getting up " of societies merely for strikes."

It is one of the disabilities of public men—a disability that cleaves in some degree even to Royal Commissions of Inquiry—that they hear most on questions of this kind from the busybodies and organised agitators of the Unions, and least from the great mass of the Unions themselves. Mr. Hughes and Mr. Harrison allow that "it not unfre-"quently happens that men are excluded from employment "because they cannot earn the Union standard of wages;" but this did not strike them as any evil, because—and here follows the usual cool excuse of ignorance—"no tangible "objection has reached us from the side of the men who "are supposed principally to suffer." Isolated, injured, and suffering men throughout the country were expected to come up to Westminster to enlighten Mr. Hughes and Mr. Harrison as if they were a consolidated body, with plenty of funds and active officers and leaders! Could not Mr. Hughes and Mr. Harrison have gone down to the country, and found out the case for themselves? Might they not at the very least have read the replies to "queries" sent in by many Unions who did not appear, and never appear before Commissions as witnesses? The Journey-men Curriers could not have given the decisive utterances above-quoted on piecework, maximum wages for weekwork, and getting up strikes, unless there had been greatly more foundation for them than Mr. Hughes and Mr. Harrison, giving ear to the Trade Union demagoguery, must have supposed when inditing their "Detailed Statement."

To fix "a limit on production" is admitted "to exist among some classes of colliers and unskilled labourers," and if in any respect true of Unionism, to be "very partially true." But Mr. Hughes and Mr. Harrison do not weigh the evidence on the other side, and dismiss the subject without the consideration it requires in the interest of Union workmen themselves. "Resistance to Machinery" they believe to be a decreasing evil, and to be no more a cha-racteristic of Unionists than of non-Unionists. The practice of the Unions as regards "apprentices" is not only treated in the same easy spirit, but is sent away with a fallacious reason annexed.

K

THE GLASS-MAKERS AND THE APPRENTICESHIP QUESTION.

Selecting a case of "the closest limitation on new incomers" to a trade, viz., the glass-makers, Mr. Hughes and Mr. Harrison confidently conclude that the Union's restrictions on apprentices have had no effect in reducing the supply of labour below the adequate demand, because in this instance of the glass-makers "the Union has a number of its members constantly out of employment." Applying this reason to the facts, let us ask why so many of the members of Unions are always out of employment? From no cause to be discovered but that they are on strike-pay. Strange as it may seem, this is specially true of the greatest and most businesslike Unions, esteemed to be much less prone to general strikes than the colliers and other misguided and reckless bodies, and to be models of good, practical, and skilful management, on a par almost, as Mr. Hughes and Mr. Harrison would have it to be inferred, with our banking, insurance, and other trading companies.

Mr. Allan, of the Amalgamated Engineers, submitted to the Royal Commission an abstract of payments for what he strictly defined as "Donation, or Out-of-Work Pay" from 1851 to 1866. In one year they amounted to 46,670*l.*; in 1858 they were 35,390*l.* ; and in the seven years from 1861 to 1866, the aggregate payments under this head amounted to 145,520*l.* The expenditure of the Carpenters and Joiners in 1866 for "trade purposes and expenses of management" amounted to 9,138*l.*, out of a gross income of only 16,539*l.*[1] In recorded accounts for the two following years, 1867 and 1868, which must have been under the eye of Mr. Hughes and Mr. Harrison, when composing their "Detailed Statement," the lavish disbursement of the funds of these Societies on other than the "friendly benefits" appears to still worse account. It would be the simplest delusion, therefore, to suppose that great Unions like the Engineers and Carpenters and Joiners, though retired for a

[1] Appendix to Eleventh Report, vol. ii. pp. 195, 218.

time under motives of prudence or security from the organisation of general strikes, have in any degree departed in their daily action from the strike policy, or that in the pursuit of this *ignis fatuus* they may not be wasting the funds and deluding the hopes of their members quite as much, or nearly as much, as the more demonstrative colliers, of whose movements Mr. Hughes and Mr. Harrison betray a latent suspicion.

As for the case of the glass-makers, on which they base their conclusion with respect to " Apprentices," it is the case of a trade wholly under Union influence, and yet by reason of its apprenticeship restrictions, unwillingness to adopt mechanical improvements, and general obstruction to what the employers perceive to be necessary to an extension of the trade, has not been able to keep possession even of its own home market against foreign ware. The imports of foreign glass ware increased from 92,040*l.*, in 1854, to 791,882*l.*, in 1867, or about 800 per cent., while our exports of the same ware only increased 40 per cent. in the same period. On what a cloud of misconception, therefore, may not Messrs. Hughes and Harrison stand when they declare that, since in this Glass-makers' Union there are always from 30 to 140 members on the unemployed list, the limitation of apprentices, and, indeed, all the other " practices " of the Union, have had no injurious effect either on the members of the Unions themselves or on the public?

It were almost idle, in the hazy atmosphere of semi-philanthropy and semi-thinking which Trade Union philosophy has gathered round the true interest of the working classes, to speak of the old Radical doctrine of the right of labour, the right of people to be employed, and to find in the industrial sphere, without let or hindrance, a free and available occupation of their faculties. Yet it may be worth while to observe how Messrs. Hughes and Harrison dispose of " the practice of the Unions " towards " non-Unionists." " It is clear," they say, " that it is a very general practice for " Unionists to refuse work in company with non-Unionists, " but this practice is far from being universal." And this

K 2

odious and revolting practice, though a very general
practice, yet, because it is not a universal practice, is a
practice, in the opinion of Mr. Hughes and Mr. Harrison,
to be lightly passed over, if not to be admired and en-
couraged.

It is unnecessary to follow the remarks of the Dissentient Commissioners on (6) "the general purpose and
origin," or on (7) "the collateral functions of the Unions."
The question at issue is not whether Unionism be wholly
bad, but what of the system is bad and what good, so that
there may be a reform, and the Unions be placed in a
relation more lawful to the community and more beneficial
to their own members. That Trade Unions collect useful
reports on the state of trade and the rate of wages, send
unemployed workmen to places where their labour is most
in demand, assist emigration, and give members aid from
the funds when on tramp, can be no reason, however useful
such operations may be, why they should do many other
acts which are either an aggression on the rights of others
or a fraud upon themselves. In so far as the "collateral
functions" of the Unions extend to the assurance of friendly
benefits, Mr. Hughes and Mr. Harrison have displayed a
laxity of opinion as to the fidelity of insurance engagements
that rather dispenses with criticism ; and in arguing so in-
geniously that a separation of the trade and benefit funds
is impracticable and impolitic, they will hardly convince
any one of the truth of such peculiar views, or lessen the
example of those Unions which have found neither difficulty
nor impolicy in what is only an honest method of book-
keeping, and of debtor and creditor account.

"EFFECT OF UNIONS ON TRADE."

On (8) "the effect of Unions on Trade," Mr. Hughes
and Mr. Harrison could not be expected to be particularly
luminous where the whole Commission were in some uncertainty, and refrained from any positive conclusion on the
subject. But if the evidence tendered in the inquiry proved
too little to warrant the Commission to report that Unionism

had been directly and grievously injurious to trade, Mr. Hughes and Mr. Harrison, on the other hand, proved too much for the opposite conclusion they sought to convey. They would not allow that shipbuilding on the Thames had been injured by Unionism, on the grounds, viz., that the Unions on the Clyde had been as active and powerful as ever they were on the Thames, and that wages had fallen, or had not been advanced, on the Thames for many long years, while they had been more than once advanced on the Clyde. Supposing this state of things to be true, and supposing it to continue—wages falling, or tending to fall, on the Thames, while rising on the Clyde—the Thames will have a fair chance of getting some of the trade back ; and shipbuilding having been ruined once on the Thames, may be ruined on the Clyde a second time. The action of the Unions, which in its more excited forms becomes intensely local, sectional, and narrow in its range of view, may thus be helping other causes, and more especially the irresistible tendency of capital to seek out the most profitable sphere both as regards labour and materials, to drive branches of industry from one part of the kingdom to another. But such displacements, in so far as they are hastened or forced by Union strikes and disturbances laying capital under abnormal disadvantages in one place as compared with another, must be injurious to trade in general and to the Unionists themselves. For the rest of this branch of the subject, Mr. Hughes and Mr. Harrison contented themselves with quoting from the returns of exports, the increasing quantities of iron and steel, steam engines, and machinery of all sorts sent abroad in the five or six years preceding 1868. There had certainly, for a longer period than quoted, been a remarkable and steady increase of metallic exports from the United Kingdom. But does this feature of our export trade lessen the effect of foreign competition as regards the general manufacturing industry of this country ? Does it not foreshadow an imminent period when the question may be not the displacement of trade from one part of the kingdom to another, but out of the kingdom into foreign parts ? Could anything teach more cogently the need of the utmost prudence on the part of the Unions as to how they act, and of refusing to believe those who tell them that capital and trade may be domineered and knocked about without limit in the interest of the workmen? There is a grim irony in the congratulations of Mr. Hughes and Mr. Harrison over the increased exports of iron, steel, and machinery when one considers the heavy clutch which the action of the Miners' Unions laid a year or two afterwards on all this great part of our trade, and the results of which, were Mr. Hughes and Mr. Harrison quoting the statistics of export now, would disclose the reverse side of the picture in a great decline.

"PRACTICES OF MASTERS' ASSOCIATIONS."

The Dissentient Commissioners, before passing to a graver subject, amused themselves by drawing an exact parallel between " the practices of Masters' Associations " and the practices of the Unions. Everything bad and coercive in the latter they found closely imitated in the former, but as they condemned everything of this nature in the practices of the Masters' Associations, and had denied up to this point that there was anything either bad or coercive in the practices of the Unions, we are at a loss to know what the position of the two Commissioners in this passage may be. It is more like an acrobatic performance than anything else. The question, however, deserved to be treated more seriously. The defensive and retaliatory measures of employers point very distinctly, in connexion with their counterparts, to the ruinous character of the Union idea that the conditions of trade and industry are to be ruled by great combinations of labour on one side, and of capital on the other, and that these monster leagues are to be in a state of perpetual and desperate war with each other. The country has borne with this idea, thinking that it was contributing in some way to a free readjustment of the relations of capital and labour ; but the idea in practice has frequently led up to scenes of devastation, which have caused many to reflect whether such things lay within the toleration of any civilised State.

Of the power of workmen and employers under hostile
Unionism to injure each other, and to involve innocent
masses of the community in loss and ruin, there has been
more than abundant proof; and if there is any utility in
writing on this subject, it must be to hint as strongly as
possible the necessity of finding some departure from a
course of action that has been a source of common detriment.

" PROPOSED AMENDMENTS OF THE LAW."

On " Proposed Amendments of the Law" the two Commissioners, if on any part of the inquiry, should have been
able to deliver a weighty and suggestive conclusion. Both
are gentlemen learned in the law, and might be excused
some crudeness of opinion on laws of trade and economy,
with which they had probably little theoretic and no practical familiarity, providing only they had proved themselves
wise in the law, and wise reformers of the law. Yet on this
part of the subject, on which they had a presumed special
and technical skill, their defect was most signal.

There were two courses, either of which Mr. Hughes and
Mr. Harrison, with the memorandum of Sir William Erle
on the State of the Law before them, might have rationally
pursued. They might either have accepted the Memorandum
as a true exposition of the law as it stood at the date of the
Report of the Commission, and proceeded to demonstrate
the respects in which it was unjust to the Trade Unions,
and how it might be amended in their favour with advantage
or no great injury at least to the community; or, they
might have disputed the accuracy of the Memorandum
on some points, contended that it gave a too lax and
colourable view of the equity with which it bore on the
action of the Unions, and proceeded in this way to establish
certain desirable amendments. But they took neither of
these courses. They preferred a third course which cannot
be characterised by any milder epithet than disingenuous.
They accepted " the exhaustive paper prepared for the use
of the Commission by the Chairman" to which they were
unable to add or subtract anything—" we do not presume,"

they say, " to make any comment whatever on the views which it expresses "—and, after this ample indorsement, they proceeded to give the Memorandum an interpretation which it does not bear ; and through this back door arrived at their "proposed amendments of the law " on a wholly so-phistical basis.

The following were the results of the law, in their most general and essential form, which they professed with all modesty to have learned from Sir William Erle :—

" 1. At common law every person has a right to full freedom in dis-posing of his own labour, or his own capital, according to his will ; and every obstruction to the exercise of that right in such a degree as to cause damage to him thereby, *even by means not otherwise unlawful*, is a wrong.

" 2. A combination by many to do a wrong, in a matter where the public has an interest, is the substantive offence of conspiracy, and a crime."

The words in italics are theirs, not ours, and are intended to cast a stigma on the Common Law, and to import that a person dealing with his labour or his capital in his own way must not be obstructed by another person, even though the method of obstruction may be not otherwise unlawful ! This would, indeed, be an anomalous state of the law ; it would imply that if a tailor sell trousers at 18s., another tailor who presumes to sell trousers at 17s. is liable to him in damage ; and if such be Mr. Hughes's and Mr. Harrison's conception of the law, nothing more can be needed to account for the zeal without knowledge with which they have thrown themselves into the cause of its amendment. But, seeing they have professed to sit at the feet of Sir William Erle in the matter, it must be safe to hear what the master himself says :—

" Every person has a right under the law, as between him and his fellow-subjects, to full freedom in disposing of his own labour, or his own capital, according to his own will. It follows that every other is subject to the correlative duty arising therefrom, and is prohibited from any obstruction to the fullest exercise of this right which can be made compatible with the exercise of similar rights by others. Every act causing an obstruction to another in the exercise of the right comprised within this description—*done not in the actor's own right, but for the purpose of obstruction*—would, if damage should be caused thereby to the party obstructed, be a wrong to be remedied either by action or indictment, as the case may be."

A tailor selling trousers at 18s. could not possibly lay an action of damages against a tailor selling the same garment at 17s. under this definition of the law by Sir William Erle, as he could clearly do under the definition given by Mr. Hughes and Mr. Harrison, while professing all the time to take the law from Sir William Erle's own lips. The one tradesman might no doubt be injured and damaged by the other, but the other would be acting *within his own right*, and there would be nothing of the nature of obstruction in the case.

When a Trade Union, or any combination of working men strike, and suspend their labour, they inflict much damage upon others than themselves or their employers, which the law does not recognise as an injury or damage to be remedied by action or indictment, because the men striking and suspending their labour are acting within their own right. They may give or withhold their labour as they please. Unionists should look more than they do at this side of the case, in which the law is practically neutral as regards the enormous injury which their action often inflicts on other persons than those immediately implicated, that is, themselves and their employers, and on large bodies even of fellow-workmen, who have had no part or say in their action whatever. A strike in one department of a branch of industry often throws hundreds and thousands of working men into enforced idleness in a dispute in which they have had no concern, and which has proceeded throughout against their will. For all this kind of injury the common law appears to have no remedy. It is silent on the whole subject. Our jurists may not have seen in its full magnitude the mutual responsibility and dependence of the industrial relations that were to arise. But it does not follow that the law will be always silent in this direction, which reaches the highest idea of all—the idea of the common well-being

—and it were surely incumbent on the Unions, on seeing
how free the law has placed them in regard to all interme-
diary, secondary, and indirect damage arising from their
procedure, to recognise and respect the strictness with which
the law forbids them, after having exhausted their own full
right, in small numbers or great numbers, of disposing of
their labour as they please, to obstruct others in the exercise
of precisely the same right.

The little play on words in italics, by which Mr. Hughes
and Mr. Harrison sought to convey a perverted interpretation of the law, and to father the perversion on Sir William
Erle, was weak on the part of gentlemen of their learning
and capacity, because it is not only known to lawyers, but
to all persons of ordinary intelligence, that acts " *not otherwise unlawful*" become grossly unlawful and even criminal
when associated with an unlawful or criminal purpose.
There is nothing unlawful in taking your neighbour a drive
into the country, giving him plenty of bread and ale, singing
to him, and doing all in your power to make him happy.
So far from being unlawful, this is one of the most pleasing
duties of humanity, and one that may probably be not so
much practised as it ought to be. But if your object is to
abduct a voter from the poll, or a witness from a pending
trial, the act assumes a wholly different complexion. And
so if workmen spirit away other workmen from their labour
by highly festive temptations and liberal gifts of money
with the intention to damage the employer, or by " picketing," under the pretence of moral suasion, obstruct workmen in going to or coming from their labour, threatening
them, or, as often happens, falling upon them and beating
them, the law will hold an offence to have been committed
according to the circumstances. It is the purpose of the
actors, and the wrong ensuing, and not the means alone,
that constitute the unlawfulness.

But not content with this obvious misstatement of the
general principle of the law, Mr. Hughes and Mr. Harrison
proceed to heap gloss after gloss upon it with the view of
making out a case of intolerable grievance. " The effect of
the two doctrines," they say, " is this " :—

"Men cannot create any legal obligation not to work, or not to employ, simply upon terms allowed by the majority. Any arrangement for that purpose is illegal ; and any attempt to enforce such agreement by what is called 'unlawful coercion,' appears to be a crime."

It would be difficult to crowd more legal obscurity into the same number of lines than is here. What is meant by "a legal obligation not to work or not to employ?" Of course, agreements between masters and workmen cannot be in question, because the law will hold such contracts binding irrespective of the opinion of minorities or majorities of the parties. What Mr. Hughes and Mr. Harrison can only be thinking of is, that when the majority of a trade resolve to work only on certain conditions, or any number of workmen resolve not to work till certain conditions be conceded, the resolution should be binding on the minority in the one case, and that it should be binding in the other case on all the workmen going into a strike as long as there is a majority for maintaining it. Mr. Hughes and Mr. Harrison seem to be of opinion that it is a blemish of the law that men cannot by resolutions of this kind "create any legal obligation." Now, what is a legal obligation? It is an obligation which the law will enforce ; and what Mr. Hughes and Mr. Harrison imply, therefore, is, that when the majority of a trade adopt certain working rules the law should enforce these rules over the whole trade ; and that when a body of workmen resolve not to work until certain terms be conceded, the law should step in and compel any of the body who may be departing from the resolution to abide by it as long as there is a majority on that side. The two learned Commissioners not only hover over, but absolutely sink into the wild conclusion of Broadhead, that in order to avert questions of "the lawful coercion" in which he was so unhappily involved, the law itself should be the coercer, and save the Trade Unions all trouble on that point. But the law, for manifest reasons, cannot yield to such tempting solicitations. In the first place the law can only recognise resolutions of the kind referred to on the assumption that they are voluntary resolutions, that they are binding only on those who have freely agreed to them, and that they are not binding on any of the number longer than they freely choose to observe them. In the second place, were the law to enforce such resolutions it would be involved in hopeless difficulties, and could only compel a minority of workmen in a strike "not to work," or a minority of employers in a lock-out "not to employ," on the condition of indemnifying out of the public purse the compelled workmen and employers for a gross infraction of the common right to dispose of their labour or capital according to their own will.

The demand of the Trade Unions to have all their resolutions against others enforced by law, which thus found ample expression in the "Detailed Statement" of Messrs. Hughes and Harrison, has always stood in curious contrast to their other demand that there should be no law or no enforcement by law between them and their own members. It must be observed in justice to the two Commissioners, with whom there has been this controversy, that when they came to practical "propositions respecting amendments of the law" they had really nothing more to propose than this :—

"Union not to be capable of being sued as a corporate body, or of being dissolved, or otherwise wound up by the courts ; and not to be accountable, *in law or equity*, to its members in respect of any rule, agreement, resolution, or act of the society."

A mountain in labour brought forth this mouse !

XI.

ARBITRATION AND CONCILIATION.

THE methods adopted by the Unions to determine rates of wages and other relations with employers have been fraught with such disastrous consequences, not only to both parties, but to the public interest, that there has been for many years no small solicitude to discover some more expedient mode of settling such disputes as may arise on these questions. This solicitude appears to be felt quite as strongly by many members of the Unions themselves as by any class of employers; and it is felt probably by the general public, and by all disinterested and competent observers of the Unionist *mêlée*, more strongly than by either workmen or employers immediately embroiled in an exciting and constant, but in all its ups and downs an essentially barren antagonism. "The strike," reported the Royal Commission, "is a very rude method of settling such a question [as "the rate of wages], and it were much to be wished that "some method could be devised, mutually satisfactory to "workmen and employers, for settling disputes on this and "other questions when they arise." The only other method, thus so desirable — apart from the natural laws of trade which, though they do not supply any practical specific for the settlement of disputes between one class of men or one party of negotiators and another, are yet entitled to infuse much calm enlightenment into such disputes—is known under the general terms of Arbitration and Conciliation, or, as it might be described, a little more reason, mutual understanding, and good temper on the part of the disputants.

DISTINCTION BETWEEN ARBITRATION AND CONCILIATION.

But it is necessary to distinguish between Arbitration and Conciliation. The medium of harmony established by Mr. Mundella between employers and employed in the hosiery trade of Nottingham and "the three counties " is called an Arbitration Board, but in reality it wields no power of arbitration properly so called, and is simply a Conciliatory Board, or such a centre of good feeling and mutual understanding between parties, with respective interests to be arranged, but having a profound conviction that they are equally necessary to each other, as may be established in any considerable and well-defined market. The evidence of Mr. Mundella is probably one of the most interesting and suggestive passages in the Inquiry of 1867-9, and one would much rather enhance than diminish in any degree its importance. But Arbitration is a different process. It implies that matters in dispute, by mutual consent of parties or by virtue of previous contract, are submitted to arbiters, with an umpire, whose award is final, and may have the force of law, like any other result of contract in the public courts, so far as it can be enforced in that way. Mr. Rupert Kettle, County Court Judge of the district of Dudley, has been the most eminent administrator of this method of introducing greater harmony into the relations of capital and labour, and averting the universally obnoxious process of strikes.

MR. RUPERT KETTLE'S EVIDENCE.

Mr. Kettle, in his evidence before the Royal Commission, divided strikes into three groups—first, disagreements upon the terms of a future contract; second, disagreement on the construction of a subsisting contract; and third, disagreement upon matters of sentiment. The second class of cases seem the fittest of all for arbitration, for when two parties in any walk of life differ as to some precise term or reading of a contract, to which both wish honourably to adhere, they can seldom do better than submit the matter in dispute to a qualified and impartial

arbiter, and this may be specially true where several employers and large bodies of working men are concerned.
Differences of this class, according to Mr. Kettle, are
easily adjusted "if people come together with undisturbed
minds." Sentimental disagreements are not so easily arranged, because it is difficult to arbitrate on differences of
sentiment, and the circumstances of many strikes that have
this origin are too meagre and intangible for so grave and
dignified a process as arbitration. It is out of the first
class of disagreements that the more important strikes arise.
The men propose an advance of wages, or the employers
propose a reduction, and the difference between them is so
considerable that the tug of war begins. But this form of
disagreement, though the source of the most extensive and
baneful strikes, is unfortunately the least amenable to arbitration, because the point to be determined is the future
rate of wages : it is not the impartial construction of an
existing contract, but the making of a new one, and arbiters
must be as much at sea as to what the future rate of wages
should be as the parties themselves, and at best can only
split the difference, or compound the dispute in some way
so as to produce agreement for the moment, which the
parties might as well have done for themselves. Beyond
setting the parties to work together again, the award can
have no effect whatever in determining the future rate of
wages, and both employers and employed reserve their
right of notice if wages, in point of fact, should tend rather
to fall below or rise above the rate fixed by the award.
Notwithstanding the disability thus attaching to arbitration
in regard to future rate of wages, Mr. Rupert Kettle addressed himself to the task of overcoming it, and from the
tenour of his evidence before the Royal Commission it may
be inferred that he had succeeded to a degree which appeared to him at that time satisfactory.

THE WOLVERHAMPTON EXPERIENCE.

At Wolverhampton there had been for some years a series
of strikes in the building trades not only most injurious

both to masetrs and men, but suspending necessary building
operations in the town and neighbourhood, summer after
summer.   In these circumstances Mr. Kettle prevailed on
the master builders and the operative carpenters and joiners
of Wolverhampton to choose six delegates respectively to
form a board of arbitration, to which all future disputes
should be referred.   The plasterers and bricklayers came
in soon afterwards, but the masons were intractable, and
stood out.   The employers appear to have entered with
unanimity into the experiment from the first, and as the
delegates of the operatives increased the delegates of the
employers were increased so as to maintain an equality at
the board; and Mr. Kettle was appointed chairman with a
casting vote.   It is the practice of this board to review a
series of rules as to rate of wages, &c., once a year, and to
make it the basis of contract between employers and employed for the year.   The employers accept the rules, and
allow them to be hung up in their shops, by which they are
held bound to observe them ; and on engaging their workmen they put a copy of the rules into the hand of each, by
which the workman is also supposed to be bound as in
contract.   The delegates of the workmen are elected in
public assemblies of Unionists and non-Unionists of the
respective trades.   Mr. Kettle not only attaches importance to this arrangement, but has great distrust of the
power of the Unions to do any good to themselves by
their own unregulated modes of action.   He is of opinion
that Unions often lower rather than raise wages in their
respective trades, while injuring the employers and the
public.   The board, having thus by an effective representative process, obtained a form of contract between the employers and the working population of Wolverhampton in
the building trades, with direct reference to its arbitration
in any dispute that may arise as an essential part of the
contract, acquires considerable power over local or sectional
quarrels, and its awards in such cases would no doubt have
much weight if they should happen to go into the local
courts against any individuals, whether employers or workmen.   Mr. Kettle's evidence proves that this board of arbi-

tration at Wolverhampton had a beneficial influence. The
main effect, however, appears to have been that there was
more quietude on the part of the Unions, less uncertainty
that operations during the building season would proceed
without strikes or disturbances, and that the native honour
of the working men breathed more freely in the larger
atmosphere that had thus been opened than it had breathed
for some years before in the narrow and distracting Union
circles. In determining the rate of future wages, or as a
legal instrument in settling disputes to that end, the Wolverhampton Board of Arbitration could have no real power.
It was soon discovered, indeed, that the petty disputes
arising in the local trade were much too numerous and too
inconsiderable severally to require the formal process of
arbitration, and a "conciliation rule" was added, which
according to Mr. Kettle "has been found in practice more
useful than the arbitration rule." The Board at Wolverhampton, though from Mr. Kettle's idea and legal processes of working called an Arbitration Board, is in substance a Conciliation Board like Mr. Mundella's Board at
Nottingham.

The futility of thinking to settle future rates of wages by
arbiters became sufficiently apparent on Mr. Kettle's examination. For example, the Board at Wolverhampton
declare a rate of wages for the season, to which the employers' and workmen's representatives agree. But if wages
rise in other districts of the country during the season, the
workmen in Wolverhampton are not in the least bound to
their employers for the season, but on "a day's notice"
may go wherever they can earn more wages. On the other
hand, if wages should fall, the Wolverhampton employers cannot run away from their workmen as their workmen may run
away from them ; they cannot bring in the cheaper labour
available ; the only thing they can do is to give their workmen "notice," and allow outside employers to come in and
take what trade may be negotiable in Wolverhampton. It
is vain to attempt to give lop-sided contracts of this kind
the force of law, civil or natural. How easily they may be
disturbed even in their attainable moral effect is shown by

L

an incident recorded by Mr. Kettle. The masons, who had stood aloof from the Board of Arbitration, waited their opportunity, and when there was a certain amount of stonework to be done in Wolverhampton that could not be delayed without throwing many of the other building operatives out of employment, threatened to strike, and on the strength of this threat obtained larger wages than the Board of Arbitration had fixed for the other building operatives. The result of this was that bricklayers and others came up, and complained to the Board that the wages had not been struck high enough, and that they were sorry they had not adhered, like the masons, to their old Union formation. "I confess," said Mr. Kettle, "that this is a very "great difficulty, and that I shall have more than ordinary "trouble to overcome it." Another phase of the difficulty is when a body of employers, as in the recent case in South Wales, resolve to "lock out" and to give up business rather than endeavour to carry on save under a reduced scale of wages. It is, happily, seldom such an extreme case occurs, and when it does occur the case is always found to be one where the Unions, having under exceptional circumstances forced up wages much above any maintainable level, have in the reaction of trade to meet the inevitable downward process. But when such a case occurs, of what avail is arbitration? When a body of employers say, emphatically, "No ; we will rather stop our business, and subject ourselves to loss of fixed capital and profits of trade," of what use can be Mr. Kettle, or any number of equally able arbitrators in such a situation? There may be room for some conciliatory efforts, but there is no ground for arbiters to stand upon, unless the arbiters are to undertake the loss arising from the operation of their decrees.

Mr. Kettle's opinion that the rate of wages, for some time future, may be determined by arbitration, rested a good deal on the particular condition of the building trades, that the employers' contracts are generally undertaken and concluded within a year. But building contracts are found in practice to end and open at all periods of the year, and it is obvious that from this, as well as other causes, wages

in the interim may either rise above or fall below the scale
fixed by arbitration for the year. The general agreement
or understanding formed by the Board of Arbitration, for
the building trades of Wolverhampton, may be very useful
as a landmark or as a bond of mutual confidence, and
under this general guide employers and workmen may enter
all the more readily into special contracts with respect to
particular works of longer or shorter duration, which contracts would have the force of law in the Courts. But
working men are naturally reluctant to bind themselves to
an employer at fixed wages for any considerable period of
time in any case, and in no case save on the condition of
continuous employment during the whole period; while
employers are as naturally reluctant to bind themselves to
this condition. They might engage themselves to this extent to a number of their men, but that they could thus
contract for the future with the whole body of men in their
employment at any particular period, is a possibility that
can very rarely, if ever, occur. The awards of Arbitration
Boards, therefore, in regard to future wages outside of
special contracts, whatever minor sphere of usefulness they
may have, cannot be put into any conceivable form of legal
obligation, were it even desirable that they should be, which
no one can say it is. This result would be too near an approach to the old system of fixing rates of wages by statute
to be favourably entertained in the interest of the working
classes themselves.

The question of wages has been knocked about so much
by Unionists, from pillar to post and from post to pillar,
that it is going round in a circle and has now arrived at a
proposal of arbitration which, if it could have any avail,
would differ in nothing from the long discarded system
under which the rate of wages and the rate of profits were
fixed by law, or by the public authorities of the day and the
place.

OPINIONS OF THE ROYAL COMMISSIONERS.

The conclusion of the Royal Commission was—" It does
" not appear that any system of compulsory arbitration is

" practicable, since there are no admitted principles of de-
" cision on which the arbitrator may proceed; and it is
" scarcely possible to bind so fluctuating a body as the
" workmen to any decision of a permanent character."
Mr. Hughes and Mr. Harrison, dealing with this question in
a passage of their dissentient Statement, say that " the fact
" [conclusion] most plainly visible is the uniform approval
" of a system of working rules agreed to between employers
" and employed; " and that " when the great advantages of
" a code of rules and prices are further supported by a
" board of arbitration, it appears to us the nearest solution
" of the labour and employment question which has yet
" shown itself." To this they add that " some facilities
" might be given to the machinery required for enforcing
" the awards of boards of arbitration regularly constituted,
" to which there had been a *bonâ fide* appeal." The code
of rules and prices thus to be made the basis of arbitration-
awards to be enforced by law, as Mr. Hughes and Mr. Harrison admit, requires to be first agreed to between employers
and employed. They must have been fully conscious that
in the codes of rules and prices of the Trade Unions, there
are many provisions, such as the hostility to piecework, the
sending " to Coventry " a non-Union workman, the right to
strike on the spot against an apprentice or a foreman, or, as
in the case of the stonemasons of Wolverhampton, the
right of prohibiting the introduction of dressed stone from
Yorkshire, &c., which no employer, or arbiter, or board of
arbitration could agree to without forfeiting all claims to
ordinary intelligence; and they may have contemplated in
this passage of their Statement an expurgation of the codes
of the Unions that would satisfy the most trenchant re-
former. But, under all this wide assumption, it is difficult
to see how any legal force or facility can be given to arbitration awards of future wages, when the workmen, on the
one hand, are at liberty to go anywhere else on the briefest
notice for higher wages; and the employers, on the other
hand, though they may not go elsewhere for cheaper labour,
are yet at liberty on the briefest notice at least to stop and
discharge their men. Mr. Hughes, pursuing this will-o'-the-

wisp idea of some solution of future wages in the courts of
law, put the following question to Mr. Rupert Kettle,—
" Would not the difficulty be met if you were to add that
" the award of the umpire might be made a rule of one of
" the Superior Courts?" To which Mr. Kettle replied,—
" The expense of that would be great, and it would
" delocalise it, which would be very disadvantageous. You
" would get a lawyer interposed. I have a great respect
" for the profession, but I do not wish to see lawyers inter-
" posed in these cases." The truth is, that neither law nor
lawyers, save under some specific and unexpired contract,
can compel working men to take lower wages than they
can obtain, nor employers to pay higher wages than they
can afford, over any future period ; and the arbitration process of Mr. Kettle, when examined, can be in reality
nothing more than a conciliatory process, like that of
Mr. Mundella.

MR. MUNDELLA'S SYSTEM.

The proceedings under the Nottingham system are of a
very homely character, and approach as nearly as possible
to the consultations that take place between buyers and
sellers in any large market. An equal number of representatives of the employers and of the workmen meet round a
table, and agree, after much deliberation, to "a statement
of prices," which is subject to review in any of its parts
under new circumstances, or on satisfactory reasons shown
at periodical meetings of the board. No appeal is made to
any authority but that of the opinion and facts of the employers and employed themselves, as gathered at these
meetings. The board has learned from experience to dis-
pense even with coming to a vote. " As chairman," said
Mr. Mundella. " I have a casting vote, and twice that
" casting vote has got us into trouble. And for the last four
" years it has been resolved that we would not vote at all.
" We said, ' Let us try if we can agree,' and we did agree."
The " higgling of the market " proceeds at this board as it
does in less formal cases, till all can rise from their seats
unanimous. Such is the amount of adherence to this system

on the part of the employers as well as of the workmen, a great bulk of whom are organised in Unions, that the "statement of prices" arranged by the board finds general acceptance throughout the whole trade.

There are occasionally, however, some few employers outside the circle, who take their own way, against whom a dispute with the operatives and a strike would be imminent. In such cases two or three employers from the board wait upon these eccentric firms, reason with them—" We have " agreed to these terms, you can do the same, they are " acceptable on the whole, and why submit yourself to a " strike, and disturb the trade?"—and, if this reasoning should fail, a hint that the board employers have empty frames for all the workmen that might abandon the eccentric firms has generally a conclusive effect. Mr. Mundella was at some pains to show that there was nothing of a coercive nature in this procedure. But his apology was somewhat superfluous, because when the general body of employers and workmen are united, partial objectors must conform or succumb in any case. If the dissenting firm be simply looking to its own business, and in its condition of profit and loss cannot conform to the general rate of wages, it is to be pitied ; on the other hand, if it is a screwing firm, bent only on squeezing as much labour out of the workmen for as little wage as possible—which, as Mr. Mundella testified, was the character ascribed by the Trade Unions, during his day, to all employers alike, as if there were no natural law, or divine law as it may be called, by which such a policy, even if universal, was sure of being circumvented—this is a kind of firm to be disregarded by the general body of employers and workmen, and to be left to the self-ruin of its own principle of procedure. Workmen will withdraw of their own free accord from such employ. ment ; all the better class of workmen will be able readily to do so ; and the screwing firm will be left in the end with the "riff-raff" of the labour market, dear and unprofitable at any rate of wages. Though in many instances combinations of large and prosperous firms with masses of workmen at their back might be much abused, yet there is little in this scheme at Nottingham, as described by Mr. Mundella, that directly conflicts with what would happen under a free and natural action of trade and employment ; and there can be as little doubt that, in the hosiery and lace industries of Nottinghamshire, Derbyshire, and Leicestershire, though of ancient notoriety for the wildest outbreaks of labour against capital, it has had a beneficial influence in averting strikes and disturbances, and in producing a much better understanding between employers and employed than formerly existed.

SPECIAL CONCILIATORY CONDITIONS OF THE HOSIERY AND LACE TRADES.

The hosiery and lace trades of the three counties, however, have some special characteristics, which have no doubt helped materially to facilitate the operation of Mr. Mundella's system.

There is not only a uniqueness of interest in these branches of industry highly favourable to a common course of action among the employers, and between the employers and the workmen, but all the labour in the trade is done by piecework from beginning to end, and there are few or none of the many smaller questions than that of wages —but nevertheless extremely vexing and prolific sources of dispute and bad feeling—that arise in trades where opposition to piecework is a leading principle of the Unions. The employer and the workmen have only to arrange the price for making a dozen pairs of stockings—steam-loom, hand-loom, silk, or cotton— or whatever the class of article may be, and their business is settled. In the steam factories there are regulations as to hours, ages, sexes, education, and other minute matters, but these are made by Act of Parliament, and when the pay for a given piece of work has been arranged, the work under all its various classifications proceeds, with a simplicity of relation between employer and workman which it would be vain to look for in trades where piecework is not only not the rule, but is systematically opposed by the Unions.

Then, the hosiery and lace trades make goods largely for foreign markets, and are closely subject to foreign competition, the bearing of which the operatives perceive and feel as sensibly as the employers. When the representatives of the employers and the workmen meet in their Board, the articles made in France or Germany are placed on the table, with the prices at which they are offered and are being sold in England. This is a demonstration which working men can fully comprehend; and it infuses an amount of reason into the deliberations at Nottingham which may not be equally attainable in branches of industry where the visible data and other means of mutual understanding are not so readily at hand.

CONCILIATION AND INDIVIDUALISM.

Mr. Mundella's process of conciliation, or, as it might as well be called, coming to market terms on a fair deliberation between employers and employed *en masse*, stands in contrast to much of the evidence given in the Inquiry of 1867-9, the purport of which may not be better described than by the term of "individualism," or the right of the employer, master of his own capital, skill, and business, to transact with his workmen individually; and the right of the workman, on the other hand, as master of his labour, his skill, and his power of making all his talents and qualities appreciable, to transact with the employer on the same basis. Mr. Nasmyth, the eminent engineer, presented this idea of the relation of capital and labour in its strongest and most concentrated form; and it is an idea so pregnant in its results that it can never be without force in the industrial system of any country that would occupy a successful, not to say a foremost, place in the business of the world. But Mr. Nasmyth's evidence, though always brilliant, practical, energetic, and reflecting much light on the springs of action and excellence in the engineering works, by which the whole labour and commerce of the Kingdom have hitherto been so eminently supported, may withal not be accepted in its leading doctrine as an absolute or universal rule. It fails in this respect, that, however individually employers may act, they have to keep a sharp eye all the while on how other employers are acting; and workmen, moving on the same individual principle, have to do the same. They are both governed to some extent in their own sphere by fellow-competitors. It would be idle to leave out of the question a general equilibrium, apart from individual motive, to which both employers and workmen have to conform. There is an element of necessary deliberation, therefore, on both sides in any case; and in whatever branches of employment such a process as that of Mr. Mundella in the hosiery and lace trades can assume an organic form, it must surely, in comparison with anything which the action of the Trade Unions has presented, be a sound and rational procedure.

RECENT ARBITRATION CASES.

The attempt to determine future wages by arbitration has had many examples within the last year or two under circumstances that must be admitted to put the process to a severe trial, but of which it should be able to bear the strain if it be in any degree a reasonable, or more than a Quixotic, mode of settling the future rate of wages.

In such a case as that of the coal and iron trade recently in South Wales, where the employers found themselves in such extremity that they resolved to close their works unless a reduction of wages were conceded by the workmen, an arbitration appears to be absolutely excluded. But employers in various branches of industry have, in the general flow and pressure of sentiment, committed themselves more or less to arbitration beyond the sphere in which arbitration can be of any practical utility. Employers and workmen, indeed, have a common facility of entering into these mimic arrangements, because the result is binding neither on the one class nor on the other. An employer cannot be compelled to continue to employ men at wages fixed by arbiters; nor can a workman be compelled to continue to give his labour under any award of that kind. A frequent result of

the more public arbitrations as to future wages has been
that where the award of the arbiters has not come up to
their expectations, the Unionist workmen have not only
individually, as the employers individually might also do,
but in a body have refused to submit to the award, and have
demanded either some new strike or some new adjudication,
as if the trade of the country could be conducted under a constant process of litigation, with its production of books and
documents, its wranglings, its distractions, and suspensions
of business, not as regards the main concern equally to
employers and employed, but as regards an entirely unsolv-
able question of *future* rate of wages. "In these days
of Union strikes and arbitrations," bitterly exclaims the
manager of a large iron-work in the North of England,
" one has hardly time to look ahead, much less to look
" back. My time has been so much occupied in getting up
" evidence and preparing cases to lay before the Arbitration
" Board, that I have had little or no time left to the business
" of iron-making."

The cases in which employers and workmen have entered
within the last year into arbitrations with a full determination to abide by the award, and in which the award, when
given, has been rebelled against by the workmen, are more
numerous than can here be dwelt upon. But take two sig-
nificant examples.

A Court of Arbitration formed in Manchester in 1869,
and embracing the Trades' Union Council of Manchester
and Salford, and the Manchester Chamber of Commerce,
broke down under a notice from the latter that as no cases
had ever come before the Court, it might as well be wound
up. A dispute between the Amalgamated Carpenters and
Joiners and their employers in the interim had been referred
to the umpireship of Dr. Watts, whose decision was re-
pudiated by the men, and another expensive and tedious
process was entered upon with professional arbitrators on
each side, leaving the final award to Mr. S. Pope, Q.C.,
Recorder of Bolton. Mr. Pope had already been engaged
in a dispute in the same trades in Bolton, and had thrice
arbitrated, and finally wrote to the Masters' Secretary that

the agreement for six months' notice of any advance had been disregarded by the men, and that such conduct rendered arbitration useless. Dr. Watts, in the Manchester case, refused concession as regards general wages and working hours, but on all other points gave an award in favour of the workmen. Mr. Pope, Q.C., increased the wages per week by sixpence, and reduced the working time per week 2½ hours; but took away other advantages to the workmen awarded by Dr. Watts!

Again, Mr. Hughes, late M.P., appeared in May last, as final arbiter with full consent of colliers and coalmasters in Somersetshire, and gave an award of 11 per cent. reduction in room of the 16 per cent. which the employers had offered to the men without going to arbitration. So far from being satisfied with this friendly award, the colliers were highly indignant at it, and demanded an appeal to Mr. Macdonald and Mr. Lloyd Jones, or, in other words, an appeal from a superior to an inferior tribunal. The collier-obloquy with which Mr. Hughes was reported to have been visited on this occasion may be a lesson to him; but the lesson should not have come from that quarter, since no man deserves more respect from the working men of the Unions, as regards all the benevolent and conscientious intention which is one of the superior tests of character, than Mr. Hughes.

NORTHUMBERLAND COAL TRADE ARBITRATION.

Of recent arbitration cases probably the most instructive, as regards the course of such proceedings, is the Northumberland Coal Trade Arbitration in March of last year. The coalmasters and colliers of Northumberland had arranged their affairs for many years on the most amicable terms. The circumstances, indeed, were all favourable to a really happy and effective deliberation on this occasion. The arbiters on each side were men of the highest authority in their respective ranks—Mr. G. B. Forster and Mr. Thomas Bates on the part of the employers, and Mr. Burt, M.P., and Mr. Macdonald, M.P., on the part of the colliers—with

Mr. Rupert Kettle over them as umpire. Mr. Kettle was
" to sit with them ; " if they came to a unanimous conclusion his office would be ended ; and if they failed to agree
his award became final. The facts of the case were that in
the prosperous and excited period of 1871-2, successive
advances of wages to the amount of 50 per cent. were
conceded by the employers, with various other advantages,
without the necessity of a single strike on the part of the
men ; and that on the rapid descent of the trade from the
inflation of 1872-3, the men were, on their part, for a time
almost as handsomely accommodating as the employers had
previously been. They accepted in April 1874, a rate of
wages only 40 per cent. above the rate of 1871 ; and they
submitted in October of the same year to a further reduction
of 14 per cent., which left them still 26 per cent. above the
rate of wages in 1871. But when the employers, in December, intimated a further reduction of 10 per cent., coal
falling heavily in demand and in price, the men began to
hesitate ; and when in January, the trade having become
still worse, it was announced that the reduction must be 20
per cent. in the soft coal pits and 16 per cent. in the steam-
ship collieries, though these heavier reductions would have
left them still considerably above the wages of 1871, yet
they could not understand such a state of matters, and
demanded an arbitration. The employers in the interim, of
course, from December 5 till the date of the award,
March 13, went on paying the 26 per cent. higher wages
than in 1871.

In laying their case before the arbitrators and umpire, a
most remarkable statement was made on the part of the
employers, viz., that while working, according to the showing
of the successive advances and reductions of wages, at
nominally 26 per cent. higher wages than in 1871, the total
sum paid in wages for a given quantity of coal had become
84·81 per cent. more than in 1871. This result was testified
by information obtained by two firms of public accountants
from the books of all the collieries in the Northumberland
district ; it was subjected to the most rigid scrutiny in the
course of the Arbitration ; and its substantial accuracy was

finally certified in the award of the Umpire. It was made clear that in this excess of 84·81 per cent. of wages in proportion to the coal produced no capital charges and no "dead" or "unproductive" work were included, and that nothing had been taken into account but "the simple amount of wages paid in bringing coal to bank."

How then, had the apparent increase of 26 per cent. in wages over 1871 swelled to an actual increase, as far as the produce of coal was concerned, of 84·81 per cent.? In the first place, the output of coal had decreased 7 per cent., (2) the number of hewers working in the pits had increased 16 per cent., (3) the number of off-hand labourers and other workmen had also been much increased, (4) under the operation of the Mines Regulation Act the number of hours the pits could be advantageously worked had been materially diminished, (5) for the increased number of men a corresponding number of cottages had to be provided, the rental of which increased the wages charge, and (6) besides the openly declared advances of wages in 1872 and 1873, the executive of the Miners' Association had been busy obtaining extra advances to individuals and to limited bodies of men, which the umpire in his award estimated in the case of the coal-hewers alone at 11·69 per cent. From these various causes an apparent increase of wages charge of 26 per cent. on the same amount and quality of coal in January, 1875, had become an actual increase of 84·81 per cent. then as compared with April, 1871. In fine, it was shown that the money value of the coal raised would only allow the employers to pay 64 per cent. more for labour than in 1871, and that as they were paying 84 per cent. more, they had acted with all moderation in proposing that the reduction should be only 16 per cent. in the hard coal, and 20 per cent. in the soft coal pits. This was in substance the case of the employers.

When the agents of the men were called upon for their case, it was found that they had no case prepared, but were merely waiting to hear what the case of the employers was, and to have time to consider what reply they could make to it. The Northumberland arbitration was not quite so flagrant, indeed, in this respect as the Durham arbitration a few weeks before, in which it appeared that the employers had simply been called up as culprits to vindicate themselves for daring to propose any reduction of wages at all !

But it may here be observed that the agents of working men in such cases, if there be any ground of arbitration, cannot but have, or should have *data* in possession to have justified their clients in entering upon so elaborate a process. They must know, for example, whether they have opportunities of earning higher wages than the employers proffer ; whether the demand for labour within their own immediate sphere is increasing or decreasing ; whether the general course of affairs, as reviewed from their side of the case, is favourable or unfavourable to what they claim ; and all this information should be so much in hand as not to have to be looked for after the arbitration has begun, or in what may be stated on the other side. Indeed, if such information exists, it is not on the other side one would expect to find it.

The law agents of the Northumberland colliers did, however, after a brief delay, produce their statement; and, as might be supposed, it added no new facts of any consequence to the question, but was simply a rhetorical discourse on what were deemed erroneous assumptions on the part of the employers. To have any ground of arbitration, it was absolutely necessary to adopt some basis of comparison, and 1871 had been accepted on both sides as a normal state of coal-mining affairs, in which the wages of the workmen were neither too low nor the profits of the employers too high. Yet the first statement in the case of the agents of the Northumberland colliers was that it must not be assumed that the profits of the employers in 1871 were fair, or that the same profits must be maintained now, as they were then, by a reduction of wages—thus departing at once from the accepted ground of the arbitration. The second statement of the case was that it was wholly wrong to assume that wages must follow the same declining rates as prices in order to maintain an equable rate of profit to capital, the clumsy sophistry of which plea may be seen when it is remembered (1) that as long as prices were rising the colliers demanded and obtained higher wages simply because prices were rising, (2) that it was only when prices fell that they demurred to any corresponding fall of wages, and (3) that it had been demonstrated in the case of the employers that profits were much lower than they had been in the nominally moderate year of 1871.

Mr. Kettle, as not unusually happens in these cases, "split the difference," and awarded 10 per cent. reduction in the soft coal pits, 12½ per cent. in hard coal pits, and from 10 to 15 per cent. on various underground and bank workers, men and boys.[1] The award did not give satisfaction to the workers; the "mechanics" in the Northumberland collieries were on strike the next week; and Mr. Rupert Kettle could hardly have reached his home after much severe work without hearing that by all his well-meant efforts he had really settled nothing as regards the Northumberland Coal Trade.

Take any supposable future course of circumstances, and ascertain what the future value of this arbitration is. Suppose matters remain for a year or two much as they were in March last, that the rates of wages remain as fixed by Mr. Kettle, and that there is a running loss to the employers, how long will they sustain that loss, and keep their workpeople in employment? Suppose there is a rising demand and advancing p.ices for Northumberland coal, will not the colliers and their agents immediately reverse the doctrine they asserted so strongly in the arbitration, and insist that wages should rise with prices? Suppose the reverse, that in the next year or two the demand and price of coal continue to fall, is any one so simple as to imagine that coal employers in Northumberland will be held bound in any degree to the award of Mr. Kettle? There are two elements wholly left out in these processes of arbitration which have a dominant force, viz. (1) the great public, that only consumes coal or anything else on terms that suit itself; and (2) an increasing working population that requires to be employed; that must be employed, whatever

[1] *Official Report of Northumberland Coal Trade Arbitration*, 1875.

Trade Unions and other interior monoplies may devise to the contrary ; and in proportion as it is not employed, the fabric that supports both the wages of labour and the profit of capital must fall away.

ARBITERS DISCUSSING POLITICAL ECONOMY.

The discussions of the arbiters and umpire in this North-umberland Arbitration case assumed at intervals a philo-sophic complexion, and from that fell into much chaffing on "the principles of political economy"—a dangerous ground to trespass upon by people who profess to fix the future rate of wages, because the laugh is almost certain to be against themselves in the end. Mr. Macdonald, for ex-ample, contended that the additional cost of labour caused by the Mines Regulation Act, which he admitted to be "very great," ought to fall on the employers ; and in the same train of thought it was maintained, in the written case on his side, that as seams of coal become thinner, or as the workings get deeper or farther away from the shaft, the cost of labour must be constantly on the increase, and that this increased cost must also fall on the employers, and must not be brought into any arbitration as to what the wages of miners should be. Under this version of poli-tical economy and arbitration of wages, the employers, of course, would very soon be wiped out altogether. Where no profit is, no capital can long remain, and the time might soon come, were these views to prevail, when there would be hundreds of thousands of miners on the bank with a supposed property in a raw material to which they could not get down, and a few hundreds of real proprietors (also on the bank) of a raw material which they could not bring up. It is capital that bridges this chasm, but capital cannot be called upon to do anything so adventurous with-out a profit, and it will certainly not be impressed by Trade Unions or arbitrations into any such service. Mr. Kettle, with probably better knowledge of economic causes and effects, kept Mr. Macdonald in countenance by remarking, "It is quite natural" [anything 'quite natural' *Scotticè* is idiotic :] "for you to say so. It is 'Uncle Public,' you

" know, who always pays." But when Mr. Forster modestly
interposed that "mines may possibly be worked at a loss,"
Mr. Kettle himself had nothing wiser to remark than that—
" Still they may probably be worked, as men train horses
" that do not always win, and yet stud and train all the
" while." There was nothing in this farrago of political
economy to guide or enlighten an arbitration of future
wages. It is clear that capital will not employ labour at a
permanent loss, and that an increasing cost of labour in
any branch of production, therefore, will not fall upon employers, but must come out of the pocket of "Uncle
Public," who consumes the product. But who is "Uncle
Public", if not the working-classes themselves? They
form the great mass of consumers all the world over.
Nothing consequently can be more certain than that in a
policy of increasing the cost of labour systematically pursued by workmen in their various trades, without respect to
the economic conditions which alone can render higher
wages possible, they may be only injuring and finally
starving each other. What increased cost of labour puts
into one pocket, increased cost of labour will take out still
more rapidly from the other pocket. Instead of being able
to consume more, the workmen will be able to consume
less, and as consumption falls away they will cease even to
be employed.

About the time the late Canon Kingsley's *Alton Locke*
appeared there was much distress among the London
journeymen tailors, and in a private discussion at that now
remote period—to which, the more remote, reference may
be only the more useful to young working men, who
pass in crowds into all the Trade-Union impolicy, since it
tends to show how completely these subjects had been can-
vassed before they were born — the following argument
ensued : — A., referring to the laws of supply and demand as the only solvent of the difficulty, contended that
the London tailors were in distress because they were too
numerous for the amount of employment. B. observed
in reply that there were tens of thousands in London who
had not a decent coat to their backs, and that the employ-

M

ment of tailors was capable of much increase. A. retorted
that these thousands had no means of purchasing coats.
Upon which B. remarked that the dilemma in that case
came to this, viz., that the misery of trades was that many
were not able to consume because they could not get work,
and could not get work because they were not able to
consume !

The law of demand for labour is very elastic, and will
cover the whole population ; but it is necessary to its
elasticity that the law of supply of labour shall be un-
restrained, because it is out of the labour of all the demand
for the labour of all comes.   The first condition of industrial prosperity is that the whole increasing population
should have free access to employment.   The second is
that the cost of production, under every aid of labour, education, invention, art, and science, should be diminished
and not increased, because this cheapness is the means of
life and comfort to the poorest, and introduces an ever-
widening circle of consumers.   Given these conditions, and
the question of rate of wages, which in nine cases out of
ten is but a nominal question, arbitrates itself, and must
always arbitrate itself more and more in favour of the working man and woman.

Arbitrations of future wages, proceeding on the assumption that all loss accruing to employers may be rolled over
on the shoulders of an " Uncle Public," who nowhere for
the time being has any practical existence, are thus found
to be hollow and insincere.

[1] Mr. Robert Wilson, of Darlington Iron Company, in a letter published in *Capital and Labour* of April 28, 1875, enforces with much
apparent reason a scheme of adjustment of wages in the finished iron
trade, under the existing Board of Arbitration, that would probably be
better than the system in practice. It may be learned from this source
that wages among the iron-workers are regulated by the selling prices
of finished iron, and that yet the cost of production is wholly left out of
the question.   Mr. Wilson gives this illustration of the unequal operation of the present system.   "For instance, if pig-iron and coals are
" so advanced in the market as to increase the cost of production
" of finished iron by 20*s*. per ton, and there is only an advance in
" the selling price of 10*s*. per ton, the puddling and other wages are

FAILURE OF CO-OPERATION IN CONNEXION WITH TRADE-UNIONISM.

With "Arbitration and Conciliation" the idea of Co-operation was prominently affiliated a few years ago ; but it would be a travesty of the co-operative principle to connect it in any form with Trade-Unionism. It belongs to a higher order of ideas than has hitherto germinated in that extensive circle. The Royal Commission had under its consideration the liberal proposal of Messrs. Briggs & Co., in their Whitwood and Methley Junction Collieries, dating from July, 1865, to give their workmen a full half-share of all profits above 10 per cent. necessary to the redemption of their capital invested. The Royal Commission, in its report, observed that the principle of Messrs. Briggs's system was "to give the workman, over and above his "wages, a share in the profits of the concern, *without sub-* "*jecting him to any liability for loss*," and that "the period

"advanced upon the additional price of 10s., whilst there may be an "actual loss to the employer in the manufacture." Mr. Wilson, pro-ceeding on the views of Mr. Barningham of the same firm, suggests that "the actual cost of production" should be taken into account, and that the wages of labour should follow more strictly and reasonably than at present the rate of profits, and not of mere selling prices. He would thus fix a minimum below which wages should not fall even when the employers were suffering loss, and a minimum above which wages should not rise when employers were making great profits, so that capital would have some chance of recovering by gains at one period losses sustained at another. There would be a large intermediate sliding scale in which wages would rise and fall quarterly or six-monthly with the rate of profits earned by the employers according to an elaborate return from all the works of the district by accountants. There can be little objection to any scheme of this kind, which aims simply at securing some steadiness of operation in great works, and Mr. Wilson has probably suggested what would be an improvement on the present system. But he does not appear to have taken into full account that there is no real test of "cost of production" unless there be absolute freedom both of labour and capital throughout the whole sphere of the industry. It would be little comfort to the iron-workers at Darlington or anywhere else to have to submit to a reduction of wages merely because the colliers and pig-iron workers of a neighbouring district had fenced off all competition of labour, and by strikes and other tactics designed to run up the value

M 2

" during which the system had been under trial was too
" short to admit of coming to a satisfactory conclusion as
" to its permanent success." The caution of the Royal
Commissioners has been abundantly justified by the event,
for the last half-yearly report of the directors of the collieries (December 31, 1874) announced that the system
had been abandoned, because the colliers had expressly
stated that they were members of the Miners' Union, and
" wished to be in future on precisely the same footing as
" the workmen employed in other collieries of the district."
In this, as in various other ways, the Trade Unions would
appear to operate as an obstacle to the progress of the
working classes in paths hitherto new, however worthy of
patient trial, and however promising of ultimate improvement and elevation to the industrial orders of society.   But
if working men will neither submit to equal freedom in their
relation with employers, nor to an association with employers in which they have a share of all the profits, and no
share of any of the losses, what is this but anarchy ?

of their labour beyond that of other people, had raised the price of coal
and pig-iron 20*s.* per ton.   The adjustment of wages by any process of
arbitration, or by any arrangement of that kind in particular trades, is
thus one of the most complex of problems.   " Cost of production," in
the books of the economists, has hitherto been conceived mainly from
the capitalist point of view, that is to say, the employer counts what his
raw materials, his buildings, and machines, and the wages of the labour
he directly employs, have cost him ; and he expects out of all these
elements to have a profit.   The "reward of production" is an entirely
different thing, and has to be obtained out of the price obtained for the
product, and this frequently neither responds to the calculation of the
employers, nor the just demand nor reward of the workman, if "costs
of production" are only to be considered.   Hence the most serious
difficulties, which are only increased, and rendered more injurious to
labour by constant efforts in particular branches of trade to stint
production and raise wages, because all branches of industry are closely
co-related, and increased cost of production thus passed on from one
branch to another, cumulates in an exorbitance of prices under which
trade breaks down, and neither capital nor labour get their reasonable
reward.   There is no ground, at least yet discovered, so sure as that of
freedom of labour and capital, the one searching out its highest wage ;
the other, its most reasonable hope of profit.   There is the other way,
indeed, of labour acquiring capital, and being its own employer ; and
that way is not closed.

ROYAL COMMISSION OF INQUIRY ON "THE LABOUR LAWS."

XII.

EVIDENCE AND REPORT ON THE MASTER AND SER-VANT ACT, THE CRIMINAL LAW AMENDMENT ACT, AND THE LAW OF CONSPIRACY.

THE legislation ensuing upon the Royal Commission of 1867-9, in the session of 1871, had brought the law relating to Trade Unions to what was deemed at the period a very satisfactory state, always supposing, of course, that the Unionists were to be content with the fullest exercise of the right of combination, now expressly protected by law, in due consistency with the rights of other persons outside their combinations, which the law was equally bound to protect. The last shade of possibility that any criminal consequence could attach to a Trade Union as being in restraint of trade, even though the action of the Unions should be hurrying the trade of the country visibly to loss and decay, was removed by the Trade Unions Act of 1871 : and in the Criminal Law Amendment Act of the same year, the most clear and in-telligible definition, and on the whole also the most equit-able, probably ever entered on the Statute Book on any similar subject, was given of acts of violence and acts of in-terference "with a view to coerce" others in what they had a full natural and legal right to do or not to do freely, which no person, Trade Unionist, or other, could commit with-out liability to criminal penalties.

Nor were the Trade Unions themselves slow to express their high satisfaction with the settlement that had thus been

accomplished. Their leaders were loud in praise both of
the Trade Unions Act and of the Criminal Law Amendment
Act, of which of course these chiefs took the chief credit to
themselves. A year, however, had scarce gone when a great
storm of discontent broke out among the Unionists against
the Master and Servant Act, 1867, the Criminal Law
Amendment Act, 1871, and the Common Law of Conspiracy
so far as it might be found applicable to any of their proceedings. There could be no peace in the country, it was
proclaimed, until these two Statutes were abolished, and
until the Unionists were made safe in their trade proceedings from all law of conspiracy to which other classes of her
Majesty's subjects in the most various spheres of action are
liable. This position was enforced by Hyde Park, and
similar processions and demonstrations throughout the
kingdom, as if it were really meant to make the country a
little uncomfortable. It is to be observed that not a word
of objection was raised to the Trade Unions Act, 1871,
and that this denotes what must be deemed the great blot of
the political agitations of the Unionists, viz., that while
accepting gracefully and silently the fullest liberty the Legislature can give them, they are not disposed to submit to
any restraint of their aggressions on the liberty of others, in
an observance of which their own liberty is indissolubly
bound up, and can only indeed be guaranteed. The two
things—liberty for ourselves, and respect for the liberty of
others—stand to each other as inseparably as the Siamese
twins, or as the obverse and reverse of a medal.

This new outbreak of discontent had the usual result in
the appointment of a Royal Commission of Inquiry into the
alleged and hitherto unheard-of grievances. The impression produced by the Trade Union agitation against the
" Labour Laws " in political and official circles must have
been profound—more profound, indeed, than can well be
fathomed on any hypothesis short of general political
" softening of the brain." One of the first acts of the Conservative Government that came into power after the General
Election in the spring of 1874, was to issue this Commission,
under command and seal of Her Majesty, " to inquire into

"the working of the Master and Servant Act, 1867 ; and " of the Criminal Law Amendment Act (34 and 35 Vic. " cap. 32), and whether any, and if any, what, amendment " or alteration in the provisions of those Acts, or either of " them, is desirable, and also to inquire whether it is ex- " pedient to limit or define the law relating to conspiracy, " either generally, or as affecting the relations of masters " and workmen."[1] It is necessary, therefore, to follow this subject a little farther, so that we may have it all before us, and know what has come of it up to this time.

REFUSAL OF THE UNIONS TO GIVE EVIDENCE.

The only difficulty encountered by the Commission was a refusal of the Societies which had stirred up the inquiry to take any part in it, or to lend any assistance in elucidating the matters to be considered. An appeal was made to the " London Trade - Union Congress Parliamentary Com- " mittee "—a body which, from the import of its title, must have had the whole case of the Unionists in hand—to produce evidence, and make any complaints they were prepared to advance. The result was a letter from the secretary declin- ing " to assist the Commission in its labours in any way," and inclosing a copy of a resolution passed by the Committee to the same effect. This course was generally followed by the Trade Unions throughout the country. Conduct of this kind was not only unreasonable and disrespectful, but it was hurtful to the Unions themselves, since it was capable of only one construction, viz., that they had little confidence, notwithstanding all the previous clamour, in the strength of

[1] The members of this Royal Commission were Lord Chief-Justice Cockburn, Lord Winmarleigh, Edward P. Bouverie, Russell Gurney, Sir Montague Edward Smith, John Arthur Roebuck, Thomas Hughes, Gabriel Goldney, and Alexander Macdonald—names, as in the Royal Commission of 1867, that must have carried full assurance to every reasonable person that evidence on the matters under inquiry would be fully elicited and well sifted, and that the report returned, including minor dissentient statements, would express the absolute truth and equity of the case as far as these could be ascertained through such elaborate means.

their own cause. This mulish spirit is the more necessary to be reprehended because it is somewhat characteristic of the Unions, and is often manifested in arbitrations demanded by themselves, where after all the troublesome and costly apparatus has been provided, they are found to have nothing to show, and have come only to hear and object. The qualification of a rather useless Member of Parliament was that he could, indeed, say nothing, but he could " always object." This, however, is not a model to which the Trade Unions, conducting what they deem a great cause before the eyes of the country, should descend.

It does not follow that the inquiry was in any degree impaired by the abstinent and surly attitude of the Unions. The information laid before the Commissioners was full enough for all purposes of reasonable decision. Mr. Shipton, delegate from the London Trade Council; and Mr. Boa, President of the Glasgow Repeal of Labour Laws Association, defined the complaints entertained by the Unionists against the laws and the administration of the laws, and not only argued these complaints with point and ability, but were prepared with cases in illustration of their arguments; some of the leading employers gave evidence on the other side; three of the stipendiary magistrates who have had the greatest experience of the operation of the Acts were examined at much length; and the Commission called for and obtained a return of the facts, depositions, and sentences in cases of conviction in the principal Courts of the United Kingdom. It is improbable that any more light would have been elicited, though the Unions had thrown their whole stores of knowledge and experience into the inquest. Still this does not excuse the Unions, after two years of agitation pitched in the highest key of social grievance, in deserting the diet they had invited; and the judgment of the working classes may be safely trusted whether a course of this kind can promote their interest, and whether it should ever be repeated, whether in great national inquiries or in the lesser arbitrations that take place between sections of employers and employed as to wages. It is preposterous to think that either the parliamentary politics or the productive industry of the country may be incessantly disturbed by an inner club of people, who, when the day of trial they have demanded comes, have neither facts nor reasons to contribute to the investigation.

FINDINGS OF THE COMMISSIONERS.

I.—THE MASTER AND SERVANT ACT.

The Commissioners show that until the reign of George II., the idea of "Contract of Service," which implies mutual and independent obligations, had not entered into the legislation of the kingdom. There were "Statutes of Labourers" from Edward III. down through the intervening centuries, in which capital and labour, employer and employed, were governed by what seems equal State license. Working people were required not to become vagrants, but to remain in the hundreds or parishes were they were born, under severe penalties, and people of substance in the hundreds or parishes are required to employ them; the terms of employment were sometimes fixed directly by statute, and sometimes under statute by the local magistrates, who in many cases may have been chief employers themselves; and many other regulations were made which in the present age are incomprehensible on the surface, and form simply a subject of recondite study in historical and social development.

These "Statutes of Labourers," must have slept more or less over long periods, as statutes often happily do. But in the 20th of the reign of George II., the relation of master and servant had become so far independent of State power, that the principle of "Contract of Service,"—or that you the master having offered so much, and you the man having agreed to take so much, any dispute between you must be referred to the magistrate on the terms of the agreement—began to be recognized. This principle, confined at first to contracts for a year or more in husbandry, handicrafts and mines, was extended eleven years afterwards in the same reign to contracts of less than a year, and by a statute

10 George IV. to labourers of all sorts. But the order of the original statute, as in the succeeding ones, was that the magistrate might decree £10 to a servant in husbandry, and £5 in case of artificers and other labourers, and levy the same in event of non-payment by distress on the goods of the master or mistress. When the complaint was on the side of the master, and was established, the magistrate might either abate some part of the wages due to the man, or discharge him from the service, or punish him, according to the aggravation of the case, by committing him to the House of Correction for some time not exceeding a month. A further statute in the reign of George IV., c. 34, dealt with breaches of contract where the servant, after engagement, failed to enter into the service or quitted it before the period agreed on had expired, and extended the period of imprisonment in extreme cases to three months, but debarred any power to order corporal punishment. Here the law rested till the Master and Servant Act of 1867 was passed.

Though the principle of contract, marking a great elevation in the *status* of the working classes, was clearly introduced in these Acts, yet the possibility of making a servant or workman liable for breach of contract in money damages does not appear to have dawned on the Georgian Parliaments, beyond abatement of whole or part of the wages due, or dismissal from the service, with terms of imprisonment, with or without hard labour, as the extreme resort. On the other hand, that these statutes were available for enforcing payment of money damages from masters and mistresses is fully established by the fact that to this day proceedings by servants and workmen against employers continue to be taken under the Act of George II. A law of contract, enforceable on the one side and not on the other, of course, is no law at all ; and it is the interest of the working classes, if the principle of contract is to be preserved, that there should be available redress against breach on their side as well as against breach on the side of employers.

The Master and Servant Act, 1867, was the result of a Select Committee of the House of Commons in the previous year, which reported after full inquiry that the law of

master and servant, as it stood, was objectionable, and
recommended that instead of a hearing before a single justice,
all cases under this category should be publicly tried before
two or more magistrates, or before a stipendiary magistrate
in England and Ireland, or the sheriff in Scotland ; that procedure should be by summons, and only, on failure to
appear, by "warrant to apprehend ;" that punishment should
be by fine, and failing payment, by distress on goods or imprisonment ; that the Court should have power to order
defendant to fulfil the contract where advisable, and to
require him, if necessary, to find security that he would
duly do so ; and that in aggravated cases of breaches of
contract, causing injury to person and property, the magistrates should have power to award imprisonment instead of
fine.   The Act embodied in effect these conclusions, and
was universally deemed a great improvement of the law, as
in various important senses it must still be held to be.
The introduction of a fine as the penalty of a contract-
breaking servant or workman was as near an approach as
could be made to the damages imposed on a contract-
breaking master or mistress, and the ultimate consequence
in both cases was the same.   If the fine or damages were
paid, the case ended ; if not, there was distress on goods
or imprisonment on the one side as on the other.   In the
provisions for a public trial before two or more magistrates ; for a civil summons before any warrant to apprehend ; for power to imprison in ordinary breaches of contract, not directly out of the breach itself, but, as a necessary
auxiliary of the jurisdiction, for disobedience to the order of
the Court ; and in the elimination of "hard labour" from
any imprisonment that ensued—there is satisfactory evidence
of a fair adaptation of the law to employers and employed,
and to the extended industrial relations of recent years,
which was wanting in the Georgian statutes, bearing as
they do a rough aspect of dealing only with a limited and
reckless class of working people, under the one redeeming
feature that where masters or mistresses broke faith with
their servants or workmen, the latter had legal means of
getting the money out of them.

But yet the Master and Servant Act was by no means a model Act. The Commissioners felt bound to report that it was " a singularly ill-drawn Act in many particulars." Not only were ordinary and "aggravated" breaches of contract, and civil and criminal conditions, too much mixed, but the clauses treating on these separate features were so disjointed and confused that magistrates were not always competent to the task of unriddling what the Legislature should have made plain and clear. The consequence was that in not a few cases the Act was administered contrary to its own intention. " We find cases," reported the Commissioners, "where imprisonment on non-payment of a fine " has been awarded for a longer period than the law allows. " Hard labour has been made part of the sentence of im- " prisonment, whereas by the 11th Section it is specially " provided that no such imprisonment should be with hard " labour. Defendants have been brought into court, the " amount of compensation, damages, or other remedy being " omitted from the summons, contrary to the direction con- " tained in Section 4, which expressly requires that these " particulars shall be stated in the summons." These are grave errors of administration which may not be confined to this department of justice, but it proves the keen and impartial scrutiny of this Royal Commission that they were found out, and were reported. The popular impression from such cases is apt to be that, whatever faults may be in the law, the magistracy must be extremely partial and un- just. But were one to go to the root of the evil it would probably be found rather that the members of the House of Commons, and even Cabinets, do not really study the reports of Royal Commissions and of their own Select Com- mittees of Inquiry as legislators ought to do, but are too often led away for political reasons into *ad captandum* enactments, which, instead of being any amendment of the law, make it on many points of detail rather worse than it was before.

It appeared from the evidence that complaints were chiefly directed against the 9th and 14th Sections of the Act—to the former because it empowered the magistrate to

impose a fine and to order imprisonment as a means of enforcing payment or fulfilment of the contract, and thus
treated as criminal or quasi-criminal cases of an essentially civil
character ; and to the latter because it dealt with "aggravated breaches of contract" without clearly defining them,
imposed a heavy term of imprisonment, and thus confused
still more what was civil and what was criminal.   Mr. Boa,
speaking in the name of 62 trades in the West of Scotland,
said that the Act was deemed "a very good Act if the 14th
clause were taken out and the 9th amended;" that the
feeling among the workmen on these points, as well as in
favour of trial before stipendiary magistrates, was strong,
and that cases of breach of contract by workmen, he
thought, should all proceed on the principles of civil law.
The employers, on the other hand, who gave evidence, held
that the Act as it stood was necessary to enforce performance of contract, and that it was mutually beneficial
both as against workmen and against employers.   This
class of witnesses also spoke in favour of such cases going
before a stipendiary magistrate when one was within reach.
Mr. Menelaus, of the Dowlais Works, thought it "lucky"
that "they had a stipendiary in his district to administer
" the law, since it removed all suspicion of partiality that
" might lie against the Justices, who were themselves em-
" ployers;" and Mr. Robinson, president of the National
Federation of Employers, observed as his experience that
Justices took a more lenient view of breaches of contract
than the Stipendiary Magistrates.

The testimony of the Stipendiary Magistrates, who were
examined, was that few convictions had issued under the
14th Section of the Act, and that proceedings were usually
taken under the 9th Section. Mr. Hannay, police magistrate
at Worship Street, said that "without imprisonment in case
" of non-payment of fine under the 9th Section it would be
" impossible to enforce the Act at all."   At the same time,
he could hardly understand what particular mischief the
14th Section was intended to meet differing from such
wilful damage to person and property as was subject to
penal consequences under other Acts of Parliament. "The

workmen," he said, when they had complaints against employers, "were very fond of this Act, and if refused a sum-
" mons under it, went away much disappointed, as the costs
" were higher and the delay greater in the County than in
" the Police Courts." Mr. Davis, Stipendiary Magistrate
at Sheffield, maintained the great utility of the 9th Section
as a means of enforcing specific performance of a contract,
"with imprisonment of course, in default of compliance."
Mr. Bridge, one of the Stipendiary Magistrates at Ham-
mersmith, proved that wages were constantly recovered by
workmen against employers " by the pressure of a summons
under the Act only."

The Commissioners, in their Report, had little difficulty
with the 9th Section, because the basis of the complaints as
to imprisonment there failed inasmuch as the imprisonment
was for disobedience to the order of the Court only, and
is not an exceptional but a universal remedy in the civil
law. In order to divest the Section of all character of
criminality it was only necessary to substitute for "fine "
compensation for damage actually assessable ; but since it
would be of no use for a Court to be employed unless it
had some means of enforcing compliance with its award,
the Commissioners could not take away the power of imprisonment, save in the mitigation that it should be in a
prison for debt only. On the 14th Section perfect oneness
of mind was not so attainable. All the Commissioners were
agreed that the "aggravated breaches of contract " referred
to in this Section were sufficiently grave to be matter of
special treatment, but the matter of doubt was whether
they should be relegated to civil or criminal process.
The characteristics of such cases are (1) that the party
breaking his contract does so wilfully, not only without just
cause, but without believing that he has just cause ; (2)
that he knows that by breaking his contract he will entail
serious injury, loss, or mischief on the other contracting
party ; and (3) that he knows he has no means of making
compensation for the injury or loss so caused.[1] Some of

---

[1] The following instances in which such breaches of contract may
arise are put in the Report :—1st. Where a man knows that his employer

the Commissioners were of opinion that it would be better that even aggravated breaches of contract should be dealt with under the civil than under the criminal law, and that it would be sufficient if power were given to the magistrates to commit to civil imprisonment for *six months* in the event of the compensation awarded in such cases not being paid. Others were of opinion that the law under the 14th Section should be maintained with the provision that it should be at the option of the party complained against to be tried by a jury. The numbers being nearly equal, the question between them as to the more dishonest and reprehensible class of breaches of contract was submitted to the wisdom of Parliament.

The Commissioners, while expressing favour for the stipendiary magistracy as a preferable jurisdiction for disputes between employers and workmen, concluded that, where such magistrates were not appointed, it would be impossible to find any other tribunal than the Justice Court before which ordinary cases could be heard with the cheapness and despatch necessary to both parties ; and they dismissed a proposition from the Trade Union side, that proceedings of breach of contract should be valid only in the case of written contracts, as uncalled for, and unsuitable to the general interest of the working classes.

has a heavy contract on, which he is bound under penalties or legal liabilities to complete, and knows that his service is necessary to enable the employer to fulfil his engagement, his place not being capable of being immediately filled. 2nd. Where a man quits his service, knowing that serious injury to his employer's property will result from his doing so ;* as, for instance, if the manager of a smelting furnace were to quit his employment, and cause the going out of the fires, and cooling of the metal. 3rd. Where the necessary effect of abandoning the service is to expose the master's property to serious injury and loss. 4th. Where the purpose for which the service is abandoned is that of unduly coercing the master in the conduct of his business. On the part of the employer, we might have a breach of contract in dismissing a workman, aggravated by attempts to prevent him from obtaining other employment." *Second Report*, p. 12.

2. CRIMINAL LAW AMENDMENT ACT.

The Commissioners, in reporting on this Act, briefly recite the previous legislation. The Act 5 George IV. made a clean erasure of all the prior Acts antagonistic to trade combinations, and gave the most extended freedom to Unionists, in all their favourite objects and modes of raising wages, shortening hours, and regulating labour, from liability to any indictment or prosecution, or to any other criminal information or punishment thereupon, whether under Common or Statute Law. But to guard this liberty against being abused, a clause was added submitting violence, threats, and intimidation for the purpose of coercion to criminal procedure, and to a penalty, in case of conviction, not exceeding two calendar months' imprisonment with or without hard labour. This Statute had no sooner become law than it was found to give rise to mischievous consequences, and in the very next session there was an inquiry in Parliament, followed by a new Act, which secured all the freedom given to the Unions by the preceding Act, but put in a more comprehensive and stringent form its provision relative to acts of coercion, and increased the penalty to three months' imprisonment. This Act 6 of George IV. remained the law of the country till the Inquiry of 1867. It was then complained of by the Unionists as being too "vague," "difficult to understand," and limiting their freedom of action in various ways too much, and too severely. Whatever vagueness or severity attached to these provisions of the 6 George IV. they were totally incompetent to prevent or check the outrages that had grown up in Sheffield and Manchester a few years before 1867, and that had shocked the whole kingdom. Parliament, proceeding on the elaborate inquiry of 1867-9, while extending the privileges and security of the Unions still more in various important respects, took up these penal provisions of the 6 George IV., revised them, made them more clear and definite, and presented them in a form more acceptable to the Unionists in what has since been known as The

Criminal Law Amendment Act. But the Unionist complaints before the late Commission on "The Labour Laws" against the Criminal Law Amendment Act were the same as against the older Statute. It was "vague," "difficult to understand," and placed the members of Unions in some degrading exceptional position under the law, apparent only to themselves.

There is thus much see-saw in the legislation demanded by the Trade Unions. Parliament goes on for a while giving them their bent of liberty ; by and by it is found that the liberty given is greatly more than can be well used : then Parliament is bound to meet the violences and invasions of right that occur by some corrective measures ; and in a year or two more, these give rise to more Trade-Union complaints, and demands for more liberty and absolution from all legal obligation. Still these provisions against criminal invasions of right Parliament never can get rid of. They may be condensed and transferred out of one statute into another, and may undergo a hundred literal transmutations from one time to another, but they will always reappear and, while the offences exist, will always command the first importance in the country. If the Trade Unionists could only comprehend that the more their liberties and powers of combination are extended and sanctioned by law, the more the law is bound to provide that these liberties and powers shall not be abused, and that such of her Majesty's subjects as do not happen to be members of a Trade Union shall not be violently and directly overridden in the exercise of their natural and civil rights—that a faithful observance of this condition by Trade Unions, indeed, is their only conceivable legal title of existence,— no doubt they would soon begin to rectify their views of the state of the law, and give Parliament much less trouble than they do, to the sad neglect of matters in which the interest of the working classes is much more deeply concerned.

The Criminal Law Amendment Act has been the subject of so much Trade-Union denunciation that it may be well

N

to give the law it conveys, as stated in the Report of the Commissioners :—

" Any person who with a view to coerce another—
" 1. Being a master, to dismiss or to cease to employ any workman, or, Being a workman to quit any employment, or to return work before it is finished ; or
" 2. Being a master, not to offer, or Being a workman not to accept any employment or work ; or
"3. Being a master or workman, to belong or not to belong to any temporary or permanent association or combination ; or
"4. Being a master or workman, to pay any fine or penalty imposed by any temporary or permanent association or combination ; or
" 5. Being a master, to alter the mode of carrying on his business, or the number or description of any persons employed by him,—
[Any person, who with a view to coerce another to one or other of these ends,]
" Shall do any one or more of the following Acts, viz. :—
" 1. Use violence to any person or property ; or
" 2. Threaten or intimidate any person in such manner as would jusify a justice of the peace, on complaint made to him, to bind over the person so threatening or intimidating to keep the peace ; or
"3. Molest or obstruct any person in manner defined by the section, that is to say :—
"*a*. By persistently following such person about from place to place ;
"*b*. By hiding any tools, clothes, or other property owned or used by such person, or depriving him of or hindering him in the use thereof ;
"*c*. By watching or besetting the house or other place where such person resides or works, or carries on business, or happens to be, or the approach to such house or place, or if with two or more persons following such person in a disorderly manner in or through any street or road —"
Shall be liable to imprisonment, with or without hard labour, for a term not exceeding three months.

To these enactments were added two important provisions :—

" 1. That nothing in this section shall prevent any person from being liable under any other Act, or otherwise, to any other or higher punishment than is provided for any offence by this section, so that no person be punished twice for the same offence."
" 2. That no person shall be liable to any punishment for doing or conspiring to do any act on the ground that such act restrains or tends

to restrain the free course of trade, unless such act is one of the acts hereinbefore specified in this section, and is done with the object of coercing as hereinbefore mentioned."

The "vagueness" complained of here by the Trade Unionists is so vaguely discernible that one must wish that one hundredth part of the statute law were equally plain and intelligible. To constitute the criminal offence it must be done (1) "with a view to coerce another," which, of course, must be to apply a force to which the will of the person to be coerced does not freely respond; (2) this coercive influence must be exerted to one or more of five distinctly specified objects in respect to which the person to be coerced, whether master or workman, has a clear and indefeasable right to choose to act for himself without external pressure of any kind; and (3), before there can be any offence, this "view to coerce" to one or more of five ends in which coercion is totally impermissible, must be manifested in outward acts of more or less violence, every one of which is uncivilised, and contrary to all the usages of civilised life. Yet the Unionists go on alleging that they do not understand this, that it is too "vague," that it is always entrapping them into criminality when they do not mean it, and that the law in some incomprehensible way is a most grievous wrong and insult to them!

The Commissioners, in weighing the complaints against the Act, resumed the principles stated in the Report of the Commission of 1867, where it was shown that the greater the numbers and power of combinations, and the more freely and fully the law sanctions the right of combination and extends the scope of combined action, the more necessary it is, and the more is the law bound to secure just and equal freedom of action to those who do not think proper to join the combination, and who choose to act for themselves; and that, in short, the power of the Unions must be exercised within the bounds of their own rights, and not aggress upon the rights of others. "To permit a body of men," say the Commissioners, "to interfere with "individual freedom in the matter of employment of labour, "by *any of the means specified in this Act*, would be to

N 2

" allow the freedom, which should be protected by law, to
" be tyrannically and unjustly violated. . . . The demands
" of a body of men acting in combination may be excessive.
" The remedy of the employer is to be found in the possible
" willingness of others to accept employment on more
" reasonable terms." This is in reality the foundation of
the right of combination itself; the Unionists cannot sap
and mine it without pulling down their own edifice; and
the reason of the case as thus stated effectually disposes of
such objections to the Criminal Law Amendment Act as
that it is specially directed against Unionists, and is invidi-
ously applicable to the case of employers and employed
alone.   For the more the law has sanctioned and covered
with its protection the action of Unions, of workmen or
employers, the more careful must the law be to repress
special crimes and offences arising out of the new circumstances. *Noblesse oblige.* The higher the legal privilege,
the more necessary to guard against offensive abuse of the
privilege.

The Commissioners, however, were disposed to think
that in a few of the cases that had come before the Courts
under this Act there was some basis for the complaint that
the provision against picketing was too general, and might
be construed to include forms of picketing that were innocent; such as when a Union on strike kept watch to see
that men receiving strike pay were not taking work from
the employers and thus defrauding the Union; or when
attempts only to persuade might be held to be "molestation with a view to coerce."   "But any such error," they
add, " would be immediately set right on appeal," as they
had been in several cases, six convictions having been
quashed in England and Wales on appeal in 1872-3, and
eight in 1873-4, out of a total of 174 convictions.   "The
" fault of such errors is not in the Statute, the language of
" which is sufficiently precise and clear." The Commissioners refer in corroboration of this conclusion to the
charge of Mr. Justice Lush in the Queen *v.* Shepherd and
others—1869 —in which he clearly pointed out the distinction between force put upon the will and persuasion

influencing the will, and the men were acquitted by the jury.

With respect to administration, the Criminal Law Amendment Act excluded from the bench any person who was a master, or father, son, or brother of a master in the particular manufacture, trade, or business in or in connexion with which the offence should be charged to have been committed. To meet an impression among Trade Unionists that magistrates who are employers in any branch of trade or business have a leaning in favour of the whole class of employers, which, if followed out as a serious conviction would seem to imply that only Trade-Unionists should be judges in Trade-Union cases, the Commissioners recommended as an improvement, as they had already suggested in the case of the 14th Section of the Masters' and Servants' Act, that an option be given to the party complained against of being tried at Quarter Sessions by a jury. With this exception they saw no reason for a repeal or alteration of the Act in question.

3. LAW OF CONSPIRACY.

The indignation of the Trade Unionists that the common law of conspiracy should be in any way applicable to them was probably the most unreasonable and most undisguisedly revolutionary feature of the open-air demonstrations that caused this Inquiry into the so-called "Labour Laws;" because by the Trade Unions Act of 1871, these bodies had been already exempted from the operation of the law of conspiracy in their capacity as Trade-Unionists. The Imperial Parliament, moreover, had been so indulgent as to make it plain that no charge of conspiracy could lie against the members of a Trade Union or any similar combination, save in direct connexion with the acts specified in the Criminal Law Amendment Act, wherein both the ends sought to be attained and the means by which they are sought to be attained are alike wrongful and criminal. An Inquiry into the subject could only expose the hollowness of the agitation, or suggest some respects in which the immunity of Trade-Unionists from the law of conspiracy had already been carried beyond the bounds of reason and equity.

The Commissioners, in their Report, give the following exposition of three categories, applicable to all classes and conditions of men, in which the common law of conspiracy becomes vital and operative :—

" First where the end to be accomplished would be a crime in each of the conspiring parties, a class of conspiracy which offers no difficulty. Secondly, where the purpose of the conspiracy is lawful, but the means to be resorted to are criminal, as where the conspiracy is to support a cause, believed to be just, by perjured evidence. Here the immediate intention of the parties being to commit a crime, the conspiracy is to do something criminal, and the case again is consequently free from diffi- culty. The third and last case is where with a malicious design to do an injury, the purpose is to commit a wrong, though not such a wrong as when perpetrated by a single individual would amount to an offence under the Criminal Law. Thus an attempt to destroy a man's credit, and to effect his ruin by spreading reports of his insolvency (though a variety of other illustrative principles might be put), would be a wrongful act, which would entitle the party whose credit was thus attacked to bring an action as for a civil wrong ; but it would not be an indictable offence. If it be asked on what principle a combination of several to effect the like wrongful purpose becomes an offence, the answer is— upon the same principle that any other civil wrong, when it assumes a more aggravated and formidable character, is constituted an offence, and becomes transferred from the domain of the Civil to that of the Criminal law. It is obvious that a wrongful violation of another man's right committed by many assumes a far more formidable and offensive character than when committed by a single individual. The party assailed may be able by ordinary civil remedies, to defend himself against the attacks of one. It becomes a very different thing when he has to defend himself against many combined to do him injury."

The Commissioners could see no reason to question the propriety of the general law of conspiracy as thus established, and were so convinced of its beneficial operation that they were glad to escape from the direction given them to consider whether it " might be limited or defined generally," on the understanding that, if it should be found desirable to alter or modify the law of conspiracy as now applicable to employers and workmen, it would be better to make such an exception to the general law than disturb and unsettle what had been found alike necessary and just as regards all other branches of jurisprudence. They had thus to examine very closely (1) whether any changes should be made in the law of conspiracy as it affects the relation of workmen and employers, and (2) the objections made to the past application of the law in this respect.

The cases in which a combination to interfere with rights of hiring and service could fall under the law of conspiracy —such as a body of workmen, some breaking their contracts and inducing others to break theirs, or quitting their employment with the intention to injure their employer, and to render him unable to fulfil his engagements ; or a body of workmen combining in like manner to break their contracts with a view to any of the purposes condemned as wrongful in the Criminal Law Amendment Act ; or a Union or other body combining to induce the workmen of a particular master to break their engagements and leave his service, &c.—were found to be so serious that no reason could be discovered why the general law should be altered to afford greater license to persons thus acting. The wrongful purpose, and the wrongful and even criminal means necessary to an offence of conspiracy, were all present in such cases. On one point alone the Commissioners thought there was some force in an objection of the Trade-Unionists, viz : "that " by the application of the law of conspiracy men are made " criminally liable for acts which are no longer penal under " the statute law, which ought not to be penally prohibited, " and in respect of which the Legislature meant to afford " immunity from punishment." This objection, which evidently rests on very narrow and shadowy grounds, appears to have been founded on some words of Baron Pollock in a charge to the jury in a case of conspiracy tried before him at the Summer Assizes at Leeds in 1874. The Baron is reported to have said that if several workmen combined not to work with another workman, and to refuse to work for an employer with whom they had an engagement unless he dismissed that workman, this act would amount to a conspiracy at common law ; and that the same principle would apply to a combination of masters agreeing not to employ a particular workman unless he left a particular society or union, or agreed to do something or other not included in

a free and honourable engagement of labour. Baron Pollock
may have been right or wrong in his view of the law as it
stood under the Act of 1871. The learned Judge was most
probably stating what the equity of England would be, as
it has come down through centuries of administration, even
were there no immediate statutes on the question ; and it
must be observed in the reason of the case that a combination of working men, calling themselves " Unionists," to
exclude by force one or more working men, who are not
"Unionists," from employment and from the means of
earning their bread, is about as cruel an offence as can be
committed, and to all persons who have any comprehensive
conception of the working class-interest in its solidarity, must
appear one of the most ugly and revolting features which
Trade-Unionism has brought into the foreground of social
and industrial life. If breach of engagement be included,
as the learned Baron appears to have implied, the offence,
of course, becomes so much the worse.

But the Royal Commissioners, on mature judgment, did
not take this line of consideration. What they concluded
on this point was, in the first place, to avoid all opinion on
the correctness of the law as reported to have been laid
down by Baron Pollock, and in the second place, assuming
the law as thus stated to be the law, that it required
amendment in this one respect, viz., that labour and capital
being alike free in their original conditions, it must be
equally free to workmen and employers, "*not under contract*," to work for or with whom they please. Therefore,
a body of men or a body of masters, free of contract, could
not be subject to any law of conspiracy in refusing to work
with or to employ this man or the other man as they
severally determined.

The profoundest legal exegesis could scarcely infer that,
in passing the Trade-Unions Act of 1871, the Legislature
had any intention to place under the law of conspiracy
such a commonplace Trade-Union procedure as the refusal
to work with non-union workmen, all its consequent hard-
ship and ruin to the latter notwithstanding, or, indeed, any
Trade-Union procedure but that disclosing itself in aggra-

vated violations of contract or in acts of personal assault and outrage. One cannot but observe that the various conundrums of legislation raised by Trade Unions, however imperfectly solved, from time to time, by a semi-stupefied Legislature, when pursued to ultimate reason, come down to very simple A B C. All is comprehended in the simple maxim, "Exercise your own right to the full, but do not infringe the rights of others." A baby, even "Ginx's Baby," could hardly lose itself in the whole question.

The substantial conclusion of the Royal Commissioners —and it is very important to mark it—was that the common law of conspiracy as applicable to Trade-Union action, had been already greatly more repealed by the Trade-Unions Act and the Criminal Law Amendment Act of 1871 than was reasonable, or could possibly be justified, and that it was necessary in reason and in the public good "to add to " the wrongful means set forth in the Criminal Law Amend- " ment Act, that of *wilful breaches of contract*," as properly subject to the common law of conspiracy.

These were the findings of the Royal Commission on the " Labour Laws." The conclusions of the Commission, as rarely happens, were practically unanimous. The only dissentient report was that of Mr. A. Macdonald, M.P., who stated without argument or reasons of any kind, but with his authority as a leader of Mining Unions (1) that the 14th section of the Master and Servant Act should be entirely removed from the statute-book ; (2) that conditions of employment requiring to be enforced by criminal law should be provided for by special statute in each trade, when found absolutely necessary, as in the case of mining operations ; (3) that the Criminal Law Amendment Act should be totally repealed ; and (4) that the Law of Conspiracy should be altered in the manner suggested by Sir William Harcourt.

LEGISLATION RESULTING FROM THE COMMISSION ON "THE LABOUR LAWS."

XIII.

THE EMPLOYERS AND WORKMEN ACT AND THE CONSPIRACY AND PROTECTION OF PROPERTY ACT.

PARLIAMENT, in the session of 1875, proceeded, on the motion of the Home Secretary, Mr. Cross, to deal with the laws which had been the special subject of inquiry by a Royal Commission. What the conclusions of the Commissioners were has been seen in the preceding chapter.

The Home Secretary, on introducing two Bills, professed to follow closely, with some few exceptions, the recommendations of the Commission. The view of the Government was that breaches of contract should be divided into two categories—one civil, and liable only to civil remedy ; the other criminal, and subject to penal consequences. To obviate all confusion of the one class of breaches of contract with the other, alleged to be the chief defect of the Master and Servant Act, Mr. Cross proposed to treat them in two separate measures, that would come in room of the Master and Servant Act. The Criminal Law Amendment Act, the repeal of which had been demanded by the Unionists, had in his opinion been greatly misunderstood, and the Government did not conceive that it could either be repealed or much amended. "It was equally necessary to "maintain the perfect free will and independence of the "workman against his fellow-workmen as it was to maintain "his freedom and independence against his employer." But, as regarded the law of Conspiracy, the Home Secretary perceived from recent cases in the Courts, as well as from the Report of the Commissioners, some opening for a modification that would meet the complaints of the Unionists. This was a fair and intelligible programme, and seemed to promise an exhaustive treatment of the question of breach of contract, in both its civil and criminal aspects, and whether on the part of employers or employed.

The second Bill of Mr. Cross, however, was found to be an unsatisfactory exposition of the law as regards criminal breaches of contract, and a rivalry ensued between the front Opposition bench and the Treasury as to which party should have the honour of doing most for the Trade Unions that had singular results on the texture of the Bill, and presented the most curious example of "legislating in a circle" that has probably ever been recorded. This will fully appear on consideration of the Bills as they now stand in the form of completed Acts.

EMPLOYERS AND WORKMEN ACT.

The Employers and Workmen Act does not expressly repeal the Master and Servant Act, but it may be assumed to come in its place, as the intention of Parliament obviously was.[1] The older Act did not apply to domestic servants, or to clerks, shopmen, and the like persons employed in trade and business. It is curious to find that questions arising with respect to these classes have been left wholly to the Common Law. The Employers and Workmen Act maintains the same distinction, and applies to "the workman," whether in rude or skilled labour, who has entered into a contract, verbal or written, with an employer. The Act does not apply to seamen or apprentices at sea. The obligation of ordinary apprentices is touched upon, though not materially changed, in distinctive clauses, the chief feature of which is that the parent or other party to the indenture may be called into Court in a case of breach by the apprentice. It is thus an Act bearing on individual workmen or hired

[1] The repeal of the Master and Servant Act is effected, with some minor exceptions, by the subsequent Conspiracy and Protection of Property Act.

servants in husbandry of every class, who have entered into
engagement with an employer; and *vice versâ*, on employers
who have entered into engagement with the same classes of
people. The distinction of classes is not very precise. For
example, it must be doubtful to the Courts whether a
kitchen-woman in a farm-house be under the Common Law
or under this Statute. The Act, indeed, embraces many
relations which scarcely come within the sphere of Trade-
Union concern or procedure ; but it is all the more important on this account since in practical operation it may
probably suggest how far laws may be wisely amended
under dictation from a totally different sphere from that to
which in numerous instances they apply.

The principle, and the whole import, indeed, of the Act is
to substitute in simple breaches of contract for some small
fine, or, failing payment, term of imprisonment, or for performance of the contract, a decree of damages in favour of
the injured party. The fine under the Master and Servant
Act was practically the same as a decree of debt only it was
more capable of being modified to the means of the defendant, when a workman or servant, than an assessment of
damages can be. But the alternative of imprisonment gave
effect to the fine, and was in its nature penal, though much
less so when under the regulation of statute and the miti-
gating discretion of the Court, than when imprisonment or
distraint ensues at the instance of a creditor. The suggestion of the Commissioners, that personal detention should
only be in a civil prison, appeared to meet the case both as
regards the leniency and the efficiency of the law. Some
time might also have been expressly allowed a workman or
servant to pay the fine under security before any imprisonment could follow. Parliament, however, disposed of the
question otherwise.

When a servant abruptly leaves his service, or a workman breaks his contract, he will now be summoned, if the
employer chooses, in the ordinary civil form, as if he had
failed to pay his grocer ; and the Court, if the summons can
be served, will assess the damage done to the employer, and
order payment of the amount with costs. The employer will

thus obtain a judgment debt against his servant or workman, which, if paid, will be a satisfaction to him. Employers, under the law as it has hitherto stood, have derived only the negative benefit arising from the discouragement given to breaches of contract by the fact that the breakers were in some cases amenable to fine or imprisonment. On the other hand, decrees of Court against employers for breach of contract, or other damage to servants or workmen, have generally been valid in a positive sense, and the injured servants or workmen have happily been able to put the recovered money in their pockets. Employers, as the law now is, will be able to obtain decrees of debt against any contract-breaking servant or workman for the full amount of damage done. The Legislature, however, in another course of enactment, in itself humane and commendable, has much reduced the value of judgment debts against poor people. Debtors cannot be put in prison unless they have means and are unwilling to pay ; and there can be no arrestment of wages. Judgments of damage to employers will often be null and void even when obtained. There is thus, in what will be found to be a large proportion of cases, a dissolution of the legal obligation of contract of work or service in the new civil form. On the other hand, there are many cases in which the operation of the Act may prove oppressive to workmen and servants. It places a great power of future annoyance to the person, against whom a decree of damages is obtained, in the hands of his employer. Working people, the few even who fall into breaches of contract, are not all waifs and strays. They seek to live in one place, to settle, and to occupy a respectable position. But with a judgment debt out against them in the hands of rigorous creditors, this will be impossible till the judgment be satisfied ; and the judgment debt based on a strict assessment of damage, may be much more severe than the fines by which the magistrates have hitherto compounded such cases.

When the damage claimed does not exceed 10l. with costs, the case may go before a court of summary jurisdiction ; but the powers given by the Act to County Courts in England imply that any amount of damage arising from

breach of contract of service may be sued for in the ordinary
civil form. The breaches of contract within the immediate
purview of this Act are no doubt breaches of the most
ordinary and simple character, where an individual workman
or servant only is concerned, where the damages can consequently seldom be of large amount, and the moral influence
of a legal obligation of contract is much the most valuable
element in the case. But the County Courts in England, the
Sheriff Courts in Scotland, and the Civil Bill Courts in Ireland are now opened to the suit of whatever amount of damage
may arise.

The most flagrant breaches of contract, without acts of
violence or direct external injury to property, occur under
the auspices of the Trade Unions, where fifty or a hundred,
or several hundreds of men lay down their tools and cease to
work on some frivolous pretext, without any warning or
notice required by the works in which they have engaged.
This is a civil breach of the most wilful and lawless character, because it is done in concert, with the deliberation
of a multitude, and there is no room for the indulgence properly extended to acts of wayward personal impulse. It is
the more inexcusable inasmuch as, by giving the required
notice, the Unionists would have full liberty to withdraw their
labour, and to do whatever they pleased of a non-criminal
character, under the full protection of the law. In such
cases, moreover, the damages often amount to hundreds, and
even thousands of pounds. In a case of this kind the remedy,
under the civil process now formulated by Act of Parliament,
would properly lie against the Union, the wilful author and
inspirer of the whole mischief. But the Unionists, who are
astute enough in matters of law, have already provided by
the Trade-Union Act of 1871, that Trade Unions can neither
sue nor be sued. It would be idle to inquire whether Parliament, which in the second Act under consideration, as
will be seen, has condoned all the most criminal breaches
of contract, involving direct and wilful destruction of property, by payment of a fine of 20l., had any idea of recovering hundreds or thousands of pounds of damage under
this Employers and Workmen Act. But, wittingly or un-

wittingly, such remedy has been offered, and it is obvious that
a suit against fifty or a hundred or more men in the Civil
Courts for damage ensuing from their combined desertion
of work, without the notice required in their engagements,
might have under the civil law very ruinous effects upon
them individually.

Another feature, and one, indeed, of the details of this
Act illustrative of the danger to the interest of working men
in specious legislation of this kind, occurs in respect to what
was a most prudent recourse of the magistrates under the
Master and Servant Act, viz., to order performance of the
contract on the simple personal promise of the workman or
servant. The Bill, as introduced by the Home Secretary,
reserved this power both to the County Courts and to the
Summary Courts. In this way a multitude of cases of
breach of contract have hitherto been settled, without either
fine or imprisonment, and in the way most easy and welcome
to the defendants, who were only required to give their own
engagements. But this would appear to have been too much
good sense to bear the strain of party rivalry in the House
of Commons, and an amendment came forth that a workman
or servant, willing to return to his contract as a settlement of
all damage pending against him, must in future give the
surety of some adequate person or persons in addition to his
own personal promise. The sole object of this too liberal
device was that the word "imprisonment" might not appear
in the Bill; but underhand, at the same time the cunning
legislators provided that the surety, whom a servant or workman in such a case may be happy enough to find, may
imprison him in recovery of the damages assessed in lieu
of performance! This unwise and hypocritical provision,
greatly increasing the difficulty of a workman or servant in
extricating himself from the bad consequence of a breach of
contract, passed even the House of Lords, and stands
part of the Statute.

The principle of the Employers and Workmen Act is
one with which no one can have any quarrel. It proceeds
on a theoretical equality always sound, reasonable, and
desirable to be realised in so far as there is a practical

equality of redress in cases of wrong. But there can be neither utility nor progress in vamping up a theoretical equality in law that is only to have the effect of relaxing the sense of contract-obligation among a large number of working people, and in many other cases inflicting worse results for breach of such obligations than have hitherto been experienced. If amendments of laws of this kind do not diffuse more widely an honest moral sense of contract-obligation, and provide in the administration that parties violating this obligation shall be more equitably treated in proportion to the wrong and to their own personal means of making honourable amends, greatly more harm than good may be done.

CONSPIRACY AND PROTECTION OF PROPERTY ACT.

This measure, without departing out of the control of the Home Secretary and Lord Chancellor, became much different in its passage through Parliament from what it was when originally introduced. Mr. Cross would probably have led the discussions of the House of Commons more effectively to a better end had he adhered in the scheme of this second Bill to what was understood to be his programme, viz. to deal with the criminal aspect of breach of contract, and to settle the criminal law with respect to breaches of contract which by one degree or more of crime passed out of the civil category. The Home Secretary had undertaken to separate the two classes of breach of contract mingled somewhat incongruously in the Master and Servant Act, and to make them the subject of two separate and thoroughly satisfactory statutes. It seemed his duty in breaking up the Master and Servant Act, to exhaust its contents, and to obtrude no alien subject until the elements of breach of contract embraced in that Act were fully examined, and either dispersed or placed in some more clear and equitable terms than they had hitherto appeared in the statute-book. There would thus have been assurance of legislation proceeding in a regular, scientific, and settled form, on this perplexed industrial relation. But the Home Secretary introduced what he deemed a change in the common law of conspiracy as applicable to trade disputes, calling his Bill a "Conspiracy Bill," and then drawing certain penal clauses bearing on " malicious injury to property" against which ample provision had been already made in previous statutes, the Bill became a " Conspiracy and Protection of Property Bill," with criminal breaches of contract proper and *per ses*—the *Prince Hamlet* of the play—left out, and disposed of by Parliament. as may be judged, in a most unsatisfactory and vagrant fashion. The erratic course thus given to the legislation by Mr. Cross was greatly increased by an Opposition amendment that the Bill should repeal the Criminal Law Amendment Act, which relates not to breaches of contract at all, but to specified acts of personal violence and molestation in which no question of contract of labour is involved ! The Government and the Opposition may equally have had some intention of 'satisfying the whole platform of Trade Union agitation in a single measure. But reasonable men of either party do not regard with much favour flighty legislation of this kind affecting the bases of the social and industrial state ; and political leaders would be wise not to indulge in such freaks. The country sees all and judges all.

Before proceeding to look how the Law of Conspiracy was amended and the Criminal Law Amendment Act was repealed by this statute, it may be well to follow out the question of criminal breach of contract.

The Bill of Mr. Cross had two clauses bearing on this question, the effect of which was that workmen employed by any municipal authority, or public company under Act of Parliament, supplying gas or water to any city, borough, town, or place, who wilfully and maliciously breaks a contract of service, knowing the probable serious consequences of so acting, shall be liable to a fine not exceeding 20*l*., or failing payment of this fine, to imprisonment for not more than three months with or without hard labour; and that employers or workmen in any other case, who wilfully and maliciously break a contract of service, knowing that the probable consequences of so doing will be to expose valuable property, whether real or personal, to destruction or to

O

serious injury, shall be liable in exactly the same penalties. These clauses remain in their original integrity in the Act as passed.

The formal distinction thus made between workmen in gas and water works and workmen in other establishments is not very clear in reason. In the one case, there is serious annoyance to the public ; and in the other, there is serious destruction or injury to private property. But both public and private interests are injured in both cases, and Mr. Cross's two clauses, more especially since they involve the same penalties, might as well have been only one. The offence in both instances implies a concert of workmen in breach of contract with the knowledge that serious injury will ensue. An individual workman in gas or water works, by breaking his contract, can inflict little or no injury. But even an individual in many other works, by breaking his contract, may inflict a great deal of injury both on his employers and on his fellow-workmen. A municipal authority or other corporate body employing men in gas or water works, knowing the serious consequence of a sudden stoppage of their works, have to be careful to have a term of service from their workmen, with formalities of notice, to which they have reason to believe that their workmen will be faithful. Other companies and firms employing workmen have to observe the same circumspection. But there is this substantial difference, viz., that gas and water companies, and railway companies (rather singularly excluded from the Act), have little or no difficulty in employing men on this understanding, whereas many great industrial establishments requiring much stricter financial calculation, and of no less importance to the country, have much difficulty in obtaining terms of service from workmen, and still more difficulty in securing their faithful observance when obtained. Nor is it to be left out of view that " minute contracts," under which bodies of workmen may lay down their tools at any moment so as to give greater scope to the action of " strikes," and to place the industry of the country more completely under the dictation of some central junta of labour, have become a favourite idea of Trade Union demagogues, who, when the subject is well riddled, are found to be the prime movers of all this legislation.

A fine of 20*l.*, or, failing payment, any term of imprisonment not exceeding three months, must be deemed a sufficient correction of any individual criminal breach of contract that may arise, involving however much damage to employers and to fellow-workmen. It would cover almost all cases in which the working classes, properly so called, are concerned. But it is impossible to eliminate from criminal breaches of contract the incident of concert, where a large number of workmen simultaneously and of set will break their contracts, and where the injury, public and private, is incomparably greater than in any individual case. The new Act has introduced a considerable innovation in this respect. The 14th section of the Master and Servant Act adjudged for such aggravated breaches of contract, involving much serious and wilful injury to public and private interests, a penalty of three months' imprisonment, with or without hard labour, but without any compounding fine. The new Act, on the other hand, adjudges a fine of 20*l.* in lieu of all penalty for the most aggravated criminal breaches of contract that may occur.

Lord Winmarleigh, one of the Commissioners on the "Labour Laws," observed when the Bill came before the House of Lords, that there were breaches of contract so injurious that he could not think that they were adequately met by Clause 5, and a fine of 20*l.* The mind of Lord Winmarleigh was no doubt well stored with the information, the cases, and the great variety of culpability and detriment in criminal breaches of contract, that had transpired in the course of the Inquiry, and hence perceived clearly enough the imprudence of visiting with a fine of 20*l.*, applicable to an aggravated case of individual breach of contract, a criminal breach of contract by hundreds or thousands of men in concert, involving among other serious consequences an enforced suspension of labour and loss of wages by hundreds or thousands more of wholly innocent working people. But what was the Lord Chancellor's reply? The learned lord, at the head of the law of England, observed

O 2

that in such cases no pecuniary compensation could possibly
be afforded to the injured parties, that the question was one
wholly of penalty, and that "the penalty proposed by the
" Bill was exactly the same as that in force under the Master
" and Servant Act." But the Lord Chancellor was in error
here at the moment on the question of fact ; because the
14th section of the Master and Servant Act, dealing with the
most aggravated cases of breach of contract, did essentially
differ from the 9th and 11th sections in that the magistrates,
where any pecuniary compensation or other remedy provided by the Act could not meet the case, might sentence
the parties complained against to the common gaol or house
of correction for a period not exceeding three months, with
or without hard labour. There is no fine under this section
of the Master and Servant Act, which appears to have contemplated breaches of contract so criminal that nothing
short of a term of imprisonment could atone for them. The
Conspiracy and Protection of Property Act departs from
this modulated legislation, condoning by a fine of 20l. the
most criminal and injurious breaches of contract to be conceived ; and it must be unnecessary to remind the Lord
Chancellor that where fifty or a hundred men wilfully and
unnecessarily violate their contracts, to the grievous loss and
injury of their employers and fellow-working-people, and
three or four of them are brought before the Courts with
hundreds or thousands of sympathising Unionists at their
back, the payment of 20l. is more likely to be a cause of de-
moralising exultation over the law than to be felt as a penalty.

The question may here be asked, why should " fines " have
any place in an Act professing to treat solely of *criminal*
breaches of contract? A "fine" in many ordinary cases
may be deemed a penalty, but it is always of the nature of
pecuniary damage for wrong done, and Parliament in these
Acts has been making a final separation between breaches
of contract for which civil or pecuniary redress may be
more or less effectively available, and breaches of contract
so uncivil, so irredeemable by pecuniary damage, and so
wholly criminal in their motives, incidents, and consequences, that there is no possible award for them but

criminal punishment. In the Employers and Workmen Act the Legislature was at extraordinary pains to exclude every-thing of the nature of penalty from civil breach of contract. In this second Act, supposed to be dealing exhaustively with criminal breaches of contract, all penalty for the most ex-tremely criminal breaches of contract is reduced to a money payment of 20*l.*

The only fruit of this inconsistency must be a new crop of grievances in the administration. Even as a Trade Union question, it is impossible to conceive any reason for the bias displayed in these Acts, because the Trade Unionists are under no temptation to violate their contracts, seeing that contract does not stand in the way of their greatest rights, not even the right of " strike "—a right that may be carried out legally and peaceably in all cases without any violation of contract. It is only the most extreme and worthless class of Trade Unionists that dream of promoting their interests by breach of engagements ; and the power of Parliament, in so far as it here encourages such violations, has been exerted in a baneful direction.

This unsatisfactory settlement of the question of criminal breach of contract was an almost unavoidable consequence of mixing up with it a modification of the Common Law of Conspiracy, and more especially a repeal of the Criminal Law Amendment Act, which belongs to a wholly different subject. The attention of Parliament was distracted from the real question under its consideration to these extraneous matters, to which it is necessary now to return.

The third Section of the Conspiracy and Protection of Pro-perty Act provides that " an agreement or combination by two " or more persons to do or to procure to be done any act in " contemplation or furtherance of a trade dispute between " employers and workmen shall not be punishable as a " conspiracy, if such act as aforesaid, if committed by one " person, would not be punishable as a crime." Of course this would be a great relaxation of the law of conspiracy if applied to all other matters as well as disputes between employers and workmen, since there is construction of con-spiracy in many cases where the thing done or procured to be done is harmless in itself, but is done or procured to be done for an unlawful or criminal end; and the Commissioners had reported that this law is so necessary an element of jurisprudence that they avoided all inquiry whether it could undergo a general modification. The Section makes no mention, indeed, of the unlawful or criminal end, and where that element is present in the " doing or procuring to be done," it may be presumed that Trade Unionists would still be liable to the law of conspiracy like other subjects of the Queen. The main interest, however, is to discover in what respect this Section of the new Act relaxes the law more as regards trade disputes and Trade Union action than it had already been relaxed by the legislation of 1871. The Trade Union Act of that year annulled the law of conspiracy in so far as the action of a Union or combination might be construed on the ancient common law doctrine to be "in restraint of trade;" and the Criminal Law Amendment Act of the same year provided that no person should be liable to any punishment for conspiracy unless in immediate connection with one or other of the acts of violence specified in that Statute. An act of violence is a crime whether committed by one or more persons ; and Trade Unionists had already received emancipation from the law of conspiracy save when an act of violence was committed. It is thus hard to see what further change of any kind this Section of the new Act has introduced. In so far as it may be supposed to bear on breach of contract, it lands in what appears to be a *reductio ad absurdum;* because breach of contract by a single person is seldom more than a civil wrong, and the Legislature has determined that it shall not be treated in any other form than under the civil law ; so that hundreds, as the Section reads in this point of view, may combine to break their contracts, and may abduct by temptations of drink and journeys to the country hundreds more from their plighted service, and yet in all this procedure the act done, if done by one, not being a crime, must not be deemed a crime when done by hundreds, and, in other words, that there can be no criminal breach of contract whatever ! It is scarce possible to believe that this was within the intention of the Legislature ; and yet some words were dropped by the Lord Chancellor which seem to signify as much. " It was " true," he remarked, " that under the existing law, if one " man broke his contract that would not be a crime, while if, " say fifty, broke their contract, that at common law *might* be " regarded as a conspiracy. Under this Bill it would not " be a conspiracy." There may be some imagined liberation of criminal breaches of contract from the common law of conspiracy, but one fails to discern how this liberation has been or could possibly be carried farther than it had been already carried by the legislation of 1871, which expressly enacted that the common law of conspiracy should nowise bear in trade disputes save in immediate relation to specified acts of violence and molestation.[1] The Trade Unionists have thrown so much dust in their own eyes on these subjects that it would almost seem to have occurred to some learned wits in Parliament to give them a little more of it.

Then, the repeal of the Criminal Law Amendment Act, though totally foreign to the Bill as a future law disposing of the question of criminal breaches of contract, was accomplished by the singular and amusing expedient of importing into the Bill the whole contents of the repealed Act, with the exception of the provision in our foot-note, which was so valuable to the Trade Unionists, and has now disappeared. Mr. Lowe began this task, and was immediately joined by Mr. Cross in its completion. Mr. Lowe proposed the following substitution for the Criminal Law Amendment Act :—

" Every person who, with a view to compel any other person to abstain from doing or to do any act which such other person has a legal right to do or abstain from doing, shall use violence to any person or any property, or shall threaten or intimidate any person in such manner as would justify a justice of the peace in binding over the person so threatening or intimidating to keep the peace."

---

[1] " No person shall be liable to any punishment for doing or *conspiring* to do any act on the ground that such act restrains or tends to restrain the free course of trade, unless such act is one of the acts hereinbefore specified in this section."—*Criminal Law Amendment Act,* 1871.

To which Mr. Cross added :—

"And every person who, with a view seriously to annoy or intimidate any other person, shall persistently follow such other person about, or hide any property owned or used by such person, or deprive him or hinder him in the use thereof, or watch or beset the place where such other person resides or is, or the approach to such place, or shall with one or more persons follow such person in a disorderly manner, in or through any street or road—"

And here followed the penalty alike of Mr. Lowe and Mr. Cross—

"Shall be liable to imprisonment, with or without hard labour, not exceeding three months."

Now let the reader please turn to the enactments 1, 2, 3, of the Criminal Law Amendment Act in the preceding chapter,[1] and say whether he can discover any difference between this substitute for the Act and the Act itself? May it not even be argued that under Mr. Lowe's brief form, all the consequences of the Criminal Law Amendment Act would have been imported into the new law, without Mr. Cross's addition, in which there is simply a more extended copy of the Criminal Law Amendment Act? Working men may thus see how little is to be gained from such chopping of law and legislation in matters of crime and offence, to which no friend of working men can readily believe them to be specially prone. The new version of the Criminal Law Amendment Act, as suggested by Mr. Lowe and Mr. Cross, commanded general approval in the House of Commons, and members on both sides of the House seemed pleased to think that in repealing one Act they had introduced its whole contents into a new Bill, treating professedly and ostensibly of an entirely different matter.

It may be remarked, as showing the danger of hap-hazard statute-making of this kind, that an important provision of the Criminal Law Amendment Act, to the effect that nothing in its contents should exempt any person from any higher punishment than is provided therein for any offence, was omitted from this House of Commons' version. It is not

[1] See page 178.

unusual in Trade Union frenzies to place explosive sub-
stances under a working man's stool or wheel, and to blow
up on a calculated accident all the apparatus of his work,
and himself as a mere appendage in the general account.
Then if A, for example,—another form of Trade Union
outrage—hires B C and D to shoot E, in order that all
the other letters of the alphabet may be, if not coerced,
inspired with a serious terror, the crime of A B C and D
is surely not to be less than murder or manslaughter at
least, or to be punished only by three months' imprisonment
with hard labour. The Bill, as amended by the House of
Commons, restricted the penalty for *all* violence on persons
and property, if it should only be done "with a view to
compel any other person to do or to abstain from doing,"
contrary to his own will and legal right,—or, in other
words, done by Trade Unionists, since this is an almost
exclusively Trade Union phase "of violence to person and
property,"—to three months' imprisonment, with or without
hard labour. Setting fire to a whole work, and even assassination, were not excepted. The Lord Chancellor appears,
from some timely hint, to have detected this omission, and
in the House of Lords' version of the Bill, and what is
now the Statute, the following further copy from the repealed Act was introduced :—

"Nothing in this section shall prevent any person from being liable
under any other Act to any other or higher punishment than is provided
by this section for any offence, so that no person be punished twice for
the same offence."

The Lord Chancellor slightly recast the comprehensive
clause contributed by Mr. Lowe and Mr. Cross, though not
in any sense to diminish the fully imported effect of the
Criminal Law Amendment Act. The conduct "with a view
to compel "—in the repealed Act it was "with a view to
coerce "— must be done, it now appears, "wrongfully and
without legal authority." But the conduct itself (1) using
violence or intimidation, (2) persistently following, (3) hiding
any tools, clothes or other property, or hindering the use
thereof, (4) watching or besetting the house or workshop or

the approach to such place, and (5) following with one or more persons in a disorderly manner through any street or road, is denominated exactly as it was in the Criminal Law Amendment Act. The Lord Chancellor gave only one original touch to the law as it was under the repealed Act, by introducing the following little qualification of "watching and besetting" :—

"Attending at or near the house or place where a person works, or is employed, or the approach to such house or place, in order merely to obtain or communicate information, and not with a view to intimidate or to deter by serious annoyance such person from doing or abstaining from doing that which he has a legal right to do or abstain from doing, shall not be deemed a watching or besetting within the meaning of this section."

"Watching and besetting with a view to intimidate or deter," and "attending at or near in order merely to obtain or communicate information," are no doubt different acts ; but it is improbable that either the law or the Trade Unionists will get out of the perplexity in which they are being mutually placed without some closer stroke of common sense than is found in this distinction. Does the obtaining or communication of information require "watching and besetting" in any form? Or are the means of persuasion, so abundantly exemplified in this country by public meetings, resolutions, advertisements in the newspapers, placards on the walls, and all the free circulation of opinion, so vague and indefinite and of so little efficacy as to be capable of being confounded with acts of "watching and besetting," of "intimidation," "compulsion," or "coercion," or any officious interference whatever of one man with another ? [1]

[1] I have had an opportunity, since writing this chapter, of reading the new text-book on *The Labour Laws*, by Mr. J. E. Davis, of the Middle Temple, and late Police Magistrate for Sheffield, and have been gratified to find from a professional authority so experienced and so justly popular, much corroboration of my purely lay conclusions. Mr. Davis, in his legal notes on the Labour Legislation of 1875, expresses (1) much doubt whether the Employers and Workmen Act, in restricting the power of the Courts to order specific performance of contract to cases where the consent of both parties is given, and in further

In concluding this review of the Royal Commission on the "Labour Laws" and its sequent enactments, there occurs not only the reflection—almost too trite now to be mentioned—how very little influence the elaborate inquiries and reports of Royal Commissions have on legislation in comparison with mere impulses and political expediencies outside the reason of the case, but also, that the whole of the questions brought under this review relate to breaches of contract and acts of violence—to offences, whether civil or criminal, to which no honest working man from one end of the kingdom to the other would lend his conscious or deliberate approval for a moment—and that consequently the manœuvres of Parliament to give a seeming encouragement to such offences involve both a humiliation of the working classes and a humiliation of the nation at the very core of its honour—the source of its laws.

requiring that the servant or workman must find one or more sureties in room of his own personal bond as under the Master and Servant Act, will operate to the advantage either of employers or employed. A large proportion of cases of simple breach of contract were settled in the Courts by order to perform in the way most agreeable and satisfactory to both parties, pp. 86, 92. Mr. Davis (2) regrets that no distinction has been left by the Employers and Workmen Act between breaches of contract in which there is a *bonâ fide* dispute, and breaches of contract in which there is every variety of groundless, wilful, or unjust motive, p. 92 ; (3) that the breaches of contract to be treated criminally under the Conspiracy and Protection of Property Act must be not only "wilfully" but "maliciously" committed, the last being a new term in this branch of Criminal Law not only liable to confused interpretations, but apt to be wholly exclusive of many criminal breaches of contract, pp. 94-5, note *g.* p. 156 ; and (4) that the same Act, in giving persons complained against option of trial by jury, no costs of prosecution are allowed or provided to the prosecutors, pp. 98-9. Mr. Davis observes (5) that under the clause relating to Law of Conspiracy "it is not improbable that cases of total irresponsibility to the Criminal Law may occur not contemplated by the Legislature, although foreshadowed by some observations and reflections in the Report of the Royal Commission," p. 101.

XIV

WHAT POLITICAL ECONOMY SAYS.

THE "dismal science" is not a favourite study of any large class of men, and of the members of Trade Unions probably less than of any equally numerous body. An appeal to political economy in a discussion of this kind, therefore, may have no more weight among the Unionists than appeal to an authority which they have already *a priori* discarded. But nevertheless most people engaging actively and extensively in industrial, commercial, and financial affairs, find not only a useful, but an indispensable guide in the teachings of political economy; and it may not be too much to infer that if capitalists, bankers, merchants, manufacturers, and others, have found advantage in paying deference to these oracles, it is almost certain that the Trade Unions, who have been adventuring as largely of late years as any other classes in pursuit of their interests, and on a new route of their own devising, will be none the worse, but all the better for consulting them also.

SPHERE OF POLITICAL ECONOMY.

To show how reasonable this is, look (1) at what political economy professes to *teach*, and (2) at what the Trade Unions profess to *do*. The great masters of political economy give or create no laws whatever; they cannot bind any class of men, or any man, or any element whether of capital or labour, or of invention or skill, or of physical or moral force that enters into the social and industrial economy, under obligation to their doctrine. What they profess to do, and what they have done, is by an immense study of facts and

experience in all past and cotemporary periods, and by much
hard and close argument connecting cause and effect at
every point in logical order, to arrive at the general principles by which the production and distribution of wealth,
and the economic progress and well-being of communities,
have been ultimately governed. Political economy, in its
highest scientific form, while extremely barren as regards the
creation of "new moral worlds" and other delectable
fantasies not under any experience, is thus extremely suggestive in a practical, business-like way, (1) of what will very
probably happen under given conditions, and (2) what cannot
possibly happen under any known conditions. This is a
source of guidance to which the Trade Unions should be
even more specially attentive than others, because they profess to do and compel where political economy professes
only to teach and suggest, and nothing surely could be more
irrational than for the Trade Unions, by a separate action,
and on a theory of their own, to attempt to accomplish what
the economists, in their sphere of impartial and generalised
reasoning, have declared to be contrary to what can either
probably or possibly happen.

VIEWS OF PROFESSOR CAIRNES.

It is unnecessary to quote largely from the best authorities
in political economy the doctrines that bear directly on the
action of the Trade Unions, and still less to weave out of them
any application of our own. The late Professor Cairnes,
in his last work—"*Some Leading Principles of Political
Economy*"—not only resumes the whole wisdom of Smith,
Ricardo, and Mill on the relations of capital and labour, and
the conditions determining the rates of profit and wages, with
many acute touches of independent thinking of his own,
which prove that the country has lost in him no mean master
of the science, but in two chapters devoted to Trade
Unionism he brings the established principles to bear on the
special subject under our consideration. No one will accuse
Professor Cairnes of any want of sympathy with the working
classes, or even with the Trade Unions. Indeed, he strains

his intellect so keenly to discover every "coign of 'vantage"
for the Unions, that the reaction sways him to a less hopeful view of the condition and prospects of the working
classes in general than many may be willing to adopt. But
any one reading Professor Cairnes's chapters on this subject
can be at little loss to know, in a condensed form, what
political economy says to the Unionists.

LAW OF SUPPLY OF CAPITAL TO LABOUR.

The principal object of Trade Unionism, at least in its
more active and ambitious character, being to divert by an
independent action of the workmen (against which there is
nothing to be said save in so far as it may be a possible or an
impossible operation), some portion of the profits of employers to the wages of the employed, the whole question
goes back at once to the conditions on which capital is supplied to the employment of labour. The hand of capital
can no more be forced than the hand of labour. There is
an average profit on which capital will be freely supplied to
any branch of industry, and there is a minimum profit on
which it may be supplied for a time, but will not be increasingly supplied, and at any rate of profit under this minimum
will certainly fall away from that branch of industry, and leave
the workmen nothing to dispute about. They will simply
in that case have to follow in their own way the movement of
capital, and withdraw their labour into other forms of employment, or endure the rigour of a branch of industry in which
the capital fund is constantly diminishing, and the constant
tendency of wages is to fall. Supposing, therefore, a Trade
Union, by a well-concerted movement, taking advantage, as
often happens, of employers under contracts requiring to be
fulfilled within a given period, or of the almost invariable
situation of nearly all employers, viz., a business requiring
to be steadily and unintermittingly pursued in order to produce profit, and having a large amount of "fixed capital"
on which any stoppage of the work must produce a heavy
loss, succeeds in obtaining a higher rate of wages, it does not
follow that the distribution of the profits of capital and

the wages of labour has been radically affected, or even that
the workmen in that branch of trade have gained any permanent advantage. They have triumphed over their employers for the moment, but the fundamental condition
remains, that if capital is left without its average rate of
profit in any trade, it will cease and fall away from that trade,
and the workmen will immediately find themselves all the
worse.

Many employers, of course, struggle under a losing trade
for a considerable period; they exhaust every means and
source of credit before they succumb; and as they fall
and close up their works one after another, new employers
and new capital come in and help to sustain a fleeting aspect
of prosperity. The fall of employers under Trade Union
action might be expanded into a sad and doleful history.
But the pleasure which Unionists seem to take in rolling
down firms is a wholly profitless pleasure so far as they are
concerned, because they only place themselves by the process
under firmer and stronger masters, and the new men and
capital coming in are under the same condition as the old
that have been supplanted—they must have a profit over
and above the wages established by the workmen.

Another ephemeral result by which Union-enforced wages
in any branch of employment may be kept in countenance
for a time is the declension that ensues in other and even
closely affiliated branches. "It is not inconsistent," says
Professor Cairnes, " with the general conclusion, that an ad-
" vance of wages in certain departments of industry should
" be effected by the action of Trade Unions where this is
" accompanied by an equivalent fall in others." The producers of coal, for example, may, by Trade Union action
under highly adventitious circumstances, raise their wages
much above the level of all other wages of labour; and
"if they can effectually exclude the competition of out-
siders," this superiority of wages may be maintained for a
considerable time. But the iron workers will immediately
find themselves all the worse placed by this elevation of
the colliers : when the effect passes on to the engineers,
it will be still more lamentable; and when the iron-

workers, the engineers, and other classes of workmen throughout the general sphere of manufacture are on the decline
because of this inordinate prosperity of the colliers, the
reaction is apt to be very severe, and the probability is
that the colliers will have no reason in the end to plume
themselves on the advantages they gained by their Trade
Union action. There is considerable temporary scope for
Trade Unions, having great organized power, and the will
to use it with sufficient inconsideration, to bring about,
under favourable circumstances, an increase of wages in
their particular sections of the industrial sphere, at the expense of diminished remuneration of labour in other branches
of employment. But to effect a general increase of the wages
of labour over the whole sphere, or even a permanent increase of the rate of wages in any particular section of the
sphere, we are referred to causes which lie outside the limited
action of the Unions, and which the tactics of the Unions
for the most part only tend to obstruct.

If the profits of capital be large in any branch of industry
open to competition, nothing is more certain than that there
will be a steady flow of capital to that industry, calling for
more labour both within and beyond its own circle, and that
the workmen particularly who are directly engaged in such
industry will have opportunities of earning higher wages and
improving their condition. This is so certain that to suppose
that any Trade Union action is necessary to render it more
certain would be as wise as to suppose that Trade Union
action is necessary to certify the thermometer. But this case
of a branch of industry in which the profits of capital are comparatively large—and in which there are both ground and certainty of an increase of wages of labour, though of frequent
example, visiting constantly, indeed, nearly all our industries
in turn under the immense, varied, and endless play of
economic forces concentrated in this country, and thus
capable, if wisely understood and improved, of being the
basis of a general elevation of the working classes—does not
carry us to the ultimate principles on which a general increase of wages depends.

CAUSES OF A GENERAL INCREASE OF WAGES.

Mr. Mill, and following him Professor Cairnes, recognising the freeness and fulness with which capital is supplied to all branches of industry in this country, and the consequent tendency of capital to fall throughout the whole sphere to a minimum rate of profit, at which it ceases to be increased, and below which it is absolutely withdrawn, have established the following conclusions :—That a general increase of wages depends (1) on the increased productiveness of labour itself, whether from the increased skill and intelligence of the labourers, or from the help of inventors, superior tools and machines, and improved processes of industrial art ; and (2) on the extension of markets for the products of labour, whether by free trade policy, the opening up of great countries like India and China, the discovery of gold mines in Australia and California, railways, steam navigation, or by all these means happily combined, creating an increased demand for the products of labour, and giving an increased supply of the materials of labour and of food and other commodities that are necessaries of life to the working classes. Now, it must be confessed that with these fundamental causes of an increase of wages much of the action of the Trade Unions cannot be reconciled. A great part of the policy of the Unions, without referring to the decaying barbarisms of machine-breaking and the like, is directed towards lessening, not increasing, the productiveness of labour ; and as regards keeping or enlarging existing markets, or opening new ones, not only do Unionists give inventors, capitalists, merchants and manufacturers, or the State, little thanks for their enterprising efforts and often costly sacrifices in this direction, but display an indifference to the whole subject resulting in Union procedure, by which markets for British goods are being constantly imperilled, and are often lost.

P

TRADE-UNION METHODS OF RAISING WAGES.

Professor Cairnes reviews the various methods of the Unions to operate on the rate of wages—(1) the direct method of calling on employers, on peril of a general strike, to raise the rate of wages, or to reduce the working hours without proportionate reduction of wages ; and (2) the indirect methods of artificially restricting the supply of labour on the one hand, and increasing the quantity of work to be done on the other, by making the curriculum of labour as tedious and restrained as possible. The Professor, of course, has, on general grounds, to condemn them all. His conclusion is summed up in the following sentences :—

"The doctrine we have been considering shows us that the ordinary motives pressing upon capitalists are always sufficient, of their inherent strength, to fill up the room constantly created for fresh investment, and do in fact fill it up [under the constant tendency of capital in this full flow to all branches of industry to fall to a minimum rate of profit] ; and this being so, where is the scope for Trade-Union action in enlarging the wages-fund ? I confess I am unable to see how, in presence of these considerations, founded as they are on incontrovertible facts, the larger pretensions of Trade-Unionism can be sustained. The permanent elevation of the average rate of wages—or, what comes to the same thing, the permanent elevation of the rate of wages in any branch of industry not accompanied by an equivalent fall in some other branch or branches—beyond the level determined by the economic conditions prevailing in the country, is, as it seems to me, a feat beyond its power. Such is the broad general conclusion to which economic principles applied to the facts of the case appear to conduct us."

But Professor Cairnes had one exception to make in favour of Trade-Union action, even in its most ambitious form of enforcing a higher rate of wages by means of strike. He did not wish to strain the general principles governing a permanent increase of wages a single iota, as to any particular action of Trade Unions, or similar bodies, beyond their own due terms ; and he supposed, therefore, the case of a branch of industry which had become, from whatever cause or causes, exceptionally prosperous, and in which the employers were making large profits, while the workmen had so far been reaping no advantage. Professor Cairnes observed that in a situation of this kind an advance of wages was certain in any circumstances, the increased demand for labour carrying its inevitable result on wages ; but as this result might not be immediate, he was of opinion that Trade-Union action had here a legitimate field of exercise, and that an association of workmen, " using its powers judi-" ciously, might determine capital at once towards those " issues which under the ordinary motives governing indus-" trial investment it would indeed in any case ultimately " reach." This is clearly a case in which the workmen have only to hold up their hands in order to obtain better terms, and which could scarcely lead to any stoppage of work detrimental to the employers or the employed ; where any Trade-Union action would be as unlike as possible to Trade-Union action of the customary character, which in its movement of forcing by great sacrifice advances of wages at one period and resisting by equal sacrifice reductions of wages at another, is more to be compared to a game of football than to anything else, were not the results so sadly unsportive. It is somewhat difficult, indeed, to follow the Professor's idea of " determining capital at once toward issues " already in full process. The employers in a trade the profits of which are large and increasing, must not only be valuing the workpeople in their employment all the more, but must be competing with each other for a larger number of workmen than they have hitherto employed, and straining their whole resources of capital to extend their operations. If the profits be so large as to invite an influx of new employers with new capital, and an opening of new works, advances of wages forced in any violent or premature way by the workmen against their present employers could only have the effect of warning away all this new enterprise, and so far from " accelerating," only retarding " issues " already sure of being realized.

It is not surprising, therefore, that Professor Cairnes should have had doubt whether, even in such a favourable case as this, to use his own words, " the Trade-Union game be worth the candle." He cannot absolve a Trade Union, even in this exceptional situation, from the responsibility of " using

its powers judiciously," and his deep distrust of the com-
petence of judgment by which Trade-Union action has
hitherto been guided, as well as his firm belief of the great
advantage that would arise were the Unions to collect
facts, and study well the principles and interests involved,
before they act at all, are equally worthy of attention.

COMPETITION OF CAPITAL.

It is constantly overlooked by the Unionists, as well as
by the quasi-economists who have hitherto kept the Union
policy in some little countenance, that there is a competition of capital with capital more keen and active, and more
flexible and facile in its movement, than any competition
of labour with labour; and that the effect of this competition is to enlarge all profitable branches of industry while
reducing at every step of the process the rate of profit of
capital to a minimum, at which the enlargement ceases and
contraction begins. They equally overlook that there is no
possibility of compelling capital to invest more in wages of
labour when this minimum rate of profit is approached or
may be in danger. When the causes that determine the
amount of wealth which falls to the share of labour, and
which in proportion to the number of labourers, of course,
determines the general rate of wages, are closely examined,
they are found ultimately to turn on the rate of profit, under
existing conditions of the productiveness of labour, that is
necessary to decide the owners of capital in their several
circumstances whether to withhold their capital or to place
it freely at the service of industrial works. If capital be
largely withdrawn, as being no longer profitably employed,
wages must fall. It may thus be judged how futile it must
be for Trade Unions to attempt on the large and systematic
scale with which the public is familiar, to force a redistri-
bution of the wages of labour and the profits of capital.
Temporary victories may be gained in one branch of industry and another, and it must be owned that Trade Unions
have a great power of cornering and embarrassing many
employers, who must either submit to their demands or be

ruined ; but the economic principles in steady operation do not permit this kind of warfare to have any permanent sway. It is certain, on the contrary, that the frequency of strikes is adding, like fires or other accidents and defaults, a new element of loss and danger in industrial undertakings, against which capital in its estimate of profit has to be insured, and is consequently pushing any extended employment and remuneration of labour so much the farther back.

The fulness with which capital is supplied to all branches of industry in this country, and is constantly bringing down in the competition of capital with capital its own profit to a minimum, while sustaining and raising the rate of wages, is proved by an aggregation of facts which it would be the merest madness for any one to dispute. It is proved by the immensity of funds, yielding to their owners a deposit interest of $1\frac{1}{2}$ to $2\frac{1}{2}$ per cent., which are placed steadily through the banks at the service of all branches of industry, and of all who are either working industrially on their own account or are employing labour. It is proved by the large amount of capital unprofitably engaged and periodically lost in the employment of labour, of which, or of the ill-fortune and distress of the families to whom the capital belonged, nothing is heard in one-sided tirades on the condition of labour. If capital be thus freely and abundantly supplied to every branch of employment, with the effect of constantly reducing its rate of profit to a minimum, and of being wholly lost to large amounts in the attempt, what can be the foundation for thinking that labour is injured by capital, or that the condition of labour can ever be improved by processes that only tend to make the case of capital much worse than it has hitherto been ?

"THE WAGES FUND."

Professor Cairnes has revived with much force the doctrine of Mr. Mill, that there is a wages fund, or a proportion of the national produce that has a necessary destination, subject to various minor influences, to the employment of labour, and can go nowhere else. It is difficult to conceive why this doctrine should ever have been contested. But it was contested by Mr. Thornton in his work on "Labour"—an unsound work in various respects, and wanting in comprehension of the ultimate operation of the principles of which it treats—and yet the curious result was that this work had some effect on the mind of Mr. Mill himself. The argument of Mr. Thornton was that a national wages fund could only be made up of several parts, and since Mr. Thornton could not conceive that any individual employer determined what proportion of his income or his capital should go to household and family expenses, to machinery and other fixed constructions, and to wages for hired labour, his conclusion was that a "wages fund" was a fund wholly "indeterminate," and being indeterminate might as well not exist as to any security of rate of wages. Mr. Thornton, in arguing from details, had evidently no conception of a general law or principle by which details on this magnitude are characterized ; he mistook the "determination" that takes place under free economic conditions for a physical compulsion operating like a fixed and arbitrary law under all circumstances, and with undeviating uniformity in every section of the industrial system ; the result being that the only "Wages Fund" which Mr. Thornton would deem worthy of the name, or which could satisfy his argument, should be a definite proportion of the whole annual produce, set apart by a decree, and divided with tolerable equality among the working classes, irrespective of all other considerations. Professor Cairnes has sufficiently disposed of this sophism, and it is unnecessary to dwell upon it.

But the grosser blindness of Mr. Thornton—a blindness which Professor Cairnes in what may be called a condescension of argument, meeting Mr. Thornton on his own ground of what may take place in the case of individual employers, has done nothing to unveil—was in failing to see that whether an employer or a capitalist lays out his available means in larger or smaller proportions in family expenditure, in buildings, or machines and other materials of trade, the destination of the capital in all cases is to wages of labour, and that this is consequently a detail which does not enter into the general question between capital and labour, nor does it touch the fact of a determinate " Wages Fund " in any degree. Mr. Mill has included in his conception of a wages fund unproductive as well as productive labour, and of the former indicated soldiers, domestic servants, and the like, who serve, but from whose labour no visible material produce comes. But if, in addition to such unproductive labour, the erection of buildings, whether they be of luxury or trade, are to be deemed a subtraction of capital from the wages fund, as Mr. Thornton appears to hold and as Professor Cairnes somewhat countenances, then it will follow that masons, bricklayers, and joiners are not workmen, but mere hangers-on of the rich, injuring by all the wages they receive some other and more proper members of the working class. If investment of capital in machines, boilers, tools and fittings, be a lessening of the wages fund and a wrong to labour, the working engineers must be drones, sucking the life-blood that should flow more directly to animate the industrial body. This absurdity might be pursued till it would become impossible to discover where the industrial body resided, or who were labourers and who were not. The distinction of " fixed " and " circulating " capital is proper enough to show the different forms of the investment of capital ; but the " fixed capital " has contributed to the wages fund, and contributes to it from year to year, as certainly as the other. There is thus much reason to protest against the principles of Political Economy being dealt with in any narrow or mousing spirit, arguing from what takes place in a supposed individual case, and refusing even to look over the boundary between one branch of labour and another ; whereas these principles are derived from a comprehensive survey as to how men will act in the disposal of their capital or labour when free to act, and as they have been found, on the general scale, from all experience to have acted.

Capital, however expended or invested, has an inevitable destination to the employment of labour, and to the wages of labour. At the same time, capital may be withdrawn from one branch of labour to another, or may be increased

in some branches more than in others, as the prospect of
profit may determine; or if there be only prospect of loss,
it may to some amount go to sleep, suspend operations for
a time, and be simply idle; in which case there will be a
pinch both as to the supply of work and the rate of wages
in the particular branches of trade thus adversely affected.
The stability of trade on the whole in this country, and the
amount of capital invested in a "fixed" form in every
branch of industry, are alike so great, that employers are by
no means either free or disposed to shift suddenly from a
losing manufacture to one more profitable. But as regards
the surplus capital, accruing from a thousand sources, it is
obvious that its owners will choose the forms of employment
that promise the best security and the most profit with
security; and that this capital will be very unequally distributed among the various trades, according to their situation and their prospects. The surplus labour, on the other
hand, is not so agile in its movement. Men bred to a
particular employment must in most cases stick to it, and in
many cases are all too unwisely disposed to stick to it, even
though it should be a permanently failing employment.
This is a natural difficulty in the case of labour, for which,
apart from a more free circulation of workmen from one
branch to another, it is hard to conceive any remedy outside
the resources, physical and mental, of labour itself. But
when we here turn to the Trade-Union policy, so far from
affording any relief from this difficulty, it is found only to
add a new and special aggravation of it; because that
policy, as we have seen, is to raise up insuperable barriers
between narrow divisions of workmen, so that one may not
pass into the sphere of another even in the same employment, and in the most closely-related trades.

The hand-loom weavers, for example, are probably the
greatest sufferers from a revolution in manufacture, and a
diversion of capital from one form of employment to
another, that may be adduced. Their hand-looms had to
compete with the power-looms, and as the struggle became
more and more severe, they put, first, their wives, and
second, their children, on the hand-loom in order to eke out

a weekly income for the present, while making at every step
the future difficulty all the greater. The history of the hand-
loom weavers has now, over near a hundred years, been a
pitiful spectacle. But there was not a time, since the introduction of the steam-loom, when labour could not have
been gradually retired from the hand-looms with a thousandth
part of the suffering with which it has been actually attended.
What prevented? This, for one cause, prevented, viz., that
under the Trade-Union instinct, tenters and others gathered
round the power-looms, and making a monopoly of their
little walk, would not leave a place for hand-loom weavers,
though these could have been employed on the steam-looms
at fifty per cent. more wages than they were earning on the
hand-looms. The inhumanity of man to man reigned
throughout.

There is a fundamental distinction, however, between productive and non-productive labour which is worthy of being
observed in this problem of the "Wages Fund," though it
may not be marked by any strongly definite line. The general
attribute of productive labour is that it restores the capital
with some profit, and that the capital fund remains intact for
the renewed employment of labour. If the labour employed,
on the other hand, be absolutely non-productive, the capital
is not restored, and cannot again be any part of the wages
fund, because it has been consumed, and has disappeared.
Now, it would be difficult to say where this distinction
begins or stops, because non-production, or consumption of
capital, adheres to many industrial undertakings of an
essentially reproductive promise, and extends to many
branches of expenditure that have no reproductive promise
whatever, and into the motives of which neither the recovery
of the expenditure nor the employment of labour enters.
The members of the Trade Unions, however, are without
exception, by profession and classification, productive workmen—an honourable or most honourable body in every
commonwealth. They are men who work under the general
condition that the capital expended in their employment
will on an average be returned to their employers with a
profit, and that the business of their several trades will thus

proceed on a secure and always extending scale. But supposing that the Trade-Union action, of which there has been so much critical note in these pages, should have the effect, in its zealous and incessant pressure, of violating this general condition in any considerable degree, and that the capital expended in their employment were not to be restored with a profit, but rather to be tending on the average to a loss ; what would the consequence be ? Would it be favourable or unfavourable to the members of the Unions, or to the cause of labour as against capital ?

In such a case the reflection of capitalists, having large funds in industrial works, would probably run in the following strain :—" We cannot make a profit in our business, " in coal-mining, nor in iron-making, nor in textile fabrics, " nor in anything else. What, then, can we do ? There is " that Foreign Loan, promising great profits, but on rather " weak security, and it may be better to keep what funds we " have to the ministration of our own pleasure. Let us " have a yacht, or add a new wing to our mansion, or " employ a larger number of domestic servants. Why not " keep a stud of horses ?—there is much pleasure, and " sometimes profit, in a stable. That flower-garden may be " much embellished ; there are some rare pictures in the " Royal Academy Exhibition which rise in value from year " to year more than anything else ; and there is the pictur- " esque little estate or shooting-box down in any shire, " which after much necessary outlay among ditchers and " dykers, and builders, joiners, plasterers, and painters, will " yield one per cent. on the whole capital, even if it should " have to be re-let. In any case, we may put business " aside, and take a tour on the Continent, and spend some " of our money on the Swiss Alps, on the shores of the " Mediterranean, or in the Holy Land." These are all commonplace outflows of the accumulated wealth of this country, apart wholly from the Trade Unions, or anything the Trade Unions can do. But they exhibit the nice balance subsisting between what Mr. Mill calls " the effective desire of accumulation," or, in other words, making profit on the capital possessed, and the desire of simply expending and enjoying one's riches without any motive of profit ; and how very easily, in this niceness of balance, the trade Unions may turn the scale enormously against their own interests, and against the permanent industrial well-being of the country. Capital cannot be absolutely bound either to productive or non-productive operations. It has always the liberty of either eating itself up, or fleeing to some more profitable shore. But in the complex modulation of this 'desire of profit' and 'desire of enjoyment,' the fact has always to be observed that capital cannot expend itself either way but in the employment of labour. Even Foreign Loans, on which tens of millions of British capital have been lost within the last few years, served for the time to stimulate British industry and sustain British wages of labour; and it is also true, as Professor Cairnes says, that a rich man of this country making the tour of Europe, can only discharge his expenditure abroad by bills of exchange drawn on British produce. Still the fundamental distinction between productive and non-productive labour remains, and it is a distinction to which the attention of Trade-Unionists may be seriously directed.

It is a result of the growing wealth of nations that a large amount of their capital fund, or the actual surplus over consumption, can be annually expended in forms, that employ labour indeed, and labour in its very highest degrees of art and genius, and that yet yield no apparent return of the capital expended. It would seem presumptuous for any one to profess to determine strictly what forms of employment of wealth are non-productive. Paintings, music, religious ministrations ; works of art, literature, and science ; the embellishment of houses, parks, and gardens; and all the elaborate ornamentations of life in which the rich indulge—who will venture to pronounce such forms of expenditure non-productive ? The fortunate possessors of so much riches may be envied by some, and in some cases they may not be remarkably worthy of their good fortune ; but the riches themselves are among the common treasures and glories of the country. No intelligent man of the working class, or any other class, will grudge the gains of a

prima donna as long as he has admission to the shilling
gallery or the five-shilling pit; or the brilliant fame and
fortune of a painter or a novelist while he can look at the
works of the one and read those of the other for nothing ; nor
will he find much ground of displeasure in the magnificence
with which a baron or a millionaire has improved, enriched,
and adorned his estate, though much of the money spent
has not been nearly so profitable financially as if it had been
invested in the Three per Cents. It is only, indeed, on
coming to what are of the nature of sensual, vicious, and
immoral uses of wealth, or such grossly unbalanced expenditure betraying an error of judgment approaching to immo-
rality, as when the cost of the mansion-house is out of all
proportion to the value of the estate, or the stables of the
owner cast affront in their comfort and luxury on the
dwellings of the tenants and labourers, that one finds any
firm ground on which to pronounce outlays of capital non-
productive, or not so productive certainly as, on the ordinary
and average prudence, they might have been. Yet it is
important on the labour side of the question, and as regards
the causes that ultimately tend most to sustain and advance
the general rate of wages, to mark the difference between an
employment of capital that gives no visible return to the
capital fund, and an employment of capital in productive
branches of labour that restores the capital, and restores it
after a more or less lengthened period with an increase. On
this latter basis the employment can be regularly extended,
and this extension of employment meets a natural increase
of the working-class population, which is always an essential
element to be taken into account. Now, it is against this
reproductive employment of capital that the elaborate and
embarrassing action of Trade-Unionism is wholly directed ;
and in proportion as this action succeeds in embarrassing, it
can only direct capital into other channels much less pro-
motive of the " Wages Fund " than those in which capital
may thus be unwisely discouraged and reduced.

It will hardly be questioned, on any side, that whether in
agriculture, mining, manufactures, trades or arts, all those
forms of employment of which the condition is to reproduce

the capital expended in them with a profit, and apart from which condition there would be no motive or inducement to conduct them whatever, are the only solid and permanent bases of the national wealth, and of the prosperity of labour. Let these be obstructed or undermined, and all other forms of employment would rapidly decline.

It thus never can be the interest of the working or wage-earning classes, as the Trade-Union policy assumes, to impede or run out capital specially in its reproductive and profit-bearing destinations. On the contrary, this policy has been, and always must be, adverse to the end proposed.

THE SUPERIORITY OF CAPITAL.

It may be freely acknowledged that there is an inequality in the condition of capital and that of labour which political economy cannot wholly remove or bridge ; and the reason of this would seem to be that this inequality is founded not only on economic elements, but on a moral difference in which the economic elements have their origin. Political economy cannot make a man who has never saved money or acquired property as strong as another man who has done one or both, or to whom some inheritance, whether of money or property, or of commercial or manufacturing means and *prestige*, has descended. It cannot even make one capitalist of superior wealth as strong as another of much less wealth. Firms flourish in the same business in which other firms of older standing, and greater resources, decline. There may be no superior moral quality in the persons who have possession of the greatest capital power, and who are or have been most successful. This is not the question. The play of fortune has a great deal to do in these matters. But on strict analysis it is found that this superiority of capital over labour, as a separate interest in the social system, has its origin in a moral quality—in the quality of abstinence, and of denying oneself present enjoyment for sake of a future gain. Political economy cannot import a virtue of this kind into one man more than another, or one class of men more than another ; but taking the broad and unalterable facts of social and industrial life, viz., that there is capital willing to give wages to labour with some ultimate profit to itself, and that there is labour willing to be employed for wages, political economy has great claim and prerogative of showing the principles on which these two factors may be combined with the highest advantage to both, and to the highest good of the community.

JUSTICE TO LABOUR.

Now, substantial justice to labour in its relation to capital seems, on economic principles, to be fulfilled by two conditions : 1st, that the supply of capital for the employment of labour be abundant or superabundant, and that in all the various branches of industry there be an active competition of capital with capital ; and 2nd, that the working or wage-earning classes have the same inducements to save, the same legal and institutional facilities of saving, of becoming capitalists, and of joining in the movement and partaking of the profits of capital, as any other part of the community.

If, as the economists hold, capital be abundantly supplied to all branches of productive labour in this country, with the constant effect of reducing its own rate of profit to a minimum, while extending the employment of labour, the first of these conditions would appear to be pretty well satisfied. It is certain that in the greater freedom and resources of capital, and in its greatly enlarged application to industrial and commercial pursuits through free trade, scientific inventions, and other means, labour has found all its advantages during the last thirty or forty years. But it may not be supposed that the end of this progress has been reached ; and any reform, any development, or any amendment of the law by which capital may be more freely directed towards spheres in which the profits of capital are high, or an impulse may be given to the productive energies of labour, must be sound and wholesome, and of essential benefit to the working classes.

The second condition has so far been fulfilled that great inducements have been held out by the State itself, and by other more private organizations, to the working classes to save, to gather capital or invest in property, and to become

earners of profits as well as earners of wages. The depositors in the National Security Savings Banks obtain a higher
rate of interest than the depositors in any other banks; and
it has been secured to them up to this time by a loss of
three or four millions sterling to the State. In other cases
millions of the savings of the working classes have been lost
through defective institutions, and other misappliances. But
there may be as little reason to suppose that this condition
of justice to labour has been exhausted as the other. There
is probably a great and hitherto unopened sphere of right
and good to labour in the application of a sound saving and
reproductive system to the working-class condition.

Professor Cairnes, as already mentioned, in his intellectual
struggle with the economic elements of the labour question,
fell into a somewhat hopeless view of the prospects of the
working man. "The remuneration of labour," he said,
" skilled or unskilled, can never rise much above its present
" level." This gloom might have been somewhat relieved
if the Professor, besides the hopeful glance he cast at co-
operation, had looked steadily, on the one hand, at the
power of saving and the profitable application of the savings
of the working classes; and had taken into account, on the
other hand, the losses, the misfortunes, and vicissitudes of
other classes of society. It is certain that nothing can be
more unreasonable than for working men to waste their
thoughts and passions in exclamations against "the tyranny
of capital" while wasting the means by which they may
become capitalists themselves. Let us not, until at least
every proper means have been adopted, harbour the anti-
social and anti-Christian idea that a working man may not
be as happy, intelligent, honourable, and as well-conditioned
a man as any man of any other class or rank of life.

Three centuries even ago Montaigne could write, " I have
" known in my time a hundred artisans and a hundred
" labourers wiser and more happy than the rectors of the
" university, and whom I had much rather have resembled;"
and in these present days it may well be considered whether
depreciation of the working man's condition has not been
carried to an unphilosophical and morbid extreme.

XV

CONCLUSIONS.

THE aim of the foregoing pages has been to elicit the policy of the Trade Unions from the most authentic sources, and to examine this policy in its contact with right, with rights of capital and rights of labour, with law, with trade, with principles of political economy, with the interests of the Unionists themselves, and with the conditions of public well-being. The task in no case could be a light one, because Trade-Union action, and the Parliamentary inquiries and reports and legislation thereon ensuing, must be deemed among the most elaborate and important proceedings in the country during the last eight or nine years ; nor could any one, making the attempt, profess to have either exhausted the materials or the argument. But the whole ground having been surveyed, with whatever merit or imperfection, it remains only to state briefly what appears to be the practical conclusions of the discussion.

I. The Trade Unions should place themselves in full conformity with the law. They may think the law by no means perfect, and may reasonably seek to have it further amended, as others do. But their rules, their relations between themselves and towards others, and their methods of action, should be placed in strict consistency with the requirements of the law as the first condition of improvement and of all proper dignity of association.

This advice may be urged on various cogent grounds.

In the first place, the law not only sanctions the Unions as lawful bodies, but gives them great power and liberty of action. A combination of working men may do under the law, with all the advantage of united force, what any individual workman may do; in short, may do anything they please, at whatever damage to others, short of breaking a contract, of directly encroaching on the equal right of others, or committing some violence that under any system of law would be a criminal offence. Our law gives both sanction and legal powers to Trade Unions which are not accorded to similar bodies in any other country in the world ; it has been largely modified of late years to suit them ; and they have thus abundant reason to be satisfied with it as a basis on which to conduct their proceedings.

In the second place, and what cannot but address itself with much force to intelligent working men, conformity to law is absolutely necessary to give full efficiency to the functions by which the Unions best promote the good of their own members, and may best extend their influence among the working population. There has been much dissatisfaction in the Unions that their funds should not be sufficiently protected by the law ; it is still a moot point among them whether they should be societies capable of suing and being sued at law; and it has been a Trade-Union grievance that they have not all the registration and other rights of the Friendly Societies under the Acts applying to these bodies. It may be doubtful how far these complaints should be treated seriously. But how, it may be asked, can the law protect funds, save from burglary, which no care has been taken to place on any legal basis ? What more protection of funds, or right of suing and being sued, can be given on the Union basis than have been more than even fully accorded by the Trade Unions Act of 1871, unless it be desired that a Union should have the power of suing and forcing its own members to some end to which they are not bound of their own will, and cannot be bound by law ? And how can a Trade Union be legally recognised and registered as a Friendly Society when its funds collected for friendly insurances are expended by rule and intention on other purposes ? How, in short, can the law extend the legal rights of association to societies which will themselves come under no legal obligations, even of the most simple,

Q

universal, and fundamental character? The law has given
the most ample powers of civil transaction and civil suit to
the Unions and officers of the Unions, and the only grievance is that of members of the Unions who may have often
just grounds on which to desire to have powers to sue the
Unions and their officers; yet how can the law, even in such
cases, help men, however much aggrieved, who have gone
into a one-sided compact with their eyes open? The
whole of this series of troubles arises not from the law, but
is the creation of the Unions themselves, which have never
condescended to place their affairs in any legal shape.

It will serve to illustrate this constitutional defect of the
Unions to observe how the question of registration has been
disposed of by the Legislature. The Royal Commission
of 1867-9 recommended, that in order to give Trade
Unions capacity for the rights and duties of corporations,
their registration should be effected through the Registrar of
Friendly Societies, on conditions that have been transcribed
in a former chapter.[1] The Unions might have strong views,
for example, as to the number of apprentices, the evils of
machinery, the inexpediency of piecework, or the crime of
working in common with non-Unionists; but they could
not expect the law to give its *imprimatur* to such views, and
could only be content to advance them in free deliberation
with employers and with public opinion without the vantage
ground, from the outset, of express legal sanction and
approval. So also one or more Trade Unions might be
chivalrously disposed to support another and unconnected
Union on strike; but this generosity could not be exercised
out of funds which the law by registration became bound to
protect for entirely different purposes, and it could only therefore take the form of special contributions, as in the case of
all similar benevolent and chivalrous efforts. This was the
view of the Royal Commission. The Act of 1871, following
on the Report of the Commission, provided a method of
registration for Trade Unions so easy that it may be carried
out on the quest of seven members of any Union, giving all
the legal powers and facilities to trustees and officers of the

------

[1] See page 118.

Unions as in the case of other registered societies, and
without any one of the restrictions which the Royal Commission sought to interpose. Yet this same Act ordains
that any agreements of Trade Unions "to provide benefits
to members" shall be null and void in law, neither enforceable nor recoverable by damages in the courts. There
is thus much legal strengthening of trustees, officers, and
governing bodies of the Unions in legal powers, side by side
with a legal nullification of the most common rights of
the members of the Unions. The situation thus produced
is perplexing and contradictory, but the mystery may be
explained in a few words. The Unions insist upon mixing
up the most different and separable objects in the same
compact, and on having legal and organic powers of enforcing this compact, while refusing to submit to the conditions without which their heterogeneous demands can,
neither in law nor in equity, be conceded. The law can
give them all the rights and powers of corporations, as it has
already given them by the Act of 1871 beyond even the due
reason of the case ; but the law in giving such rights is
bound to require corresponding obligations, the obligations
in particular of a corporate body to its own members, and
this is a necessity of the law which the Unions will not
submit to. Hence the humiliating concession of the Act of
1871, that any agreement of a Union "to provide benefits to
members" shall be of no legal force in any court.

The absolute condition, it is true, on which the law has
been enabled to give so much scope to the right of combination, clearing it from all ambiguity that might arise on
the common law doctrine of "restraint of trade," is that
the combination shall be a voluntary combination, that no
one shall be coerced into it and no one coerced from going
out of it ; and that, as regards parties outside the combination, "full liberty be left to all other workmen to under-
"take the work which the parties combining have refused,
"and no obstruction be placed in the way of the employer
"resorting elsewhere in search of a supply of labour." But
this principle may be well obeyed by the Unions to the end
of giving great additional strength and justice to their internal

arrangements. When a member leaves a Trade Union of his own will, he leaves his contributions behind him, and cuts himself off from all participation in the funds, as in the case of a person failing to pay his premium of insurance. The Union has no debt to enforce against him, and he has no further claim upon the Union. When a member of the Union departs from a strike the Union cannot compel him to return to the strike, or punish him for not returning, by any means which the law can ever give. If they compel or punish him at all the Union must take the law into its own hands. These are unalterable conditions of the case. On the other hand, if a member or members of a Union are extruded against their will, without any breach of the regulations on which they became members, why should they not have legal redress? If a Union breaks up into two parties, one adhering to the officers who have possession of the funds, and another forming round other officers or leaders who have no possession, in that case the Union will either be a lawless body, and a great wrong will be committed on one side or the other, or it will be a legal body, and its financial affairs receive a legal and equitable adjustment. The Trade Unions may acquire most substantial advantages, and become much stronger because juster in their constitution, and be of much greater utility to their members than they have hitherto been; but to reach these ends requires conformity to the law, and to the essential legal principle of all Trade Union combination.

II. The benefit funds of the Unions should be fully reserved for the purposes for which they are contributed.

As regards most of the Unions, including the largest, the term "trade and benefit funds" is a misnomer, because they have in reality no "trade funds"; and the fact simply is that funds are collected in the name of benefit, on a seemingly insurance basis, and are expended freely for trade and "strike" purposes. The most plausible defence offered for this astounding practice is that the Unions, though dealing among their members in matters of business requiring strict financial accuracy and good faith, are yet, after all, only free clubs of

fellow-workmen, who are thinking primarily of trade purposes, and care comparatively little for insurance of benefits;
but that, at the same time, the pledge of benefits has so
great an effect in increasing the members and funds of the
Unions that it would be highly detrimental to introduce any
other arrangement.[1] This defence, of course, is full to the
brim, not only of sophistry, but of palpable dishonour,
placing on the Trade Unions a character of knavery, indeed, which no one would like to attribute to them. But it
may be observed that it surely rates much too low the intelligence of members of the Unions, and that in any case it
throws their permanent interest to the winds. Why should
the Unions be at enmity with fundamental principles of law,
and with common integrity among themselves, by adhering
to a financial perversity of this kind? Their present plan
is to levy contributions for " benefit purposes," and to spend
the funds thus obtained on strikes and trade purposes, and
when the fulfilment of the benefits is in danger to make
" special levies " in that first interest. But just turn the
system gently the other way; suppose funds paid for benefit
purposes to be reserved for benefit purposes, and funds
required for strikes and other trade emergencies to be raised
by "special levies;" and see how easily by this change of
"right shoulder" instead of " left shoulder " forward, the
whole movement would fall into order—into conformity with
law, with legal privileges to the Unions, with honesty between
the Unions and their members, and with a due maturity of
consideration in exercising the often self-hurtful power of
" strike."

III. There would follow from these changes an erasure
of various rules from the codes of the Unions, of the nature
of those indicated by the Royal Commission when tracing
the conditions of registration, the emblazonment of which
as rules is simply a needless offence. since they can have no
force as rules till they are agreed to by employers. " Limiting the number of apprentices," for example, the Unions

---

[1] Mr. W. Allan's Evidence (Q. 7505-7, 7593). Report of Royal
Commission (87).

are in no position to make a standing rule, seeing that they
have no common proportion or principle by which the limit
is to be regulated, and the question, even as a matter of
practical adjustment between masters and men, presents
itself under entirely different conditions in one trade as compared with another, and in the circumstances of the same
trade at different periods. Rules "to prevent or limit the
use of machinery" would perhaps be readily condemned by
most of the Unions, but Unions that made and acted upon
such rules should be cut off from the fraternity, and not
allowed to disgrace the general body of workmen. The
members of a Union may have strong views, correct or
erroneous, on matters of this kind, but they must know that
their views are only to be advanced by rational deliberation,
and by the fitness and expediency with which they commend
themselves increasingly to employers as well as employed.
To inscribe them in their books, often in the most vague
and unregulated form, does not make them rules, but is only
throwing a firebrand into the workshops of the kingdom,
and multiplying those partial strikes, which are constantly
breaking out like crackers on a Queen's birthday, and which
give the head-officers of the Unions so much toil and travel,
as they affirm, in attempting, often vainly, to extinguish or
compose them. That Trade Unions should weaken and
compromise their position under the law by a *brutum fulmen*
of this kind, to which publication gives no real force, and
in favour of which, so far as it was just or reasonable, they
would retain in any case all their powers of persuasion and
judicious action, must be pronounced in every point of view
imprudent.

IV. As few strikes as possible ; or, even better, none
at all.

The more intelligent, thrifty, and far-seeing members of
the Unions themselves must be heart-weary of the constant
turmoil and loss of the war of strikes and lock-outs, whether
on the petty or gigantic scale, by which the working classes
are grievously impoverished, and the productive industry of
the country is subjected to chronic suspense and paralysis.

It is obvious, that were the Unions to abstain from including in their so-called rules various obnoxious declarations which have not only obtained no manner of assent from employers, but are contrary to public policy in the most liberal and enlightened form hitherto conceived, three-fourths of the minor strikes would disappear, and the administration of the Unions assume not only a more consistent, but an incomparably more effective and beneficial method. It is no less obvious that were the Unions to adopt the ordinary financial integrity that funds subscribed on due scientific calculation for benefit purposes should be sacredly reserved for these purposes, and should not be appropriated to other purposes in the prosecution of which the benefit liabilities of a generation may be dissipated in a few weeks or a few months, all the larger class of strikes would be entered upon with much more deliberation, and with so much greater knowledge and understanding of the circumstances of the trade, as well as so much greater sense of responsibility, that strikes or resolutions to strike would much more seldom fail of their object than hitherto. There would be reason to hope that the demands of the workmen in the majority of cases would be so mature and reasonable as to be no sooner made than they would be conceded.

The too simply artful coercive tactics of one section of a trade "striking" in the hope of being subsisted by the contributions of other sections who remain at work, and making the war, as it were, support itself out of the "enemy's" resources, would disappear; and along with them "lock-outs" would as happily vanish from the country. In any case it would remain to withdraw labour in detail from a hard to a more liberal employer, and from a place of lower to one of higher wages, and thus keep in action, by a quieter and safer way, a wholesome competition among employers for good work.

V. Do not stimulate or squeeze Members of Parliament too much in favour of what may be only class prejudices or the grossest errors. It requires a hero-candidate to stand in the face of hundreds or thousands of working-class

electors, and tell them what their true interest is, in opposition
to what may be their own fondly-nourished prepossessions.
There are only few men of this heroic stamp in any age ;
nor is it likely that in the present age their number will
be much increased. Let not working men, therefore, be
deceived by supple members or candidates for membership. Let them honour strength and breadth of mind
and absolute independence of character, even when the
impact of such qualities seems to rub against themselves.

It is not to be disguised that the change of legal,
economical, and political attitude thus recommended would
give the Unions more the character of Friendly Trade
Societies, securing mutual help to the members on an
assured basis, while affording means of a full and calm discussion of all trade interests ; and less of the character of
Fighting Unions contending pell-mell, and often blindly, for
indefinite trade purposes to the utter sacrifice in many cases
of the funds and well-being of the members. This, on the
contrary, is the sum of the lesson to be conveyed, and almost the last word to be said. Because it is in their
character as friendly societies of mutual help and of industrial and intellectual culture that the Trade Unions, greatly
marred as this character must be admitted to be by the
enormous waste of funds and turbulent contentions of late
years, have been most beneficial from the beginning of their
history until now ; and it is in their character, on the other
hand, as fighting societies that they have been most baneful
to the interests of the Unionists themselves, and to the
interests of the general community on which all amelioration of the condition of the working classes must stand
for ever.

LONDON : R. CLAY, SONS, AND TAYLOR, PRINTERS.